JOHN PETER KENNEY is Associate Professor of
Religion and Humanities at Reed College.

D1213994

MYSTICAL MONOTHEISM

John Peter Kenney

MYSTICAL
MONOTHEISM

A STUDY IN
ANCIENT PLATONIC THEOLOGY

BROWN UNIVERSITY PRESS
Published by University Press of New England / Hanover & London

BROWN UNIVERSITY PRESS
Published by University Press of New England

© 1991 by the Trustees of Brown University
All rights reserved. University Press of New England, Hanover, NH 03755
Printed in the United States of America   5   4   3   2   1
CIP data appear at the end of the book

For Anne, Madeline, and John Edward

CONTENTS

Preface   ix

Introduction   xv

1. The Foundations of Hellenic Monotheism   1

1. Degrees of Reality   3
2. Divine Ideas   15
3. The Emergence of Hellenic Monotheism   32
4. The Demiurgic Theology of Plutarch   43
5. Early Platonic Theism   54

2. The Demotion of the Demiurge   57

1. Numenius and the Degrees of Divinity   59
2. The *Didaskalikos* of Alcinous   74
3. The Exemplarism of the Athenian School   85
4. Middle Platonic Theology   88

3. The Mystical Monotheism of Plotinus   91

1. Divine Simplicity   93
2. Intellect and Ideas   112
3. Hid Divinity   128

Conclusion: Mystical Monotheism   150

Notes   157

Bibliography   187

Index   209

PREFACE

This is an essay in philosophical theology and its history. It is the initial study in a broader inquiry into the foundations of Western monotheism and represents an effort to reflect anew upon our theistic patrimony. I have not undertaken this research on a formally historicist basis, nor indeed have I done so because of an obscure nostalgia for the august fabric of some primordial theology. Mine is a simpler excuse. In studying the Western theistic tradition, I have been struck by the pronounced extent to which the metaphysical bases of theology have shifted over time. This observation has led to the judgment that unhistorical appraisals of Western theism neglect too much of significance and subtly alter the scope of theological commitment. Some of the variegated richness of the tradition is thereby lost, and understanding is foreshortened. Thus, I resolved to look into the development of philosophical monotheism, beginning with its original sources. Some might consider this historical essay to be but a mosaic of escape from current issues in philosophy of religion deemed to be more pressing. I can only say that I find a sense of prodigal adventure in this endeavor. I have become convinced that ancient theism merits more than just antiquarian interest and that contemporary philosophical theology can profit by revising the surface tale of its neglected past.

The proximate focus of this study is the development of philosophical monotheism from the late Hellenistic period through the death of Plotinus in 270 A.D., the period of its initial coalescence.

Platonism dominated this process of conceptual articulation, as the resources of classical metaphysics were employed in the service of divine transcendence. While Platonism was never the sole basis for this development, it was nonetheless critical to it. In order to understand this emergent theism, it is therefore necessary to assay several versions of Platonic theology, sorting out their divergent concepts of deity against the background of their common metaphysical assumptions. This is my fundamental intention: to examine some salient varieties of Platonic theology prior to Plotinus and then to focus analysis on his novel theism. Alternatively put, it is the theistic transformation of Platonism that is under conceptual review. However, it should be understood that my primary concern remains conceptual, not historical; I am fundamentally concerned to understand the metaphysical bases and systematical character of these early theologies, especially that of Plotinus.

Some of these authors are, to be sure, storied figures, and I shall be basing my reflections upon antecedent histories of Hellenistic and Late Antique philosophy, an area of scholarship that has been considerably advanced by classicists in this century. There is, nevertheless, much more to be said about this thought, especially from the standpoint of philosophical theology. My own approach owes much to contemporary Anglo-American studies in philosophical theology. I must admit at the onset that ancient philosophical theology is perhaps not readily accessible to us and that it can sometimes produce a marked sense of conceptual dislocation. I hope, however, to exhibit that this theological tradition can be made intellectually tractable and to allay the suspicion that it was largely incautious speculation by minds freed from the reins of conceptual probity.

There are two principal reasons for my interest in this period and subject. As I have noted, there is my lingering suspicion of neglect: that our understanding of classical theism suffers from the restricted nature of our vantage. This perspective has itself been variously conditioned by the inertial vision of ecclesiastical orthodoxy, by the unrecognized accretions of medieval scholasticism, and by the self-conscious revisionism of modern theology. I fear we have lost or ignored valuable aspects of the original, especially the realist metaphysical foundations of early philosophical theism as well as its pervasive contemplative and apophatic character. I want to focus upon these elements within ancient philosophical theism: its combined emphasis on the existence of the divine intelligibles as well as on the conceptual transcendence of divinity. I suspect that no reader of ancient philosophical theology can fail to notice these paradoxical features, and yet our analyses too often leave them out of account.

This delimited appraisal of ancient theism has resulted in an impoverished understanding of many important figures in Western theology, especially the Neoplatonists and their Jewish, Christian, and Islamic successors. In extreme cases, authors such as Eriugena, Ibn 'Al 'Arabi, and Meister Eckhart have seemed somehow fugitive and their conceptions of deity liminal. Such an approach might perhaps be countenanced were it not for the pervasiveness of mystical or apophatic theology throughout the history of the Western monotheistic traditions. Having attempted to understand this theism according to one restricted but predominant paradigm, we are left in vain for some excuse before a historical progression of Jewish, Christian, and Islamic Platonists who should not have belonged, by such interpretive standards, within the theistic traditions that they in fact inhabited and significantly influenced. Indeed, we may be missing as well one important dynamic of theistic traditions as such: their capacity to develop or at least to retain several different readings of their most basic credendum. I think we must therefore resolve to revise by extension our understanding of Western theism to include its mystical and apophatic dimension; only when informed by its overall scope can we hope to evaluate it fairly. Hence, the present project of historical restoration. I believe that a fuller treatment of ancient philosophical theology will begin to strengthen our grasp of the rich dimensions of Western theology as a whole, sustaining a more catholic reading of ancient theism and restoring thereby many worthy members lost under the reprobations of a narrower theological canon.

I must also admit to an additional motivation for this inquiry into ancient philosophical theology, one that is, I suppose, natural for a student of religions, and that is an interest in comparative religious thought. Each of the Western monotheistic religions has engaged in a prolonged process of philosophical self-definition, and for each this endeavor has been rooted in ancient Greek metaphysics. The mark of this foundational reflection continues to obtain throughout

the texture of their theologies. Thus, clarification of theological con-
sonance and divergence across the monotheistic spectrum can be
enhanced by analysis of ancient philosophical theology. This should
improve our comprehension of their joint endorsement of theism
and provide grounds for further analysis of its separate appraisal
within each theological tradition. Though doubtless at times arcane,
I hope that this study in ancient Platonic theology will contribute
to rational reflection upon theism at the close of a century too often
riven by the maniacal forces of denominational intolerance and athe-
istic totalitarianism.

One significant matter of scholarly policy should be noted initially. Because my interests are philosophical, I have kept doxographical and philological considerations to a minimum. Beguiling
though source criticism may be in the history of ideas, it is not
my primary concern, and so such issues are entertained only when
apposite to theological analysis. Ancient philosophical doxography
sometimes seems to be a 'wilderness of mirrors'; I have been afraid
throughout to become lost in it. My discussion has been based upon
the major authorities in this field, and I have referred the reader to
their works when it seemed necessary. I have tried at the same time
not to encumber the book with extensive notes, having attempted
to thread a responsible line between pedantry and scholarly indif-
ference.

Prefaces are by convention a chartered locus in which one can
acknowledge one's debts. Mine are too extensive to mention, except
for the most immediate. I should like to recognize posthumously
my gratitude to Horst R. Moehring for the benefit of his direction
in the study of Hellenistic religious thought. I owe as well a special
debt to A. H. Armstrong for his generous attention to this research
as it has developed over the years. John Dillon was kind enough to
comment on an early version of chapters 1 and 2. David Burrell and
Robert Berchman were also very helpful in providing suggestions
at various points. It is probably gratuitous to issue ritual injunctions
against imputing responsibility to any of these; if not, let this notice
suffice.

Portions of this research were revealed at various academic soci-
eties and meetings, including the American Academy of Religion,
the American Philosophical Association, the International Society

for Neoplatonic Studies, the Colloquium Origenianum Quintum at Boston College, and the International Patristic Conference at Oxford University. The 1987 Conference on Comparative Religious Thought sponsored by the University of Chicago and the University of Notre Dame was particularly important to the development of this project. I should like to thank the participants on those occasions for their comments. Mention should also be made of several institutions that have provided important assistance: Brown University, where this work was initially drafted as a dissertation in 1982; Harvard University, where it was revised during my residence as a Visiting Scholar in the Divinity School; and Reed College, which provided research and sabbatical funding. I must register particular thanks for the opportunity to study and write during the 1984–1985 academic year to the National Endowment for the Humanities and so ultimately to my fellow citizens of this republic.

My thanks also to Karen Bondaruk of Reed College for her help in preparing the manuscript and for her patient instruction in the mystic world of computer software.

Finally, I am indebted to my family for their support of this prolonged inquiry into the remote origins of our theological heritage. This book is specially dedicated with gratitude to Anne, and to Madeline and John Edward.

October 1990   J.P.K.
Portland, Oregon

INTRODUCTION

Realist theology is rich in its ancient lineage. The transcendent existence of forms or divine ideas was long central to philosophical theology, with many variant accounts of the degrees of reality serving as the bases for contrasting theologies throughout late antiquity and the early Middle Ages. A gradual transition ensued, however, in the later medieval period, signaled by the rise of nominalism,[1] which significantly reoriented our approach to divinity, producing a manifest divergence between modern philosophical theology and the ancient realist tradition. This essay is concerned with that older theology, which entered the high Middle Ages in a philosophical form very like its antecedents a millennium before but which subsequently dissolved. That ancient theology, the *via antiqua*, is now largely neglected. It is with later medieval and Reformation thought that contemporary philosophical theology seems comfortable, for we can enter into its characteristic notions without too marked a sense of conceptual dislocation. We feel, in short, comfortable with this theology, for we are its direct heirs. At the same time, our sense of removal from earlier figures in philosophical theology, such as Plotinus or even St. Augustine, is considerable; their metaphysical assumptions seem alien to us, and thus their works are frequently ignored in our own deliberations on the coherence of theism. In many respects this neglect is not surprising, given the atmosphere of philosophical strangeness which that older theology can sometimes convey to us, although this intrinsic distance should not be an excuse for wholesale dereliction. These are, after all, the thinkers who initiated Western theism, and so it is incumbent upon us to re-construe their metaphysical assumptions if we wish to understand theism in its original form.

The most important conceptual factor effecting this estrangement is probably the realist character of ancient theistic metaphysics. The central feature of late antique and early medieval philosophical theology is a fundamental reliance upon degree of reality meta-physics, the basis of which is usually some sort of Platonism.[2] These Platonisms were grounded in the notion that reality is hierarchi-cal in character, so that it makes sense to talk about degrees of 'being.'[3] This is not a natural metaphysical move for us, and neither is the consequent theological perspective or the kinds of issues it raises. We must nevertheless resolve to consider ancient philosophi-cal theism in light of this central metaphysical thesis; absent it, much of the ontological import of this theology is lost to us. We will be able thereby to get beyond discussion of 'classical theism,'[4] that maligned generic construct that has fared so badly in the often mock combat of modern academic theology. We can expect to see ancient theistic metaphysics for what it was, with some of its major presupposi-tions in view, and can thus hope to conceive better the conceptual framework that established its theological parameters. Beyond this there is the additional promise of achieving some understanding of the multiple concepts of deity that have been absorbed into the homogeneity of 'classical theism' so that its varietal character may become more pronounced. Thus, we need to begin by reflecting in a preliminary way on realist theology, and then we can approach the principal issues in the development of Platonic theism upon which we shall be concentrating.

1. Realist Theology

To look into early theistic philosophy is to find a hierarchical uni-verse, graduated by degrees of reality. This is the central feature of realist theology: the conviction that there is a divine world more real than our own. We must realize, however, that there was much more involved in ancient realist theology than just a thesis regarding the independent existence of universals; indeed, this was usually not a particularly important element, strange as that may seem. Rather, the motivating idea behind this theology was the broader claim that some transcendent entities have more being than do those of the sensible world. For moderns, this is the really difficult point, since a relative status in being between two sets of entities, between two worlds, is thereby postulated. I might illustrate the point informally by noting that a narrower, logical realism would address the existence of universals and would countenance an ontological difference between two types of reality, namely, universals and particulars. This sort of realism falls short, however, of the degree-of-reality thesis, the hallmark of ancient Platonism. The more enriched position, which originated in the dialogues of Plato's 'middle period,'[5] held that there are not only different sorts of reality but that one class of entities, particulars, is at a lower level of reality than another, that of universals. The basis for this claim seems to have been the assumption that forms or universals are the metaphysical causes of particulars, so that there is a one-way relationship of ontological dependence between these levels.[6] This key development, which made forms into constituents of a grade of reality superior to their ontological products, fundamentally altered the character of the logical thesis, widening it into a broad theory regarding the structure of reality itself. It is upon this metaphysical theory that realist theology depended. While the logical element of the thesis was important as a conceptual catalyst, what truly mattered in theology was this divine realm of 'being,' transcending the world of contingency and change. Indeed, some ancient Platonists evidently considered admitting forms of individuals in the world of 'being;'[7] the foundations of their Platonism plainly lay elsewhere.[8]

The primary intuition of realist theology was its recognition of an ontologically more fundamental realm, a world of perfection and power, whose presence was manifested by the fact and character of our common world of appearances. The major feature distinguishing realist and nominalist theology was thus their variant positions on the hierarchical character of reality and on the postulation of a world of 'being' and divinity, more real than the manifest facticty we identify as the sensible world. For theological realists these degrees of 'being' were correlated to the notion of divinity, whereas for nominalists this basic metaphysical model was denied in favor of some version of the claim that there are only different types of reality, including both the earthly and the divine. But in realist theology, the concepts of 'reality' and 'divinity' are conjoined, and both admit of gradation: the world of true 'being' is preeminently divine, while whatever is deficiently real also lacks divinity.

Within such realist theology the issue of the relations between reality and divinity naturally emerges, and the character of this association certainly seems to have been subject to negotiation in antiquity. As a value concept, divinity might be retained in its proper sense only for true 'being' and might be applied analogically to lower levels. Alternatively, it could be said that reality and divinity are strictly correlative concepts, both subject to corresponding gradation. In any case, realist theology has always been required to account for significant gradations along this scale of 'being' and to explain those major calibrations that resulted in important differences in that hierarchy. Reality may have been arrayed along a continuum, but it did not lack for points of discrimination, and neither did divinity. Our world of change and qualitative opposition was resolved into a deeper one of stability and symmetry; thereby was a crucial point of delineation identified. To assess the nature of divinity against the emergence of such points of ontological demarcation was of necessity a principal issue.

Another related consequence of this hierarchical model was the mediated view of reality that resulted. While this was also a theme open to variation, there was a common emphasis upon the interrelationships that were held to obtain among the various levels. Higher levels were usually viewed as being causally productive of lower ones, while there was often a concomitant force postulated that motivated these lower entities to imitate or even somehow 'return' to their superior ontological causes. Reality thus evinced a broad pattern of causal activity over against a fundamentally fixed hierarchy, so that the sense of separation among levels could be balanced by the complexity of their associations. It seems always to have been clear that the constituents of higher levels merited that status because of their superior power and their relative surfeit of 'being,' so that no real reciprocity between levels was possible. Higher levels had nothing at stake in their production, and their capacity for this activity was usually construed as being relative to their own standing in the hierarchy. Realist theology thus posited a mediated universe, although it was one in which a deep asymmetry obtained between ontological causes and effects, whose relations were never reciprocal.

Perhaps the most frequently discussed feature of ancient realist theology is the static character of its highest principles, the powers that exhibit true 'being' and divinity. While there is much in this issue that requires careful explication, it is true that the wholly real and divine realm was one whose nature was often seen as largely fixed and was thus a level upon whose efficacy one could rely. We shall examine this theme in some detail because it lies at the center of one of the most pressing problems faced by ancient realist theologians, the question of the ultimate status of intellection. The motive character of mind and of many mental activities posed a whole host of difficulties for Platonists: how should intellection be accounted for in relation to the fixed nature of true 'being' and of the forms? Should it be debarred from a place of preeminence in reality and treated as a parasitical product of lower activities? If it should be admitted to have some place within that world, is intellection something whose motivity affects all of 'being' or only some forms? Do the forms each exercise intellection, as separate monodic minds, or do they do so only jointly? Or is intellection a power to be reserved and located as a separate entity, different in its changing character from the forms but like them in being fundamental and ultimate to reality? These are the sorts of problems that became prominent in ancient realist theology and upon which the early theistic debate focused. It is this thread of discussion that I propose to follow in considering the development of ancient Platonic theism.

2. Mysticism

It is now a commonplace in religious studies to remark on how especially vague is the term "mysticism." This is certainly true: ghosts, occult phenomena, and St. Paul's conversion on the road to Damascus might all be colloquially described as "mystical." There are clearly opportunities here for the academic revisionist; many have seized them, and so the current literature on the subject is sizable. The use of so suspect a term in my title, even if in an adjectival mode, invites queries on its meaning and demands reference to recent scholarship.[9] I should like to begin, curiously enough, by taking refuge in this adjectival usage of the term "mystical." Its point is to call attention to one particular type of ancient theism, distinguished by its emphasis upon the hidden character of the deity. I want to be quite restrictive in my use of this term, attempting to preserve some of the original resonance of the Greek adjective *mustikos*. This was a word that retained throughout antiquity a sense that was close to our terms "secret" or "hidden," hence also "mysterious." I shall use the adjective "mystical" in this way, as a modifier for "monotheism" or "theology," keeping in view its ancient lexical association with *mustērion* (a mystery or revealed secret) and ultimately *muein* (to close or shut). Hence, the conjunction of "mystical" with "theology" or "monotheism" marks an emphasis upon the intrinsically hidden character of this subject matter and its ultimate referent. I shall thus employ this adjective to indicate a type of theology or a particular conception of the divine. I have also used the term "apophatic" (from *apophasis*, a denial; *apophēmi*, to deny) in a similar fashion, to emphasize the conceptual inaccessibility of the ultimate divine reality.

My approach to the mystical aspects of ancient theology makes common cause with recent developments in the study of mystical traditions that have sought to rehabilitate analysis of their conceptual and theological components. Broadly put, this alteration in outlook has been based upon a rejection of the claim that there is only one valid method for the study of mystical literature, one that seeks to identify a single common experiential core for all "mysticism," or failing that, perhaps a limited class. This 'common core' hypothesis has promoted the view that the theological elements found in mystical literature were impositions upon certain universal or nearly universal experiences and were thus largely distortions based upon some previously held theological scheme extraneous to these experiences. In order to be properly assessed, it was maintained that mystical thought must be purified of those elements that produced such interpretive distortions and, further, that these intrusions must be 'bracketed' in order to restore, by conceptual distillation, the original and unmediated core of mystical experience. Mystical theology was on this basis frequently devalued, since it was seen as being the product of a process that systematically distorted genuine mystical experience by means of external interpretation, and was in addition viewed as the belated translation of such experience into an inappropriate and fixed theological language acceptable to some prevailing religious orthodoxy.

Many contemporary philosophers of religion would now eschew such a universalizing approach, with its exclusive experiential focus, and insist instead upon a more 'contextual' understanding of mystical writings. I find myself in pragmatic agreement with this 'contextualist' school. This is not the place to argue the methodological case for such 'contextualism,' one which is itself difficult to specify and open to significant qualification. But it can, I think, be said that this school of analysis has drawn attention anew to the modes of thought found within mystical traditions and to the writings themselves and that this is in itself salutary.

Whatever one might think of the new edicts and proscriptions that have been issued against typological or comparative approaches, and academic skepticism seems in order here as well, there has been a liberating effect upon the study of mystical theology. Admitting the significance of the theology found in mystical literature and relating this thought to the philosophical and religious traditions in which it developed seems a sensible method, one that holds significant promise of clarifying what are often obscure writings. These writings cannot be treated only as a collection of disguised reports, requiring only husking in a quest to reveal the raw data of mystical experience. If such a process of analysis were theoretically defensible, there would still be no compelling reason to accept such reductionism at face value nor to admit this as the sole valid approach to the comprehension of mystical theology. Much depends upon what one wants to understand, psychological experiences of a certain type, or claims about the nature of reality recorded by mystical writers. Such literature nearly always involves much more than just a record of intense spiritual experiences; one usually finds a complex set of statements grounded in a religious tradition, often modifying certain of its conventional tenets. Mystical theology emerges within a religion and so incorporates a religious metaphysics, which is both the basis of this thought and in many cases the subject of radical revision. To ignore these facets of mystical literature on the basis of antecedent methodology is to run the risk of excerpting these writings from the very contexts that promise the keys to their intelligibility. This seems at best extremely restrictive, legitimate perhaps for the psychologist of mysticism, but at worst endemically distortive when applied as an exclusive methodological rule. I have, therefore, no quarrel with those intent upon this quest for a 'common core,' provided that no methodological reductionism is therein implied with respect to mystical theology. I would reject, however, any approach to mystical literature that both limits attention strictly to this alleged experiential core and denigrates the conceptual import of theology. The present study therefore rests upon this irenic methodological judgment: that while an 'experentialist' approach, seeking a typology of the common characteristics of mystical experience across religious traditions, might be valid and might prove to be persuasive, it can, nonetheless, provide no warrant to foreclose the theological study of mystical literature. And that is, in part, the subject of this inquiry.

3. Monotheism

Theism is a promiscuous concept, indiscriminate in reference but frequent in use. It is similar in this respect to other concepts of deity, for example, pantheism or monism. Their employment is often vague and even pejorative; when they are encountered, I am sometimes reminded of the perhaps apocryphal saying attributed to Dean Inge: "Any stigma is good enough to beat a dogma." We are in need of some help if we are to make responsible use of this terminology, and so some stipulation is in order.

At its most general, the term 'theism' denotes belief in a deity or deities and is opposed to atheism. It thus includes both monotheism and polytheism.[10] In its more common, narrower usage it is restricted to the belief in one deity and is equivalent to 'monotheism.' We should distinguish first of all between philosophical and nonphilosophical contexts for the use of all such concepts of deity. Our discussion here is concerned with philosophical theology, and so we are interested in theoretical and articulated systems of beliefs, in reflective theology. Hence, monotheism and polytheism need to be taken as referring to positions in formal theology, rather than as terms that refer to ritual or religiously colloquial beliefs. Given this initial restriction, I will treat theism as a variant term for monotheism, which is defined simply as the thesis that there is an ultimate divine principle transcendent of the physical universe. Polytheism would hold that there are many ultimate and transcendent divine principles.

Inclusion of the notion of transcendence distinguishes both concepts from pantheism, which would maintain that everything is divine. Taken distributively, this would suggest that divinity is a constituent element in the world; while taken collectively, it would entail that the whole of reality is divine. In neither case is divinity a power distinct from the world, for it is either a common immanent aspect of the universe or an alternative description of the system of reality as a whole. Monism is probably best treated in relation to pantheism, based upon an additional ontological assumption: that there is only one reality and that the multiplicity of the phenomenal world is illusory. There seem to be two common understandings of monism, each based upon a type of pantheism. One version of monism begins with collectivistic pantheism, the thesis that the universe as a whole is divine, and stresses the sense of uniqueness involved, concluding that there is only one single ultimate principle. All multiplicity and difference are merely apparent and unreal. This is a numerical reading of monism, focusing as it does upon the singularity of what is real and divine. There are no grounds for any recognition of genuine degrees of reality nor for the logic of divine transcendence; such concepts wither before the intensity of the utter and total uniqueness that is the single, divine reality. The other common type of monism revises distributive pantheism and its notion of divine immanence by affirming that there is only one kind of reality—namely, divinity—and denying that any other quality is real. This qualitative monism shares a common rejection of divine transcendence with numerical monism; there is, after all, nothing distinct from this one reality to transcend. The ontological modalism of monism, its treatment of all plurality as only illusory modes of the one divine reality, precludes any claim of real divine ontological separation from the world. Since Plotinus and the Neoplatonists have often been viewed as monists, we need to be clear on this denial of transcendence in monism. Ontological transcendence is a shibboleth of theism.

Monotheism is also subject to considerable variation of its core thesis, and care must be taken to avoid premature determination of its implications based upon cultural habituation and precedence. To assert that there is one ultimate divine principle is to stake a claim about the structure of reality while leaving much unsaid. A key issue is the sense of oneness involved. On a numerical reading, this core thesis would be taken as endorsing the uniqueness of this divine principle. There is a single deity; the class of divine beings has only one member. This is the dominant thrust of what might be called "exclusive monotheism," with its emphasis upon the uniqueness of the deity. But there is another way to construe this monotheistic thesis, one that turns on a qualitative understanding of oneness. On this account, monotheism would be principally concerned to support an ultimate divine unity behind, but distinct from, the world. This unity might be thought of rather as a special type of reality different from and superior to all others. It would be seen as a unique kind of being rather than as a unique being. It would thus not be initially envisioned as a numerically single principle. There is, then, in this qualitative monotheism a final divine unity beyond the multiplicity of the world, a deeper unifying nature behind the cosmos. Divinity seems thus to be the final inclusive unity behind the manifest plurality of the world's plurality, the ultimate completeness that transcends but resolves its fractured multiplicity. I shall refer to this approach, which emphasizes divine primordiality, completeness, and ultimacy, as "inclusive monotheism."

In noting these logically possible approaches to the monotheistic thesis, I should hasten to add that they have often been closely interrelated in the presentation of philosophical theism, and this is probably because, taken discretely, there seems to be something incomplete about each claim. Exclusive monotheism has the burden not only of articulating the fact that there is one deity but of explaining why this is so. This type of monotheism would not suggest an endorsement of an accidentally unique being; that there happens to be just one God seems not to be its real point. Exclusive monotheism needs, therefore, to explain the numerical uniqueness of the deity and to indicate that the nature of divinity is such that there can be of necessity only one such instance. There is thus some considerable conceptual pressure within exclusive monotheism to develop an account of the nature of divinity construed in a qualitative way. The object is to show the special character of divinity and its unique position in reality so that the fact of a single deity excluding all others seems to follow conceptually. Inclusive monotheism has, on the other hand, the problem of explaining what the nature of this special underlying quality might be. How is this transcendental substance, divinity itself, to be represented? The qualitative uniqueness of divinity is thus in question, and so there is a need for a theoretical discussion of the unique type of being that God is. These two readings thus tend to dovetail and so knit together these conceptually distinct approaches to monotheism. Nonetheless, one can discern in certain theological traditions a disposition toward one or the other version of monotheism, and we must be aware of this possibility as we begin to review the historical record.

Before taking up our main historical project, we also need to recognize that, like all philosophical concepts of deity, monotheism is not suspended free from many metaphysical assumptions, which are usually so deeply imbedded as to be barely separable conceptually from the core monotheistic thesis. We have already noted this in the case of monism; its modalistic ontology was central, helping to mark it off from pantheism. The same is true of monotheism with respect to ontological derivation or generation. It might be possible to construe either exclusive or inclusive monotheism as being neutral on the question of ontological generation or derivation. On this view the transcendent divine principle would be just another constituent, albeit a preeminent one, within the inventory of reality. It might be claimed alternatively that God is a unique entity distinct from all others or that the divine is a special property unlike any other. One would simply prescind from any notion of ontological derivation so that God would not be an answer to questions regarding the ontological basis for other sorts of things. These might be treated perhaps as too lacking in proper form to be meaningful. Now this is admittedly an eccentric sort of monotheism, counterintuitive because of our ingrained disposition to conjoin monotheism with a theory of ontological derivation for the universe. There may be more in this conceptual strangeness, though, than mere habit. Given the pressure already noted to account either for numerical or qualitative uniqueness, there is a clear benefit to be accrued for monotheism by setting the divine principle apart from all reality as its unique source or ground. By settling upon the divine principle the role of an onto-logical power that generates all consequent beings, its special status can be more readily construed. As the necessary and sufficient con-dition for all subsequent beings, the divine first principle can be considered to be numerically unique by position or distinctive in character because it functions as the unitary source for the universe. Its distinctness and transcendence of its products are underscored as well. This seems to be one important reason behind the tendency for monotheism of whatever sort to include the articulation of an ontological derivation thesis. The drafting of this important codicil to monotheism occupied many of the early theists whom we shall be reviewing.

For purposes of conceptual relief, it might be a help to note that polytheism could also be set out in terms of ontological de-pendence; minimally, two necessary divine principles would be in-volved, neither being sufficient for ontological production of the lower universe. Because it specifically excludes a claim of divine numerical uniqueness, polytheism is not concerned with endorsing the ontological sufficiency of a single deity. Hence, the stakes for demonstrating the exact line of ontological derivation are less. Freed from the requirement of accounting for numerical uniqueness, poly-theism is under less pressure to settle exactly the issue of ontological origins. Since any polytheist must still account for this commitment to a class of divine beings, ontological derivation may remain sig-nificant for an explanation of the nature of these gods. A theory of divine production through the conjunction of the gods may in-deed help to underscore their joint separation from all consequent beings, thus supplying a minimal, functional characterization of the nature of divinity as such and ascertaining commitment to this class of divine beings. As in the case of inclusive monotheism, there is no constraint to use such a derivation thesis to certify the numerical uniqueness of God. It should not be surprising then that ancient philosophical polytheism may seem, from the perspective of our cultural monotheism, to be shockingly uninterested, even cavalier, about ultimate divine production, leaving its theological universe littered with sundry powers. For a philosophical polytheist, though, this is rather a matter of disinterest; it is simply not the burden of such theology.

We must realize, then, that monotheism can admit of a plethora of variations upon its core formula, and many of these have been developed through the history of Western theism. We need to insist upon a continued catholicity in our approach to theism, given our historical intentions, so as to improve our awareness of the ancient discussion. For the logic of transcendence differs within each theism, and we must remain attentive both to the range of theological divergence and to the common problem involved, that of articulating the ultimate divine unity. Special care must be exercised in a few areas. We should be clear that a theist may adopt the common thesis of ontological derivation but nevertheless remain neutral on the question of temporal generation. The choice of cosmology—between eternalism and creationism—while often important, is not conceptually central to monotheism. What matters for monotheism is not whether ultimate divinity produced the universe in time or whether the universe is an eternal system; its special characteristic is ontological dependence upon a necessary and sufficient ground of being. The ancient and medieval cosmological debate on this question should not be taken as having divided theists, who endorsed creationism, from adherents of an essentially different concept of deity, which included an eternalistic postulate. Similar circumspection is in order on the question of the nature of the divine mind. Whether intellection is an activity of the ultimate deity or something that emerges at the level of the deity's ontological constituents, this is an issue upon which theists can also disagree. It is natural for theism to utilize this notion to support its claim of divine uniqueness and transcendence, and there are usually very specialized reasons for qualifying or even denying the ascription of intellection to divinity; but this remains, I think, a quarrel within the theistic camp. Likewise for the scope of providence: to deny that the deity exercises providence or to locate this power at the level of lesser derivative powers is not a matter of essential difference for theism. Deism ought really to be seen as a variation of monotheism.

The reason for this latitudinarian edict on the concept of theism is quite straightforward. We need to be fairly flexible if we are to understand the historical development of those forms of philosophical theology that would gradually coalesce in late antiquity and the early Middle Ages into the stable model that by convention we call 'classical theism.' The complete classical theistic position would maintain "belief in one God, the Creator, who is infinite, self-existent, incorporeal, eternal, immutable, impassible, simple, perfect, omniscient and omnipotent." [11] This is a very complex thesis, one that was worked out over many centuries in Christian, Jewish, and Islamic scholasticism. But the historical incipience for this trajectory in philosophical theology can be identified in late antiquity, although in virtually all individual cases before the fourth century some feature of the composite model is lacking. To insist upon completeness and to deny that earlier figures, such as Philo, Origen, [12] or Plotinus were theists seems unnecessarily restrictive. It also obscures much of the intent of their theology, which frequently centered upon working out the core theistic position on divine unity and transcendence in the face of various sorts of cosmic pantheism and dualistic polytheism. I would prefer to say that the foundations of theism were laid in this period while the details were settled later, and so these early inventors are best seen as full members of the movement they initiated. Comparing earlier positions with later ones is natural in the history of ideas; it is invidious, though, if those subsequent, more refined views are used normatively to exclude earlier ones from membership on grounds of immaturity. It seems better, then, that we broaden the notion of theism and concentrate upon its main thrust. In this way we can study the rich variety of ancient theology without prejudice and treat these theologies on their own terms, admitting in the process what a messy business the history of ideas is.

There is another reason for treating theism in this rather blunt fashion, and it again has to do with the cultural force of classical theism. As I have noted, monotheism can be developed in ways other than just exclusive monotheism, with its tendency to accentuate the numerical uniqueness of the deity. Qualitative unity is another approach, and we can find this, I think, within ancient theology, especially with 'pagan' or Hellenic figures who were concerned to articulate the divine unity behind the gods and their cosmos. This 'Hellenic theism,' with its focus upon the ultimate divine unity, is an important alternative tradition within the philosophical theology of the period, one in which I hope to locate Plotinus. If we allow the more common numerical emphasis in classical Western theism to dominate our understanding, then we are in danger of missing this other dimension. A good deal of perplexity seems to have been attached to the theology of Plotinus and some other Hellenic theologians; part of this stems, I think, from an inability to recognize the genuine tenor of this theology, especially its preoccupation with an inclusive and primordial divine unity. I am suggesting, then, that we attempt to extend our understanding of ancient theism beyond our culturally freighted one; thereby might we restore a partly lost school in theological history, one whose depiction of divinity was later subsumed into the medieval scholastic effort to justify the unique existence of a monotheistic deity understood in more exclusivistic terms.

4. Mystical Monotheism

Titles of books often say too much or too little. Mine does both. Its point rests upon the adjective, for I am primarily interested in one particular aspect of early theism. For that reason this is not a complete study of the many varieties of ancient philosophical theism, one that takes account of the whole range of theological issues (e.g., providence, theodicy, etc.). But neither is it a systematic analysis of ancient mystical literature. My intentions lie modestly between these two extensive subjects. I will analyze several versions of ancient theistic metaphysics, basing this taxonomy upon theological features that we know to have been under dispute in the period, including the nature of divine unity, the scope and significance of divine intellection, the character of the intelligible world, and the conceptual transcendence of ultimate divinity. Even these topics can be pursued in only a limited fashion in this preliminary study. My ultimate goal is to clarify a developing feature within ancient theism, one that would remain pervasive if sometimes recessive, throughout the history of Western theism. The term "mystical monotheism"[13] is meant to refer to this persistent theological theme: that divinity should be understood as an ultimate and inclusive unity, transcendent of 'being' and intellection and so beyond human knowledge as it is standardly understood. It is this developing mystical dimension within the early stages of Western theism that is my principal topic. Such an abbreviated treatment has a claim nonetheless to significance, since it will allow us to chart some salient varieties of ancient philosophical theism. There is much at stake here. What has become the normative tradition in Western theism had its origins in late Hellenistic theology, and so no serious appraisal of the conceptual development of classical theism can neglect it. This is the point at which ancient philosophical theology took its 'theistic turn,' one of the great peripeties in Western intellectual history. For this reason, the present analysis of this development, even if restricted in scope, can stake an independent claim for the reader's attention.

This incipient study can promise an additional benefit for the historical study of Western philosophical theology, and that is an enhancement of our understanding of the Neoplatonic theology of Plotinus. If we can reconstruct the theological discussion in which Plotinus's own thought developed, if we can catch again some of the conceptual and religious force behind his views, then we will be much better able to represent with cogency his religious metaphysics. Given the confusion among students of the philosophy of religion regarding Plotinus, this stands as one important desideratum in the study of Western philosophical theology.[14] This essay into the critical foundations of Plotinus's thought is intended to help locate his views within the ancient theistic spectrum. I plan, then, to concentrate upon the early treatises of the *Enneads*, where we can still discern Plotinus's efforts to separate himself from various Middle Platonic and Neopythagorean doctrines. By establishing this critical trajectory for Plotinus's theology, the contours of his mystical monotheism will emerge, a concept of deity that would become widely influential in later Jewish, Christian, and Islamic philosophical theology.

The plan of this volume follows its two intersecting purposes. In chapters 1 and 2 the development of several varieties of realist theology from the first through the third centuries A.D. will be reviewed, concentrating upon those that defined alternative types of theism and thus were precedents for Plotinus. Chapter 3 will focus upon Plotinus's criticisms of these antecedents and his construction of his own Neoplatonic monotheism. The essay will close with a discussion of the significance of mystical monotheism in Western philosophical theology.

studied, with special attention to apophatic theology and the rejection of dualism among Neopythagoreans (1.3). By contrast, the early Middle Platonism of Plutarch is reviewed, with its emphasis upon the role of a demiurgic deity (1.4). The chapter closes with a brief review of some aspects of early Platonic theism (1.5).

1. Degrees of Reality

Realist theology began its long career with Plato and his articulation of degree of reality metaphysics, and so it is there that our inquiry must begin. There is, however, the very real danger that the present investigation might end there as well, for Plato scholarship is vast and rich, its issues as notoriously vexed as they are fundamental in their significance. Since our interest is not in solving the enigmas of Plato's own thought, a sensible course will be to sketch out some themes in Plato that are apposite for the study of subsequent theology; this will provide the foundation necessary for analyzing the structure of Middle Platonic theology.

Plato does not use the term "degree of reality" as such, although the concept is central to the middle period dialogues, such as the *Phaedo* and *Republic*.[6] It might be possible to argue that in earlier dialogues the forms are presented as a type of reality distinct from particulars but not yet viewed as constituting a superior level.[7] In the *Phaedo*, however, it seems clear enough that the *anamnēsis* argument implies the view that forms are transcendent of the sensible world and of higher ontological import.[8] It is only because of the soul's acquaintance with these forms during a preexistent state of disembodied purity that we can come to recognize their morphic presence in the changeful sensible world. Knowledge of forms, if it is meant by Socrates to count in favor of the soul's preexistence, must have been the result of the soul's previous condition outside the world of flux. The *anamnēsis* doctrine suggests, then, a separate existence of forms construed not only as logically different from particulars but also as occupying a different level of reality entirely.[9] In the *Republic* this two-world thesis is articulated as "that which is entirely real" or "purely real" is contrasted with "that which is in no way real," while between them is an intermediate state, "that which is both being and non-being."[10]

This arresting thesis was perhaps the most important foundation of ancient philosophical transcendentalism, establishing as it
did some conceptual warrant for a realm of deeper import behind
the manifest image of the sensible world. Its tacit adoption in late
antiquity often masked its complexity, for this theory of an intelligible world was a highly economical answer to several conceptually
distinct questions.[11] At least in the middle-period dialogues, Plato
used the theory of forms to address problems in logic, epistemology,
ethics, and aesthetics, among others. Upon inspection, these may
not be entirely compatible uses, a fact that seemed to have troubled
Plato, to judge from later dialogues such as the *Sophist* and *Parmenides*. Since later Platonic theology evinces a largely silent selection
from among these aspects of Plato's thought, we need to reflect on
this issue.

Plato's hierarchical metaphysics may be said, in broad terms, to
have rested upon two distinct bases: the logical-epistemic and the
valuational.[12] The former dimension of the theory was probably the
result of Plato's reflection upon Socrates' definitional inquiry;[13] Plato
came to recognize a class of entities, universals, distinct from sensible particulars, that could serve as a priori notions independent
of conceptualization,[14] as paradigms for predication,[15] and so on.
What motivated the further degree of reality hypothesis seems to
have been the cognitive surety that was attached to such universals. Plato seems to have considered forms as being more real than
sensible particulars because they were cognitively more reliable. As
paradigms of predication, forms defined the terms by which they
were identified. Knowledge of a form thus had an apodictic character unlike that of sensible particulars, qualified as knowledge of
these was by perspectival confusion and the possibility of change.[16]
Indeed, Plato seems frequently to have thought of forms not just as
universal standards but as really possessing the properties that they
serve to define. As such, each was a perfect exemplar of its special
quality or property. This exemplarist understanding of forms was
based on an apparently self-predicational interpretation of statements like: "the good is good."[17] As *Protagoras* 330d–e has it: "What
else would be holy, if holiness itself were not holy?" The form de-
served its attribute or description preeminently.[18] This tendency to
render absolute each form is especially clear in the famous speech of

Diotima at *Symposium* 210eff., where the wondrous nature of beauty is described at the apex of the lover's ascent. Beautiful particulars are subject to generation and destruction, increase and decline, and are qualified by predicative opposition, for each may be beautiful in one respect but not in another, at one time but not at another, with respect to one thing but not to another, or from one perspective but not another. The form of beauty would by contrast be purely beautiful (211e); each form is "self-same and by itself and an eternal unity" (211b1).

Logical and epistemic considerations evidently helped to lead Plato to postulate a realm of universals that were perfect exemplars, occupying a higher level of reality. His treatment of forms as *aitiai*,[19] as metaphysical causes of sorts for particulars, underscored this two-world hypothesis. As perfect and absolute standards that sensible particulars share in or imitate, forms define the possibilities of the sensible world.[20] Their complex interstitial relations, whose entailment patterns are discernible through *diairesis*,[21] establish the boundaries of the ontologically deficient world of fluxation. It must be noted, though, that while forms are ontological causes necessary to 'becoming,' they are not construed by Plato in the middle-period dialogues as sufficient for this derivative realm. This sets up at least one of the problems addressed by the cosmological treatment of the theory of forms in the *Timaeus*: What conjunction of forces beyond the forms is necessary for the existence of 'becoming'? We shall return to this problem when the *Timaeus* is considered.

Why a logically and epistemically based distinction between paradigmatic universals and particulars should have led Plato to this degree of reality hypothesis is a question outside our focus here, although some brief, speculative reflections on this issue may be of profit to our theological investigation. As moderns, we often have difficulty coming to terms with the Platonic notions of 'being' and the forms; our tendency is to settle for a distinction of ontological type between universals and particulars and to find the concept of degrees of reality to be quite odd. This may well be due to differences in our fundamental understanding of notions like 'being' and 'existence,' so that Plato's move toward a hierarchical metaphysics may have been rooted in some basic conceptual dispositions of classical Greek thought and language. Indeed, surprising as it may seem, for Greeks of the classical period there was no easy way to formulate the notion of existence. As Charles Kahn has shown, "the fundamental value of *einai* ('to be') when used alone (without predicates) is not 'to exist' but 'to be so,' 'to be the case' or 'to be true.' "[22] The Greeks were therefore without a sense of existence that is removed from any reference to the nature, quality, or essence of a thing. In classical Greek, 'to be' is always dependent upon some implied context or sense of prediction or upon a veridical claim, so that 'to be' always relies upon a predicative background. While for moderns, existence is a strict sortal concept (i.e., either including or excluding), the Greek notion of 'being' was more latitudinal. Degrees of existence is, from our contemporary standpoint, at best a paradoxical notion. For the Greeks, degrees of 'being,' with this implied background of qualitative predication, was quite intelligible, so that ranking entities in terms of their 'being' seemed an acceptable procedure, though it is one that we must struggle to apprehend by a forced alteration in our normal conceptual procedures. Unlike ancient Greeks, modern usage tends to distinguish sharply between existence and nonexistence, so that we do not say, for example, that "humans have more existence than plants." Both plants and people exist, and though we may wish to import other evaluative criteria to gradate them, this is not reflected in our usage of 'existence.' In addition,[23] we might say that universals like 'justice' exist, but this is not usually taken to confer separate existence upon an abstract object; in common discourse it amounts to a disguised reference to the extension of the concept, to its instantiation. We might, in philosophical contexts, wish to challenge this usage, but it prevails in the common language nonetheless. It is possible to say that justice exists to a greater extent in one nation than in another, but what we mean by this is that justice is more perfectly instantiated in one place than in another. This is, once again, not a violation of a disjunctive attitude toward 'existence' but a linguistic usage that does duty for some evaluative distinction. We are merely talking about degrees of justice among certain recognized entities, not of degrees of reality.

My point then is not that Plato thought that there were some things that had more existence than others but rather that Greek usage allowed him to conjoin evaluative notions with what we would call existence and, on this basis, to discuss degrees of 'being' in a way with which we are not immediately comfortable.[24] The theory maintains that things in the world of becoming existed; it is just that they were deficient in many respects. This value judgment relied upon the descriptive instability of sensible particulars, and so in assigning these entities to a lower level of 'being,' Plato was relying upon the implied predicative or qualitative background of Greek usage of 'being.'

It should be made clear that this is not a case of conceptual determinism but only an attempt to understand how conventions in language and conceptualization may differ and, by recognizing this divergence, to come to recognize somewhat better how Plato's metaphysics worked conceptually. Whatever may be said of Greek common language ontology, it is clear that Plato did operate with a notion of degrees of 'being' that relied upon an implied descriptive foundation, and it was for this reason that forms were centrally important to him. Forms were predicatively stable, and in a philosophical ontology influenced by a veridical or predicative background it is understandable why pride of place should be given to that which is predicately secure. 'True being' is an epithet that belongs to that which 'is what it is' without alteration, cessation, or relativity, and so on this ontology it belongs to forms as Plato understood them. Those entities that exhibit complete predicative stability have the strongest claim to metaphysical preeminence, and this entails, on Plato's analysis, that they be transcendent of this world, qualified as it is by instability and flux.

It is understandable, then, why Plato placed so much emphasis upon the cognitive surety of forms, as are his repeated attempts to articulate their qualitative sameness. His focus upon the absoluteness of a form and upon its self-sameness[25] are all part of an effort to establish an analysis of forms that would secure their ontological status. Similarly, Plato's tacit self-predicative interpretation of forms is an element in this general approach and a natural outgrowth of his ontology. The importance of self-predication in the case of forms is understandable only if one recognizes the overall context of the theory, that is, as a special development of an ontology requiring that metaphysically preeminent entities be describable by, or hold, the predicates they serve to define, for their ontological status depends on their genuinely exemplifying these qualities. The concept of degrees of reality depends upon an understanding of 'being' that keeps the qualitative nature of a thing in view, and in this sense Plato's metaphysics is 'essentialistic.' It is not dependent upon a claim that there are degrees of existence but is in fact an analysis of reality that conjoins certain value notions with a recognition of the logically different sorts of things that are to be found in our experience. While it is a way of analyzing the world that is different from modern conventions, it cannot be dismissed outright as fundamentally absurd; indeed, some have seen certain merits to this approach.[26] What is most important for our purposes is that this degree of reality metaphysics, with its bases in logic and epistemology, became normative for later Platonic theology, even if the conditions that occasioned its initial adoption might have ceased to obtain.[27]

While the concept of degrees of reality in Plato's dialogues is characteristically articulated in terms of this logical-epistemic criterion, the moral, aesthetic, and religious aspects are equally significant. Unlike the logical-epistemic criterion, this is a much more elusive element in Plato's thought, lacking the same degree of exact theoretical development, though it is no less significant for that. I should like, then, to review this other notion of the 'more real' in Plato, summarizing it with a view toward completing our appraisal of the grounds for degree-of-reality metaphysics.

Throughout the dialogues, the spectrum running from 'being' to 'non-being' is represented as having strongly evaluative overtones. As we have seen, the very concept of 'being' is based upon a conceptual backdrop that holds predicative or qualitative stability to be preferable to their opposites. This component of the theory is, however, expanded greatly in many passages, which indicates that Plato attached even stronger evaluative and religious associations to this position. There are, for example, contexts in which it is clear that what is less real is somehow debased: The discussion of art at *Republic* 599a–b suggests that the production of what is less real, of phantoms, is not a matter of serious concern. This is in keeping with Plato's general view that what is less real is of little worth. This tendency to depreciate lower levels of reality over against 'being' in a fairly radical fashion is not uncommon in Plato. In the cave allegory, the reoriented spectator discovers that his former objects of interest were just nonsense compared to more real things.[28]

Terminology of this sort is also related to the language of religious initiation and contemplation in which the doctrine of forms is frequently cast.[29] In the *Phaedo*, this type of thinking coalesces around the purgation of the body as a necessary condition to the apprehension of being. Only through purely intellective knowledge can the forms be known, and in this process the body is a hindrance, a source of confusion to the soul in its search for truth and intelligence. Contemplation of reality and 'being' is taken, then, to entail moral purgation as a necessary condition, so that wisdom amounts to purgation. At the same time, the objects of wisdom, the forms, are considered to be divine.[30] This approach is not confined to the very dualistic *Phaedo*. Much the same attitude toward forms in their contemplation can be found in the *Republic* and the *Phaedrus*. At *Republic* 490b, the true lover of knowledge is represented as striving after 'being' and coming into contact with it through his soul, in this case through a part of soul that is akin to forms. Only through such a relationship with 'being' is the inherent travail of his soul eased. Later (at 500cff.), the philosopher who is fixed upon forms is treated as one who would attempt to emulate the values they possess: "As he looks upon and contemplates things that are ordered and ever the same, that do no wrong to, and are not wronged by, each other, being all in a rational order, he imitates them and tries to become as like them as he can" (500c2–5).[31] Lest this assimilation to higher value seem uncertain in import, its religious character is ascertained at c9–d1, where the values of the order of 'being' are termed 'divine,' and the individual's approximation termed 'divinization' up to the degree permitted.[32] The discussion in Book 6 of the form of the good situated at the apex of the hierarchy of forms serves to establish it as the foundation of 'being' and value for both the intelligible and sensible worlds. Degrees of 'being' and value are thus conjoined for the good itself is a thing of inconceivable beauty, the source of knowledge and truth, and yet it surpasses them in beauty (509a).

We find in the *Phaedrus* (247cff.) the same theme of the divine status of forms and the religious value that accompanies contemplation of them. In this case it is said that real 'being' is the soul's true object and that reason alone can apprehend it. Most important, reason directed upon 'being' is that which nourishes the gods as well as souls (247d1–2). This contemplation is the life of the gods and of souls that are capable of following the gods. This, of course, implied that the status of gods is dependent upon, or at least related to, their contemplation of forms, a theme that we will see developed in the *Timaeus* account of the demiurge. Hence, the religious value of forms is very great indeed, since their significance is such that both gods and mortals contemplate their natures. 'Being' is therefore treated here as a concept of overwhelming significance in evaluative and theological terms. It is clear at 249c1–8 that this is no isolated theme. Plato, in a striking passage, maintains that a philosopher's soul may recover its wings and have vision of the perfect mysteries (i.e., 'being' and forms), a vision of nearness that makes gods divine: "Therefore, it is meet and right that the soul of the philosopher alone should recover her wings, for she, so far as may be, is ever near in memory to those things a god's nearness whereunto makes him truly god. Wherefore if a man makes right use of such means of remembrance, and ever approaches to the full vision of the perfect mysteries, he and he alone becomes truly perfect."[33] There is then no depreciating the theological significance of 'being,' and this is reiterated as the discussion continues, with mystery language being repeatedly used in reference to forms and their contemplation. Forms are referred to as "sacred objects" at 250a4, and as "honored and prized possessions" at b2, while our glimpse of beauty is termed "a blessed sight and vision" at 250b6–7. The same parallelism seen in the *Republic*[34] between the state of the beholder and the status of the beheld objects is then set out (250b–c). In this case, the elements of 'being' are said to be "whole and unblemished, tremorless and blessed apparitions" (250c2–3). Similarly, the discourse of Diotima reported in the *Symposium* (especially 210aff.), with its transformative ascent from physical to spiritual beauty, makes evident yet again the overwhelming evaluative force of the theory.

It should be noted that forms in the middle-period dialogues were objects of contemplation not only because they were standards for value predicates. This was true of any sort of predicate. The force of the theory rests on the fact that forms were the perfect instances of any property in question. To the extent that each form was the perfect paradigm of its respective quality, there was a certain absolute value attached to each form, derived from this logical and epistemic function. Contemplation of any form—that is, of the absolute instance of any quality, however trivial or debased—would always be the apperception of a perfect object. The logic of perfection is, in this sense, neutral with respect to the evaluative import of any form. But there was clearly much more to the nature of 'being' itself than this logical or epistemic analysis would suggest, as Plato's language of religious contemplation just reviewed indicates. Knit into the theory of forms in the *Phaedo*, *Republic*, *Phaedrus*, or *Symposium* is a tacit selectivity based upon a further value thesis: that 'being' is a realm populated by objects of intrinsic moral or aesthetic value. This is assumed, not argued, and how it could be presented with cogency is irrelevant for us. But it should be clear that a blessed vision of forms of disvalue was hardly what contemplation of true 'being' was meant to entail in these middle dialogues, for 'being' and value were so allied in Plato's hierarchical model as to be inseparable. To contemplate this deeper level of reality was, for Plato, to apperceive a realm evaluatively perfect in the strongest possible sense, whose absolute objects were instances of all true value and only true value.

The conflicted foundations of this hierarchical metaphysics were not lost on Plato; later theological Platonism seems, however, to have focused on a reading that principally recognized forms of moral and aesthetic value. For this reason we cannot pursue the matter in detail. But we do need to recognize the importance of this particular abridgment. A realist thesis that hypostatizes absolute objects on the basis of logical and epistemic criteria alone is very different from one that further restricts the scope of 'being' along valuational lines.[35] Plato certainly recognized this, although his own solution, if he had one, is obscure. The broadest statement of the logical-epistemic criterion is found at *Republic* 596a, 5–7: "We are accustomed to assuming one form in each case for the many particulars to which we give the same name." On this version there would be forms corresponding to all common names. That Plato ever rejected this position is not obvious.[36] The major locus of discussion is *Par-*

menides 130a–e, where Parmenides criticizes the youthful Socrates' theory. There is general agreement on mathematical forms[37] such as likeness and unlikeness, unity and plurality (130b). This would be in keeping with the list from *Theaetetus* 185aff., which included likeness and unlikeness, sameness and difference, unity and plurality, odd and even, and number in general, though 'being' and 'nonbeing' are included in that group as well. It is important to note that Parmenides and Socrates seem also to be agreed (130b) upon all the terms in Zeno's preceding argument, which had included motion and rest (129e). This suggests, then, that the consensus extends to these as well, which puts this discussion into accord with the inclusion of motion and rest among the "greatest kinds" at 251cff. of the *Sophist*.[38] Next we find that valuational forms are accepted as a class at 130b (rightness, beauty, goodness and "all such things"). It might be concluded therefore that these seem to be the sort of forms about which Plato was most convinced and which were the subject of general theoretical ratification by the Academy.

Discussion now turns to the sorts of forms about which there is some doubt for Socrates. The first group under question (130c1–4) are forms like man, fire, or water, that is, forms for living creatures and the four elements. These were not represented in the early discussion of the theory but are found in the later dialogues as Plato's interest in natural philosophy developed. *Philebus* (15a) discusses the species man and ox, and *Timaeus* (51b) includes all natural species within the intelligible living creature. The *Sophist* (266b) treats man, all other living creatures, and the natural elements as the results of a divine craftsman, which may suggest, should the cosmology of the *Timaeus* be interpolated, that this production would be based upon corresponding models which are forms. The evidence of the *Timaeus* alone (assuming that it is a late dialogue, as is the traditional view, and probably later than the *Parmenides, Sophist, Philebus* group[39]) suggests strongly that Plato did not abandon such forms of natural species, which feature so significantly in his later cosmological efforts.

There is also doubt expressed in regard to forms for hair, mud, dirt, and other objects deemed trivial and undignified (130c5–7). The objections of the young Socrates seem not to be based in this case on theoretical objections to forms of disvalue but rather on the apparent absurdity of such a postulation (d5). Parmenides, in his reply, seems to assume the same, since he suggests that Socrates' doubt is based upon a youthful concern with common opinion (e4). In favor of such forms, Socrates does, however, weight a theoretical claim: that what is true in one case (i.e., for other common predicates) should be true in all (d5–6). Resolution to these difficulties is given by Parmenides himself, who maintains that the youthful Socrates has not yet achieved the philosophical outlook of which he is capable, one that will presumably allow him to ignore public attitudes to follow a more universalizing theoretical path. This suggests that both forms of natural kinds and those of more trivial common objects have a warrant that is recognizable upon independent reflection, so they need not be rejected. Hence, the evidence of the *Parmenides* points in the direction of a fairly broad theory. Nonetheless, the *Parmenides* does not discuss some other types of forms that might be troublesome and that might also limit the theory's scope; these must be examined as well.

The consideration of natural kinds and elements suggests the problem of artifacts and their formal bases. While there may be doubts drawn from external evidence,[40] forms of artifacts are represented in the dialogues whenever the standard imagery of the craftsman and his model are employed. At *Cratylus* 389b1–d3, a shuttle is discussed, while *Republic* 596b3ff. is concerned with a bed; in both cases the imagery implies a corresponding form.[41] Similarly, forms that would clearly conflict with the valuational and religious aspects of 'being' seem to be countenanced at a variety of different places in the corpus. We find impiety at *Euthyphro* 5d2–5;[42] the unjust and the bad, along with their opposites, at *Republic* 476a4–7; injustice at *Theaetetus* 176e3–177a2 and at 186a8 the dishonorable and the bad, again with their opposites. These passages indicate recognition of forms of disvalue on a par with more evaluatively positive forms, and there seems to be no decisive rejection of them. The logical-epistemic aspect of the theory, which we saw articulated at *Republic* 596a5–7, is present throughout the dialogues, and if anything, Plato's later interests in cosmology and dialectic led to a continued and broadening appreciation of the range of such entities.

While final determination of Plato's own position on the question remains outside our scope, the basic issue is clearly significant for the study of later Platonic theology. If true 'being' is understood as a hypostatized realm inclusive of the perfect instances of all properties, then the notion of degrees of reality is fundamentally altered. 'Being' itself would simply reproduce in an absolute fashion the full scope and texture of 'becoming';[43] its constituent forms would be superior to the instances of 'becoming' because they would be everlastingly,[44] complete and unchanging self-exemplifications. There is still an evaluative component to this hierarchical ontology, with its preference for changeless stability, that would require defense, but its real force is based upon the logical and epistemic notions of necessity and certainty, concepts that are bound up with Plato's perspective on forms as a priori, self-predicative universals. Such a version of the theory suggests the possibility that contemplation of the forms could yield a terrible vision of supreme evil itself or of many individual vices or negative qualities in their absolute, hypostatized versions. True 'being' would be rich with many depravities, and the philosopher would indeed endure a tremulous vision of perduring evil in all its perfection, beyond the passing and derivative terrors of 'becoming.' Some might well see in this a moral *reductio* of realist metaphysics, rather in the way that the more horrendous versions of predestinarianism seem to be an affront to the insights of ethical monotheism. The position might be supported, however, by insisting that admission of these forms of disvalue provides the basis for a different account of the significance of such properties, one that is more adequate than the restricted thesis. These dark forms might be seen ultimately as resolvable into some deeper pattern within 'being' itself, one that has as a whole a positive value. Such an 'ultimate harmony' thesis would be available to a theological realist, but it would have to be argued in such a way as to blunt the enormity entailed by the admission that perfect forms of evil are fully real. Though speculative to say, it could be that this problem may have been behind the discussion in the Academy of a metaphysical dualism.[45] Two opposite principles, sources of value and disvalue beyond the level of forms, might provide a way to address the problem of the evaluatively mixed character of true 'being,' suggesting a more ultimate level into which the level of 'being' and its complexity could be resolved. However this may have been, later Platonic theology tended to feature the restricted version, pollarding forms of disvalue and establishing 'being' and value as correlative in the metaphysical hierarchy. The theological treatment of this model is thus very different from what would have been the case had the broader thesis been retained. It is to this question of the theological development of the degree-of-reality thesis that we will shortly turn.

2. Divine Ideas

Few notions are more important to the tradition of Platonic theology than the doctrine that forms are divine ideas or thoughts.[46] Few are more difficult to trace. We must perforce pay some attention to the problem of the origins of this concept in the present section, although our main interests remain analytical. I shall begin with some remarks on the theology of the *Timaeus* and then turn to a review of the early evidence for the thesis and to an examination of its function in Xenocrates, Plato's student in the academy, and in Antiochus of Ascalon, commonly viewed as the initiator of Middle Platonism.

If one adopts a realist ontology along the lines iterated in the middle-period dialogues, then several critical theological questions naturally emerge. These hinge on the causal efficacy of the forms and the degree of intentionality involved in their instantiation into 'becoming.' It is clear from the *Phaedo* that forms must be viewed as *aitiai*, as 'natural causes' necessary for the intelligible structure and pattern of their instances. But are they sufficient for the existence of these instances? Are other powers necessary as well, whose association with forms generates 'becoming'? And does that class of additional causal powers include an element of planning so that intentionality might explain that a given form is instantiated in time and space? Does this intentional or thinking power only select from among the forms for the production of 'becoming' or does its mental efficacy affect the character of the forms themselves? Has the shape of 'being,' the constituency of forms, been molded or selected by an intellect? These are the questions that seem to have imposed themselves upon Plato and other members of the Old Academy as they turned their attention to issues of cosmology and theology. They represent issues endemic to the developing trajectory of Platonic theology.

Plato and his associates certainly had as part of their agenda an effort to address what was by their time a set of problems established in pre-Socratic thought. Assuming the existence of self-instantiating and ontologically separate forms, several problems of pre-Socratic cosmology were thrown into a different relief, especially questions regarding the ultimate constituents of reality, the bases of causality, and the origins of the visible world. This cluster of related issues is discussed by Plato, especially in the *Timaeus* and *Laws X*. The introduction of the 'receptacle,' the principle of spatial extension and fluxation, indicates that the forms were not viewed as sufficient for the production of 'becoming.' The same is true of the 'demiurge,' a power of cosmological agency whose efficacy unites forms and receptacle in order to produce the world's soul, the world's body, the gods, indeed, all of the aspects of 'becoming.' The introduction of a divine agent, whose intervention is critical to the instantiation of forms, clearly raises the issue of the character of this relation of 'being' to divine intellect. Two basic approaches, with significantly different theological implications, seem to have been entertained by Platonists prior to the period of Plotinus: (1) forms are thoughts existing in the mind of the demiurgic intellect, the 'divine ideas' doctrine; and (2) forms are paradigms independent of the demiurgic intellect, what might be called 'paradigmatism' or 'exemplarism.'

Although long read into that dialogue, the *Timaeus* does not support the claim that the forms are the derivative thoughts of a divine mind. Quite the contrary: the *Timaeus* maintains that the forms are paradigms independent of and distinct from the divine intellect. There are obvious interpretive problems in reading the details of this 'likely story,'[47] but it seems certain that part of the point of the cosmology rests upon the distinction between the demiurge and his model. After an initial and strong statement of the two-world thesis (28aff.), attention is drawn to the question of the character of the model used by the 'maker and father of the universe.' The conclusion drawn (29a2–b1) is that because this demiurge is good—indeed, the 'best of causes'—he would assuredly look to the best model, one that is everlasting and stable. Regardless of whether Plato intended this to be a literal question of cosmogonic generation in time or not, the philosophical point seems clear: that power that acts as an efficient cosmological cause within the universe does so on the basis of an everlasting model, independent of itself. This sense of separation is written directly into the imagery, for it is *toward* (29a3) the everlasting model that the demiurge must look. This is then expanded at 29d7–30c1, the principal text on the demiurge and a probable source for the mistaken divine thoughts reading. It is reiterated that the demiurge is good, and so in consequence he must be free from any Olympian jealousy; thus, he desires to make his product as much as possible like himself (i.e., good). Hence, he looks to order, which he judges to be better than disorder, in his act of construction. It should be noted that this desire to make things like himself has been taken to mean that the demiurge himself is the model. That is surely a mistake. Timaeus's point follows from his preliminary argument that a good craftsman will look to a good model. A desire to produce the good leads the demiurge to resort to only a worthy model; the assumption is that choice of another model—that is, one that exhibits the confusion of flux—might be a possible option were it not for the character of the demiurge. There is no doubt, however, that the model and the demiurge are distinct; otherwise there would be no point to Timaeus's whole discussion.

There has been a tendency for modern readers to slip anachronistically into a theistic approach to these passages based in particular upon the notion of the craftsman's goodness. Since the maker desired to make things good like himself, then he might seem to be the real beneficent source of the order and goodness within 'becoming.' Hence, he might be identified with the paradigm. This exegetical inference is unwarranted. The notion of goodness involved is based on the craftsman image; it has a strong component of teleology and utility. The demiurge is good at his craft, which has as its goal cosmic production. The concepts of altruism and deontology are not implied. One must remember that Timaeus accounts for evil based upon some receptacle of disorder, upon the exigencies of necessity. This cannot be attributed to the craftsman, whose actions must be established as being pursuant to order. This seems to be the reason for the emphasis upon his character as a craftsman; for if reason is to overrule necessity, as the basic argument of the dialogue will hold (48a), then the demiurge must be the most effective agent possible. In saying this I do not wish to suggest that this imagery is quite antithetical to any suggestion of divine beneficence in cosmic production, only that the concept of goodness involved does not include this notion and so offers no foundation for identifying the demiurge, the beneficent craftsman of the world who makes it like unto himself, with the paradigm of order.

The significance of this separation of the principle of cosmic ordering and his paradigm becomes somewhat more perspicuous as Timaeus explains the nature of this model. At 30c1–31a1 we are told that it is an intelligible living creature, one that contains all intelligible living creatures and that serves as the demiurge's archetype for the living creatures of the visible world. Subsequently, Timaeus indicates that this is the unique and all-inclusive model of the demiurge (31a2–b3). None of this description implies that the model should be identified with the cosmic craftsman. By suggesting that the model is intelligible, Timaeus indicates that it is an objective entity that can be apprehended by the mind of the demiurge, but there is nothing to suggest that such rational apprehension is responsible for the model's existence.[48] Quite the contrary, for the whole force of the imagery establishes the perfection, completeness, and independence of this 'living creature,' an entity that exists in its own right. While an object of intellection for the demiurge, it is not dependent upon his thinking.

There seems no doubt that Plato used the 'intelligible living creature' as a cosmological image for the intelligible world of forms. There are problems, of course, with the membership in that realm in the *Timaeus* since the initial discussion of the range of intelligible creatures contained in this collective paradigm includes only those of living creatures: the heavenly gods (i.e., earth, planets, stars), birds, fish, and animals (39e).[49] But given the cosmogonic topic, this is not surprising and cannot detract from the main point, that the intelligibles collectively are used as an independent model by the power of cosmic production in ordering becoming. There is therefore no textual reason to identify model and maker in the *Timaeus*. As already noted, that the demiurge desired to make all things like himself (29e3) indicates only his intention to act as an agent who brings order and reason into chaos.[50] Thus, demiurge and paradigm are the active and passive aspects of the principle of order or reason, although they remain nonetheless distinct. Similarly, it is said at 36e5–37a2 that the world soul is the "best of things brought into

being by the best of things intelligible and everlasting."[51] This as-
signs the demiurge to the status of an intelligible and everlasting
being, that is, one that is not visible and not generated.[52] It does
not identify him with the paradigm. This may suggest grounds for
claiming that the demiurge is an intelligible entity and that it should
be one of those contained within the intelligible living creature if this
model is to be complete.[53] But this is an extrapolative argument, not
something to be found in the dialogue or supported by it. Finally,
the conclusion of the *Timaeus* (92c7) holds that the visible world has
been made as an image of the intelligible world,[54] that is, of the
forms. To press the relation of demiurge and paradigm further is
to collapse the structure of the *Timaeus* cosmology; there may be
cogent philosophical reasons to do so, but these are not considered
by Plato.

One further point should be borne in mind. There is hostility in
the dialogues to an interpretation of forms that construed them only
as mental concepts. *Parmenides* (132b) discusses this issue, and conceptualism is not endorsed. Yet the divine thoughts thesis would
require an argument in the *Timaeus* for what amounts to a theological conceptualism, with the intelligibles treated fundamentally as
divine thoughts, parasitic upon the mind of the 'father and maker' of
the cosmos. As I have suggested, the weight of exegetical evidence
is strongly against this reading. While the *Timaeus* is enigmatic, the
main lines of its philosophical argument can be discerned; conceptualism of any sort does not seem to have been among them. Language of volition or decision (29e, 30a, 41a) is never developed in the
Timaeus with respect to the demiurge and his thoughts, as one might
have expected on a theologically conceptualist reading. The divine
will is operative only in relation to production of the world soul,
the celestial gods, and the elements of 'becoming.' It is never applied
to the world of intelligible being. It is to be admitted, though, that
there is one passage in another dialogue that can be taken to suggest theological conceptualism. *Republic* (597bff.) can be construed
to suggest that the form of bed is produced by a divine craftsman.
But the context mitigates this evidence. Plato is concerned to depreciate the mimetic arts based upon the view that such art produces
objects that are twice removed from the truth. A painting of a bed
is once removed from a phenomenal bed and twice removed from

the intelligible bed, while the artist is similarly once removed from the bed maker and twice removed from the divine artificer. Symmetry for polemical purposes seems central there, not theology. In any case, there is no reason that this should be read into the later discussion of the *Timaeus*. The detailed discussion of the issue in the *Timaeus* supersedes and outweighs this passing reference.[55] If there is indeed any indication of ontological derivation of the forms in Plato, it is upon the form of the good at *Republic* 504e7–509c4. This justly famous passage cryptically suggests that the good, as the apex of the hierarchy forms, is beyond 'being' in dignity and power. Just as the sun provides the conditions for the perception and nourishment of visible things, so the form of the good furnishes the intelligibility and existence of the other forms. Whatever is to be made of this discussion, it is clear that the ontological dependence of forms, if countenanced by Plato, would appear to involve at least one special form, the good itself, and not a demiurgic intellect.[56]

As for subsuming the demiurge into the intelligible world, we must not forget that a principle of cosmic production shows up repeatedly in the middle and late dialogues. In the *Republic* there is brief mention of an artificer born of the senses and of the heavens (507c6, 530a6). In the *Sophist*, it is suggested that the coming to be of things from 'not being' is due to a divine artificer (265c3–5), and at *Statesman* 270a3–5, the world is described as guided by a divine power and given its life and immortality by a divine artificer (cf. 273b1). Plato evidently took this notion quite seriously, using it to address the question of the production of a lower ontological level from a higher one. Along the same lines, the *Philebus* (23c–30e) maintains that *nous* or intellect is the demiurge and cause of the mixture of limit and unlimit, a conjunction that produces 'becoming.' I would conclude, then, that Plato was working out in various ways an explanation for the order of the universe, based both upon the rational structure of the intelligible forms and upon a rational power of cosmic ordering, one that imparts formal patterns into a chaotic substratum. He seems to have recognized at *Sophist* 248cff. that this principle of intellection and cosmic causality had a place outside 'becoming' and among the everlasting intelligibles,[57] although that provides no basis for simply subsuming it into the class of forms so that its independence is compromised.

Evidence external to the *Timaeus* suggests, then, that Plato seriously entertained the notion of an independent cosmological agent separate from the forms but also closely related to them in the production of 'becoming.'[58] The exact details of this later theology are admittedly hard to specify, no doubt because Plato's explicit recognition of the intrinsic difficulties of this subject (*Timaeus* 28c) led him to address theological or cosmological issues in a limited fashion appropriate to the subject matter. Nonetheless, these late dialogues evince a repeated recognition of a demiurgic power that imposes order on disorder. Plato's interest seems to have been to consider a theological understanding of the order and beauty of the universe or, conversely, to explore a cosmological understanding of divinity. This effort culminated in *Laws X*, where the classic design argument for divinity was initiated. In view of the generation of the world soul by the demiurgic intellect in the *Timaeus*, no equation of the 'best soul' of *Laws X* with the demiurge of the *Timaeus* is possible, even if such a dubious, conjunctive approach to the reading of these texts were countenanced.[59] Yet if such a reading were allowed and if this conflation of world soul and demiurge were accepted as a serious position entertained by Plato in the later dialogues, there would still be no cogent basis for collapsing the paradigm and this world soul–demiurge. The cosmological thesis repeatedly discussed in the late dialogues remains clear: an independent pattern of reality is used to bring order to an opposite principle and to produce 'becoming' through some divine agency. There is no evidence to suggest that the paradigm's independence of the demiurgic intellect was abrogated. Let no one join together what Plato has put asunder.

The exemplarism of the *Timaeus* gives no credence, then, to the divine thoughts doctrine; indeed, it marks off an important alternative position. Two related points are at issue: the causal relation of intelligible 'being' to 'becoming' and the ultimate status of intellection. At a stroke the thesis of the *Timaeus* addresses both, establishing as central a power of cosmic production that is responsible for the patterns of order that obtain in 'becoming.' Alternative approaches were certainly available. Forms might have been treated as monadic powers each capable of direct structuring of disorder, an approach that will be later endorsed by Plotinus in a modified version. Some sort of theological conceptualism, subordinating the intelligible world to the divine intellect, would also have been possible. To these the exemplarism sketched in the *Timaeus* represents a significant alternative. We must remember that the structure and value of the known world rest upon the intelligible forms. Exemplarism is one way to vouchsafe their integrity, for the constituents of true 'being' can thereby never become "changeable things plastic to the will of a Governor; they are standards to which a Governor of the universe must conform." [60] If forms are made subordinate in nature or content to the demiurge and if the range of demiurgic production is allowed to include 'being' as well as 'becoming,' then the entire force of realist theology is altered. If the very character of 'being' is dependent upon the mental activity and volition of a divine mind, then there has been no small theological shift. If the mentalist or volitional aspect of this divine thoughts thesis were to be pressed,[61] and the divine mind licensed to conjure up whatever forms it might wish, then the very point of realist theology has been abrogated. 'Being' must be accorded a sufficiently independent status, external to the intellection and the imagination of the demiurge, else the whole structure of realist theology collapses into a volitional monarchianism. The force of realist theology, with its emphasis upon the immutable divine paradigms of order and value, once secured by exemplarism, would now be lost, and the focus of theology would shift to the divine mind, the intellective source of true 'being.' I mention this rather extreme sort of theological conceptualism only in order to suggest that the forms' relationship to the divine mind is clearly a central issue, since the whole import of realist theology rests in the balance. We shall see that there are less extreme ways to introduce a divine ideas interpretation of forms, ways that will not have these subversive implications. Nonetheless, the exemplarism of the *Timaeus* certainly represents one of the strongest positions by which to avoid the possibility of such conceptualist theology's arising.

If it was not position that was entertained by Plato in the dialogues, then when did the divine thoughts doctrine emerge? Of this we cannot be sure. Surprising as it may seem, the clearest and most explicit evidence for the doctrine comes from the first century A.D.[62] It was certainly much older, for there are traces to be found earlier on, although the reasons for its adoption remain obscure.

For our purposes it is the latter issue that is more important, but because it cannot otherwise be considered, we must look into some of the early doxographical evidence of this doctrine. It should be noted that it may well have been the case that there was no aboriginal version of the divine thoughts doctrine and that there were a number of routes taken at different times by various thinkers for distinct reasons. Upon inspecting the evidence one does not find a single theological position being handed down intact but rather a series of related positions often significantly different because of their surroundings and the conditions of their use. If we bear this possibility in mind as we reflect on this strange trajectory, we can avoid needless confusion.

There is good reason to suspect that treating the forms as divine thoughts goes back to the Old Academy. We can be certain that there was debate about conceptualist interpretations of the forms among Plato's associates; that much is indubitable, given the rejection of this view at *Parmenides* 132b. Alkimos, a Sicilian historian of the fourth century B.C., also gave evidence of this view when he reported that "each one of the forms is everlasting and a thought."[63] Whether there was any attempt, however, to locate these mental concepts fundamentally within the divine mind is uncertain. This bit of evidence from Alkimos is insufficient to draw that conclusion. To call a form a *noēma* need only be a way to contrast it, as an immaterial entity perceived by the intellect, with material objects.[64] Although it is probable that Alkimos meant that a form was primarily a mental concept, there is no reason to suppose that he meant a divine mind was doing this thinking. Again, because he reports that a form was considered to be everlasting does not require that it be located within an everlasting divine mind.[65] Alkimos may indeed be familiar with a divine thoughts doctrine; we cannot exclude that possibility, but neither must we infer that it is the only possible reading of this evidence. There was nonetheless ample conceptual warrant for associates of Plato to drift toward a theological conceptualism. After all, the figure of the cosmic craftsman in the *Timaeus* suggests that the demiurgic intellect thinks about the external paradigms,[66] thereby suggesting the possibility of a conceptual image of these paradigms within the demiurge's mind. It would be an easy and natural move for someone who took the conceptualist line discussed in the *Parmenides* to develop a divine thoughts position. It is possible that such reasoning prevailed among some members of the Old Academy, although most of the evidence which suggests this approach comes from much later and indicates a further desire for eclectical accommodation with the views of other schools, especially Stoicism.[67]

The best evidence of Old Academic origin for the divine thought doctrine is found in the fragments of Xenocrates, although again there is reason for caution. It is quite possible that Xenocrates did indeed develop some version of the divine thoughts thesis, but I do not think we can be certain that he did, nor can we assess with any cogency his argument for this view.[68] That it would fit into his metaphysics quite nicely is true enough. It seems clear from the evidence we have[69] that Xenocrates endorsed a dualistic system of two opposite principles, a monad and an indefinite dyad. This looks very much like the metaphysics attributed to Plato by Aristotle in *Metaphysics* I. 6.[70] I think we can discern both in this evidence from Aristotle and in what we know of Xenocrates a common concern to emphasize the success with which the principle of order, limit, or unity imposes itself on disorder and plurality. Xenocrates' dualism, like Plato's,[71] had a theological asymmetry to it, for it was the principle of order that was theologically primary. This fits the plot of the *Timaeus*; in Xenocrates we can see it in his description of the monad, which he called 'Zeus,' 'intellect,' and 'the supreme god.'[72] But in Xenocrates the dyadic principle may have been identified with the world soul, further underscoring her subordination to the monad[73] and suggesting in opposition to the *Timaeus* that the world soul itself was not derived from the conjunction of the principles of order and disorder.[74] But in view of Plutarch's discussion of the formation of soul in Xenocrates,[75] it is unlikely that Xenocrates simply identified the world soul and the dyad; even so, the secondary and subordinate character of the dyad is evident enough.

It was from these two principles that lower levels of reality were derived, and it appears that Xenocrates was quite thorough in articulating this derivation system.[76] For our purpose the key question is, where did the forms fit in? There is no ready answer. Xenocrates defined a form as "a paradigmatic cause of naturally constituted phenomena," also considering it to be "a separate and divine cause."[77] This indicates that he opted for a conception of forms that was weighted in favor of a fairly strict, valuational criterion. The definition was presumably meant to rule out forms of artifacts and unnatural perversions.[78] He also collapsed Plato's distinction between ideal and mathematical numbers, although the reason is obscure.[79] From these countable but ideal numbers a Pythagorean system of derivation ensued: lines, surfaces, solids, and so on, down to sensible and physical things. It is interesting to note in this context that Xenocrates defined soul as a "self-moving number,"[80] to which Aristotle replied that this was "much the most unreasonable thing said about it."[81] Plutarch suggested that Xenocrates was following in this the proportional construction of the world soul in the *Timaeus* (35a ff.), although as Plutarch notes, Plato never actually called the soul a number, only that soul was constructed according to a numerical formula.[82] Even so, what could Xenocrates have meant by this claim? I suspect that the key lies in the mental capacity of soul, its ability for intellective motion. Soul would therefore be a noetic principle, one that is somehow in motion in an intellective sense and thus capable of an intermediate role between the other idea-numbers and the types of physical motion that would emerge at lower levels.

From this meager evidence a number of different accounts of the intellect–ideas relation can be constructed, all of which are conjectural:

1. Assuming that the world soul was not identified with the indefinite dyad, then the idea-numbers, including the soul, would be located after the one and the indefinite dyad and before lines, surfaces, sensibles, and other entities that depend upon the idea-numbers. The intellective motion of soul would be a constitutive feature of the intelligible world, as in the *Sophist*, and it would help to explain both the general fact of active generation of lower levels and the specific generation of physical motion. Xenocrates might then have construed the relation of intellect to paradigm as occurring at this level after that of the one-dyad. Of course, the language of temporality and generation cannot be taken literally, as Xenocrates was aware, but only for the purpose of instruction or representation.[83] Thus construed, ideas or numbers would be secondary to the monad and dyad in the ontological hierarchy, the everlasting para-

digms of sensible things. Nowhere is it suggested that the inclusion of soul as an intellective number makes the forms dependent upon this intellection. As I have suggested, its presence, like that of the demiurge in the *Timaeus*, helps to suggest how the intelligible forms or idea-numbers are productive ontological causes. This seems to me the most plausible reconstruction of Xenocrates' views on the location of the ideas.

2. If one were to accept the association of the dyad and world soul, then the construal just presented would be modified so that the idea-numbers would then be located within this soul-dyad.[84] Forms would thus be the thoughts of the world-soul dyad. This seems very doubtful, not only because the conflation of dyad and world soul is questionable but especially because of the fundamental inclusion of the intelligibles within a negative principle of disorder. The indefinite dyad is, after all, the power of irrational and disorderly motion that requires intelligible structuring, not the seat of the intelligible world. This reading therefore makes no philosophical sense that I can discern; it is the product of doxography run amuck.

3. A very interesting final possibility remains, one that has been put forward by Dillon. This reading of the evidence has Xenocrates endorsing a divine thoughts doctrine that makes the idea-numbers the self-contemplative content of the monads intellect:

We recall that Xenocrates' supreme principle is an Intellect, and an Intellect necessarily thinks. One may suppose that he is engaged in self-contemplation, but even so, what are the contents of this self? It seems inevitable that what Xenocrates' Monad contemplates is the sum-total of the Idea-Numbers, which form the contents of his mind. The doctrine that the Ideas are in the mind of God may thus with great probability be attributed to Xenocrates. By the time of Antiochus, at any rate, it is established doctrine, and it was certainly not devised by the New Academy.[85]

The doxographical imperative here is clear enough and compelling; indeed, this position would make good sense conceptually. It might be possible to extend Dillon's argument by reflecting upon Aristotle's account of the monad and the dyad and their generation of numbers at *Metaphysics* I, 6(987b18–22). "Since the Forms were the causes of all other things, he thought their elements were the elements of all things. As matter, the great and small were principles;

as essential reality, the One; for from the great and small, by participation in the One, come the Numbers."[86]

This passage suggests that the primal Pythagorean numbers (one, two, three, and four) are not derived from the dyad in the usual way, through the imposition of limit by the monad. They would therefore be inherent somehow in the monad and derived directly from it. Xenocrates, as we have seen, made the monad explicitly an intellect and identified ideal with mathematical numbers. A further modification may have been his treating all of the idea-numbers as thoughts of this monadic intellect, thus developing the implied inherence of these primal principles in the monad. Whether this would have been seen as violating the monad's unity is unknown.

It is possible that Xenocrates did develop his views in this way, but I do not think we can make any certain judgment from the evidence. As I have indicated, while this last option has its attractions, I lean toward the first view, that he treated the idea-numbers together with the world soul at a separate level in his derivation theory below the monad and dyad. Even so, we cannot be sure what the relation between the world soul's intellection and the other idea-numbers was, although no subordination of these paradigmatic causes to such an intellect is evident, nor was it likely. As for the stronger divine thoughts doctrine represented by the third option, I can only confess an admiring agnosticism; this may have been what Xenocrates should have maintained, but we do not know that he did.

As the above citation from Dillon suggests, the trail is cold until we come to Antiochus of Ascalon, about 100 B.C. Before examining this later, Stoicizing Platonism, we need to reflect briefly on early Academic theology. While we have found no certain evidence of the adoption of the divine thoughts doctrine, this does not mean that the theological location or status of the forms was not discussed and a version of this thesis considered by some in the Academy. Many philosophical reasons for this line of discussion can be conjectured. As already noted, the inherent ambiguity of the demiurge figure, whose thinking about the external paradigms presumably generates internal thoughts as well, could have initiated it. There is also the significance of Aristotle. His discussions of metaphysical theology

when he was a member of the Academy and the subsequent impact of his thought after he left must be taken into account.[87] An
Academic such as Xenocrates may thus have developed a system
with a *nous*-monad that contemplated the forms as its ideas. This
might have been either a parallel development or a response to Aristotle's theology of a self-directed divine intellect and also a rebuttal
of sorts against criticisms of Plato's theory. As divine thoughts of
the *nous*-monad, forms would be efficient, cosmological causes and
their transcendent or 'separate' status vouchsafed by this theological treatment. But these reasons must remain conjectural. However,
two points remain noteworthy despite this limitation. The elements
of the intelligible world, whether forms or numbers, remained for
Xenocrates and Speusippus transcendent entities, so if the divine
thoughts doctrine was entertained within the Old Academy during this time, it would have been interpreted as underscoring the
existence of 'being' as a higher level of reality distinct from the
sensible cosmos. It also should be noted that even if the divine
thoughts thesis did emerge, it is unlikely to have been construed
along strongly conceptualist lines, which would have undercut the
independence of the forms or their paradigmatic function. The meager bits of evidence we do possess, such as Xenocrates' definition
of a form as a "paradigmatic cause" or Speusippus' description of
the decad as "a most complete paradigm for the productive god of
the cosmos," indicate exactly the opposite.[88] If the divine thoughts
thesis was considered in the Old Academy, paradigmatism would
thus have been a predominant feature.

We move on now to the origins of Middle Platonism, to Antiochus
of Ascalon and the restoration of Academic metaphysics in the wake
of the skeptical New Academy.[89] Here we begin to find evidence of
a divine ideas doctrine of a sort, but everything hangs upon the
philosophical content given to the formula. The principal problem
is the transcendence of the forms. Antiochus probably used some of
Plato's language, since it turns up in later authors generally thought
to have been influenced by him, especially Cicero.[90] For example, in
a passage from the *Posterior Academics*,[91] Cicero mentions the Platonic
'idea,' defining it as "everlastingly simple and uniform." While this
sounds conventionally Platonic, there are also numerous passages[92]
indicating that Cicero construed these 'ideas' on a Stoic model as

cognitive perceptions, thus entailing a conceptualist interpretation. Ideas would be psychological constructs, general concepts that the mind generates; they would not be accorded any ontological independence. They would, in consequence, not warrant a 'separate' or transcendent status. They might, however, be everlasting, since they are always being generated by percipient subjects. It seems likely that some such Stoicizing Platonism was endorsed by Antiochus, and his version of Platonic theology was similarly modified. At *Posterior Academics* 27–28 we find a rereading of the *Timaeus* that may in outline be that of Antiochus. The Stoic categorical notion of *qualitas* is used as a description for forms, which are treated as a collective force or *vis*. This force is inherent within the world, holding it together. It is described as a sentient and immutable being in which perfect reason inheres. This immanent mind is then identified with the world soul, with perfect wisdom, and with providence; it is termed *deus*. This theology thus conflates the demiurge with the world soul and makes this principle immanent within the cosmos. It would perforce be a rarefied material or a quasi-corporeal entity[93] and would lack any claim to ontological transcendence.

While we do not have a text from Antiochus that explicitly mentions the divine thoughts doctrine, it is likely that he held it. If the demiurge and world soul are conflated and identified with the Stoic *logos*, then the forms would probably be treated as the content of this immanent cosmic mind. Given the conceptualist treatment of forms already noted, it would seem that Antiochus adopted a type of theological conceptualism as well. The ideas would constitute *logoi spermatikoi*, the sum total of which would be the *logos*. They would be divine thoughts, the ideas of a providential cosmic mind, dependent upon this mind ontologically. Antiochus could be said, therefore, either to have adopted some version of the divine thoughts doctrine discussed in the Old Academy and to have given it a Stoic reading or else to have constructed it as part of his program of reasserting a metaphysical Platonism in a Stoic environment. Either way it has little of theological substance in common with the *Timaeus*.

A certain pattern in philosophical reflection often takes hold in a given period, one that provides the basis for theological development or variation. Good evidence for what were probably the prevailing conceptual conditions in the first century A.D. can be found in Seneca, *Epistulae* 65, and modern scholarship has drawn attention to this letter for this reason.[94] I should like, then, to look at this garbled scholastic representation of Platonism in order to catch a glimpse of the theological status of the forms. Some insight can be gained by examining this scholastic representation of causality, which is clearly intended to have cosmological and theological significance. The list of causes is given in the form of prepositional terms, a common practice which Theiler called the 'metaphysics of prepositions.'[95] Seneca is discussing Stoic and Aristotelian causal theory; he describes four Aristotelian types of causality, as well as a fifth type that he rather eccentrically states was added by Plato, in the following terms:[96]

1. "materia, sine qua nihil potest effici . . . ," "id ex quo."

2. "opifex," "artifex," "id a quo." Seneca's discussion suggests not only efficient causality and the agency of a craftsman, but the later context (7ff.) indicates that this sort of causality is meant to include the theological principle that the demiurge represents.

3. "formax," "id in quo," which Aristotle described as the "idos." This is the immanent form.

4. "propositum," the "causa propter quam," "id propter quod"; that is, final causality construed as the purposes or intentions of the causal agent.

5. "exemplar," 'idean,' "ad quod respiciens artifex id quod destinabat effecit," "id ad quod." This is a final cause construed as an archetype.

What is important about this scheme is the fact that it allows us to see what the conventional interpretation of Platonic theology was for an informed student of philosophy, since Seneca is probably following a philosophical handbook of some sort.[97] Its putative origins in the dialogues, especially the *Timaeus*, the division of causes in *Laws* X, etc., are outside the scope of our concern. What bears notice for our inquiry is the fact that the natural location of divinity in the scheme is in the category of *artifex*, that is, it is the demiurgic function that is construed as being the sort of causality that is fundamentally that of the divine. In addition, Seneca locates the *exemplar* within the divine mind, so it is clear that this must have been taken to be the standard interpretation of ideas: "God has these exemplars of all things within himself and the numbers and designs of all things which must be produced he embraces within his mind; he is full of these geometrical figures which Plato called ideas, immortal, unchanging and never wearing out." [98] The sort of Platonic theology sketched here is not the exemplarism of the *Timaeus* but rather the divine thoughts doctrine. While the forms lack their former independence from the demiurge, they have still a significance that calls for their specification in such a causal listing. They remain that to which this god refers, even if this is an act of introspection. This suggests that while treated as internal divine principles, they have not become purely conceptual products subject to change at the behest of the divine intellect. What we see here is an attempt to relate these two elements of Platonic theology, the ideas and the demiurge, and to subordinate the former to the latter without actually denying the cosmological importance of the ideas themselves.

Seneca is not, of course, to be taken as endorsing this piece of Platonic scholasticism that he records. It is very likely, as has been indicated, that he would have read this theology from an immanentist perspective similar to the approach of Antiochus. Nonetheless, his introduction of this material indicates the presence of a tradition of interpretation that conventionally located the ideas within the demiurge. Despite our lack of a completely clear-cut statement from a Platonist in the period, there are good grounds to conclude that the divine thoughts doctrine, if it was not actually a product of the Old Academy or of Antiochus, was at the least such a common view that it could be asserted without argument in a summary of Platonism in the first century A.D. Hence, some type of theological conceptualism must have developed to such a degree by the middle of that century that it had ceased to be controversial. There is no indication that this tradition had come to regard ideas as concepts in the divine mind that were intentionally mutable, so a paradigmatic understanding of their function was probably also normative.[99] However, given the pervasive Stoicism of the age, it is quite unlikely that such theology was systematically free from an immanentist understanding of the divine ideas.

Where does this doxographical review leave us? It seems first that we have no evidence that approaches certainty on the development of a divine thoughts doctrine in the Old Academy. But if it did emerge, it was almost surely a version that retained the exemplarist force of the *Timaeus* theology. Second, the evidence from the first century B.C. and early first century A.D. indicates that a theologically quite different doctrine was developed, probably by Antiochus and other early Middle Platonists influenced by Stoicism. While this position retained some exemplarist features, it constituted an immanentist understanding both of the forms and of divinity. By identifying forms with the Stoic *logoi spermatikoi*, which were themselves contained within the supreme *logos* or *nous*, the forms emerged as the intradeical thoughts of an immanent divine mind.[100] Explicit evidence of the view that forms are paradigmatic ideas in a transcendent divine mind does turn up in Philo Judaeus, although the position is unlikely to have been original with him.[101]

While these different approaches to Platonic theology can be dimly discerned through our meager evidence, they established important precedents for later Hellenic religious thought. Both conceptualism and examplarism will surface again, defining significant options in later Platonic theology against which early Neoplatonic theism will be framed. In order to understand those subsequent developments, we must now pursue the development of Hellenic monotheism among the Pythagoreans of the first centuries B.C. and A.D. Therein lie the immediate origins of philosophical monotheism.

3. The Emergence of Hellenic Monotheism

The monotheism of the classical tradition, "Hellenic monotheism," was a representation of divinity that evolved from ancient reflection upon an obscure unity behind the surface tale of cultic polytheism. It sought not to rend the august fabric of archaic polytheism but to resolve its complex tapestry of powers into a single, divine unity.[102] Its historical origins are lost to us, although some evidence for the effort to construct an ultimate ground of being and divinity surfaces in a loose cluster of Pythagoreans active in the first centuries B.C. and A.D. These have come to be known as Neopythagoreans, to distinguish their thought from the pre-Academic phase of Pythagoreanism.[103] While many of these later Hellenistic Pythagoreans continued to hold to the school's older doctrine of two opposite ultimate principles, there seems also to have been an alternative position initiated, one that resolved this dualism in a final divine unity.

The ancient dualistic theology out of which this new movement evolved is well attested. Fifth-century Pythagoreanism was based on two conflicting powers, Limit and Unlimited, or Odd and Even (*Metaphysics* I.5, 985b23ff.). As we have seen, this approach is evident in Plato's dialogues. The *Timaeus* contrasts reason in the guise of 'self living creature,' the eternal collection of paradigms, with necessity, the errant cause consisting of disorderly motion. The *Philebus* juxtaposes limit (*peras*), the principle of order, with the unlimited or formless (*apeiron*). Aristotle interprets Plato (*Metaphysics* I.6, 987a29ff.) as postulating a One and an indefinite dyad as ultimate principles. The former imposes order, form, or limit, onto 'the great-and-small,' that infinite opposite power that is understood to be a nonrational principle of limitlessness. This type of dualism seems to have occupied Plato's students in the Old Academy.[104] Speusippus appears to have held to a two-opposite principle theory, although with significant modifications. Denying that metaphysical causes are instances of the properties they produce, he held that the One and the indefinite dyad were categorically distinct from their respective derivative qualities such as 'being,' goodness, or evil. Aristotle's reprimand (*Metaphysics* XII.7, 1072b30,) makes evident that Speusippus's principles were, in Aristotelian terms, potentialities not actualities: "Those who suppose, as the Pythagoreans and Speusippus do, that supreme beauty and goodness are not present in the beginning, because the beginnings both of plants and of animals are causes, but beauty and completeness are in the effects of these, are wrong in their opinion." [105] The implication of this position for Speusippus's interpretation of the One is especially interesting, since it suggests that the One, as the cause of 'being,' is itself outside or distinct from 'being.' But unlike the Good of *Republic* 509b, it would not "exceed being in dignity and power"; it would be the seminal source of 'being' whose causal role makes it categorically distinct from its consequents. Proclus in his *Commentary on the Parmenides* represents Speusippus's view along this line in an apparent quotation:

This is also how Speusippus understands the situation [presenting his views as the doctrines of the ancients]. What does he say?

For they held that the One is higher than being and is the source of being; and they delivered it even from the status of a principle. For they held that, given the One, in itself, conceived as separated and alone without the other things, with no additional element, nothing else would come into existence. And so they introduced the Indefinite Dyad as the principle of beings.[106]

Exactly what Speusippus's own views were, or whether the 'ancients' he has in mind were Pythagoreans, is outside our purview here. Nonetheless, it does appear that he construed the One as distinct from the principles of order and 'being' that were consequent to it. We shall return to this question shortly. That he endorsed some sort of dualism seems certain, and in this respect he resembles the other prominent figure in the Old Academy, whose views we have already discussed, Xenocrates. A *nous*-monad was contrasted in his case [107] with the dyad, the everflowing or materiate power. This dualistic line in the speculative metaphysics of the Old Academy was conditioned by Pythagorean influences; this is clear from Aristotle's discussions in *Metaphysics* A and N. As a result, later Hellenistic Pythagoreans must have looked back to a tangled mass of fifth- and fourth-century Pythagorean and Academic sources, alike in their embedded cosmological dualism, however variant the details. It is against this backdrop that the emergence of an ultimate divine One among Neopythagoreans must be understood.

The usually meager record of historical evidence from this period is particularly sketchy on Neopythagoreanism. The evidence suggests a period of pseudepigraphical production from the third through the first centuries B.C., which followed upon the activities of better-attested fifth- or fourth-century figures like Philolaus or Archytas.[108] It is possible to discern in some of this pseudonymous Neopythagoreanism a monotheistic departure from the Old Pythagorean two-opposite principle theory, though it is difficult to date this development with any specificity. More troubling for our inquiry is the fact that a firm philosophical context is difficult to provide for this centrally significant thematic development, making it very hard to analyze the conceptual bases for this monotheistic revision.

Later Neoplatonists such as Syrianus report what seems to be a fairly extensive adoption within the Hellenistic Pythagorean tradition of a unitary first principle. For example, Syrianus reports that

Brotinos the Pythagorean[109] endorsed a One that was superior to intellect and 'being' in both power and eminence. This he identified with the good.[110] In the *peri archon* of Ps-Archytas, a work that has been dated to the middle or end of the fourth century B.C., we find a divine first principle that is a primary unity above both the monad and the dyad and above intellect.[111] Alexander Polyhistor, writing in Rome about 80 B.C., reports on a Pythagoreanism that endorsed a primary monad from which comes the indefinite dyad; together they are productive of the Pythagorean derivation series.[112] Sextus Empiricus also distinguishes an older tradition, which derived the numbers from the monad and dyad, from a newer school that endorsed their derivation from a single principle.[113] He relates that some held that the monad was the principle of all things; every thing participates in it, and it generates the indefinite dyad from itself.[114]

While dating of these developments can be only approximate,[115] it is clear that some sort of monotheistic Neopythagoreanism developed by the first centuries B.C. and A.D. against the background of an older, more traditional, dualistic school. Two conceptually distinct approaches to Neopythagorean theism can be discerned in the clotted mass of our sources, and these bear further reflection. First, there is a record of one position that held that the primal monad was a first principle that gave rise to a dyad. Subsequent generation was the result of the conjunction of these two powers. This is the version preserved by Alexander Polyhistor; his account is as follows: "The principle of all things is the Monad; from this Monad there comes into existence the Indefinite Dyad as matter for the Monad, which is cause. From the Monad and the Indefinite Dyad arise the numbers; from numbers, points; from these, lines; from these, plane figures; from plane figures, solids; from solid figures there arise sensible bodies." What is evident here is a modified Pythagorean derivation thesis, based upon an initial principle, that nevertheless continues to serve as a functional opposite to the dyad once that secondary principle has emerged from the monad. This means that the basic pattern of the earlier dualistic cosmology has not been changed subsequent to the critical shift to an ultimate unity. It also implies that the initial monad contains both the quality (i.e., matter, indefiniteness, etc.) that the dyad expresses in its emergent stage and the character that the monad manifests in its cosmological role (i.e., limit, rational order). Hence, the first principle might be said to be qualified by both sets of opposites. Not surprisingly, we find some fleeting references to the monad as being both male and female, or odd and even, or even matter.[116] The striking upshot of this position is that this ultimate is thus made directly into a compound of limit and unlimit, of order and disorder. It is difficult to say, given the state of our evidence, what the basis for this interesting innovation was.

The other position on the nature of the first principle in Neopythagoreanism postulated a supreme One superior to both opposites, the monad and dyad. This second approach is better attested and so more amenable to analysis. It was adopted by Eudorus of Alexander who was active in Rome about 60 B.C. and who is usually classed as a Neopythagorean. Here we find quite clearly a supreme One followed at a secondary level both by a second monad and the unlimited dyad. This supreme One is the causal foundation for all things, including both form and matter. The latter has thus ceased to be an independent principle. Simplicius, the late Neoplatonist commentator, records the following explanation of the *archai* by Eudorus:

It must be said that the Pythagoreans postulated on the highest level the One as a First Principle, and then on a secondary level two principles of existent things, the One and the nature opposed to this. And there are ranked below these all those things that are thought of as opposites, the good under the One, the bad under the nature opposed to it. For this reason these are not regarded as absolute first principles by this School; for if the one is the first principle of one set of opposites and the other of the other, then they cannot be common principles of both, as is the (supreme) One.[117]

According to Simplicius, Eudorus postulated a primal One, which is the causal foundation of a second one, the monad, and also of the unlimited dyad. All of reality is therefore derived, in an unspecified fashion, from this initial One. Rejected are the two opposite principles at the foundation of all reality, and in their stead is an ultimate unity beyond them. Corroborating evidence for this position, possibly in reference to Eudorus, is found in the *Commentary on the Metaphysics* of Syrianus (112, 14ff., Kroll): "Those men [sc. those who believe in the Ideas] used to say that, after the one principle [*archē*] of all things, which they liked to call the Good or the One above Being, there were two causal principles [*aitiai*] in the universe, the Monad and the Indefinite Dyad, and they used to assign these *aitiai* conformably to every level of being." [118]

It is critical to note that this position has several important implications. There is a final unity at the basis of reality, beyond the older Pythagorean primal opposites, and this power seems to transcend these opposites. It does not enter into any direct action in relation to them, as was the case in the other form of Neopythagoreanism just reviewed. Neither is there any suggestion that it contains or has the properties that emerge from it. The suspicion is that in moving toward such a unity beyond the opposites Eudorus or other Neopythagoreans recognized that they were pressing beyond the level of qualitative description. But given the paucity of evidence, we can only conjecture in regard to these earliest authors.

If we turn to Moderatus of Gades, a Neopythagorean active in the middle of the first century A.D., it is possible to discern with some increased clarity the structure of this Hellenic monotheism. As Dodds and Merlan [119] have shown, the doctrine depends upon a tradition of Pythagorean exegesis of the *Parmenides* hypostases prior to Moderatus, a tradition that was probably connected with Ps-Brotinos, Ps-Archytas, and Eudorus. The critical piece of evidence is a much-discussed passage from Simplicius that contains valuable information on Moderatus via Porphyry. Because of the passage's importance and complexity, I shall quote it at length in Merlan's translation:

It seems the first among the Greeks who had such an opinion concerning matter were the Pythagoreans and after them Plato, as indeed Moderatus tells us. For he, in accordance with the Pythagoreans, declares of the first One that it is above being and any entity; of the second One [that which truly is and is an intelligible] he says that it is the idea; and of the third One [that which is psychical] that it participates in the One and the ideas; of the last nature [which is that of the sensibles] derived from it that it does not even participate but rather receives its order as a reflection of the others, matter in them being a shadow cast by the primary non-being existing in quantity and having descended still further and being derived from it.

And in the second book of *Matter* Porphyry, citing from Moderatus, has also written that the Unitary Logos—as Plato somewhere says—intending to produce from himself the origin of beings, by self-privation left room to quantity, depriving it of all his ratios and ideas. He called this quantity, shapeless, undifferentiated, and formless, but receptacle of shape, form, differentiation, quality, etc.[120]

Merlan has argued that this system must have been Moderatus's own, rather than being an anachronistic projection upon his thought by Porphryry.[121] It seems reasonable to consider this general system to be that of Moderatus, though this is not crucial for us. But what is central is the character of this metaphysical derivation system, for we can clearly discern a pattern here of recursive principles, corresponding to levels of reality and dependent upon a unitary first principle. This primary One is established as "above-being and any entity," over against a second One, which is clearly identified as intelligible 'being.' From what we can discern of Ps-Brotinos, Ps-Archytas, and Eudorus, it is likely that this primary One is intended to be above intellect as well, though this cannot be stated with certainty.[122] It is, in any case, outside the standard descriptions of 'being,' for these apply properly to the second One. The term "The Unitary Logos" probably refers as well to the second One, which would amount to a principle equivalent to the living creature of the *Timaeus*, the unitary composite of the forms, combined with the demiurge. This identification of Logos with the second One is important, since it is the key to the interpretation of cosmic derivation. The third One (the psychical level) and the fourth level (the material) seem to be dependent upon the productive activity of the second principle. As lines 5ff., make clear, the unitary Logos produces lower levels of reality by a process of self-privation. The theory seems to be such that quantity is produced by the self-privation of the Logos, by the removal at this level of all "ratios (*logoi*) and forms." Both of these concepts seem, from the earlier description of the second One, to be applicable at that level. Hence, the unitary Logos, which is productive of lower levels in this direct process of self-abnegation, is the second One.[123]

The implications of this scheme for the history of Western philosophical theology are considerable. First of all, we have here a system of hierarchically arranged principles that are treated as causally related to their subordinates, and these correspond to levels of reality. Second, the first One is intended as a projection beyond the level of 'being' and intelligibility, so a realist ontological hierarchy is being employed in order to point to a fundamental source beyond perfect intelligibility or finite conceptual description. Third, and very important for our analysis, the active principle of intellection and production, indeed the central figure for such activity, is the second One or Logos. We should note that the description of the Logos (5ff.) makes reference to *Timaeus* 29e and 30c–d, specifically to the intentions of the demiurge in production. This use of volitional language indicates that the second One is being construed in the role of an intentional principle engaged in cosmic production. Finally, the character of this system is clearly monotheistic, since the principle of materiality is not viewed as preexistent and independent but rather as itself produced in the process of cosmic generation. Dualistic theology has been modified with this 'steretic' theory of production, of self-privation by the Logos, so that quantity and materiality arise through the internal activity of this principle alone. This principle is the foundation for the Ideas, the active basis for cosmic production, and the level of such intellection as is appropriate to that task. The Logos-demiurge is itself productive of the foundations of materiality, but it is not the first principle, for it is secondary to the first One, which transcends 'being.'

One can discern here the basic pattern, noted in Eudorus and some other Neopythagoreans:[124] a primary One as the foundation of a monad and a dyad; we are in a much better position with Moderatus to understand the conceptual significance of this doctrine. Above all, the metaphysics of Moderatus give us evidence of the development of a theory that reifies the primary principle of reality, locating it clearly above the forms and the demiurge; hence, this theology also begins to devalue active, intellective production by the first principle. The latter tendency, the 'demotion of the demiurge,' became central in subsequent realist theology, though we must postpone detailed analysis until we can examine a more extensive articulation of the position.

This hierarchical treatment of principles of unity, culminating in a One beyond 'being,' is a move of great, though subtle, significance for philosophical theology. Herein do we see the emergence of

Hellenic philosophical monotheism, with many of its characteristic features in view. There is, first of all, the apparent sense that earlier, more pluralistic ways of representing divine ultimacy are now falling away, the multiple conflicting powers of Olympian polytheism giving way to a philosophically articulating dualism and then being superseded by the recognition of a final unity behind all powers. But this is not some unity that is characterizable in terms of the opposites that derive from it. Rather, this ultimate unity begins to be thought of as transcending characterization: it is not male–female, or odd–even but beyond those sorts of specification. Its ultimacy is strangely betokened by its resistance to characterization, for it is beyond limit, beyond the intelligibles, beyond the opposites. It is essential that notice be taken that this Hellenic monotheism emerged out of such dualism and remains deeply conditioned by the conceptual circumstances of its initial departure. For negative theology became the token of Hellenic monotheism because of this transcendence of qualitative opposition in cosmology. The One was ultimate precisely because it could not be specified in terms of the primal pair of opposite qualities or any other subsequent predicates. Hellenic philosophical monotheism was thus fundamentally articulated in terms of apophatic theology and grounded in the degree-of-reality metaphysics that became a common property of both Middle Platonists and Neopythagoreans.

The Neopythagorean One of Eudorus or Moderatus was also a single principle: its ultimacy entailed its uniqueness, though that was not, as it were, the primary vector of this theology. What mattered most, it seems, was that the One was the primal source behind the manifest opposites, whose conflicting forces have, in their conjunction, generated the world we know. But it was thereby also unique: the inclusive character of the One suggested its exclusive status. That is a theological corollary that was evident but not central to the discussion. The resolution of the primal opposite powers was found in an ultimate unity that at once includes but transcends them. The articulation of this primordial unity was the real burden of this nascent Hellenic monotheism. Divine singularity and uniqueness were present but were arrived at not by excluding other putative claimants to ultimate divinity but by reaching the apex of a hierarchy of divine powers and finding that ultimate unity that was dimly present beyond this chain. For the Neopythagorean One was distinct from its consequents and indeed from their collective system; it could not be conjoined to them. As the inclusive origin of all, it was separate from all. It is in this sense that it was unique: unique in virtue of its ultimacy.

Two questions naturally emerge from this initial inspection of Hellenic monotheism within Neopythagoreanism: Why this rejection of dualism in favor of monotheism? Why this odd claim of the transcendency of being and characterization? To the former question there is no immediate answer. As in all cosmological arguments for monotheism, there is a tacit demand for a final answer to questions regarding the source of the primal opposites, or indeed of the cosmos as a whole. The principle of sufficient reason, the assumption that the existence of any event, state of affairs, quality, or thing must have some reason, has long been a tacit component of rational theology. Cosmological arguments for monotheism trade upon it by applying this principle to cosmology and treating the cosmos as a state of affairs demanding explanation. After all, Plato, in the ontology of the *Philebus* (26e–30e), recognizes a final unity beyond Limit and Limitlessness. Aristotle at *Metaphysics* XII, 1075b18ff. notes the following: "And those who suppose two principles must suppose another, a superior principle, and so must those who believe in the Forms; for why did things come to participate, or why do they participate, in the Forms?"[125] The tendency to assert a final causal principle as an explanation for the existence of the cosmos was clearly a recognized option. While cosmological dualism certainly qualifies as a plausible theory, nonetheless the countenancing of two powers invites their association with the class of explicanda. To assume a final principle may seem to satisfy that demand more succinctly. But to avoid a further regress of causal explanation, there is a compelling need to establish the unique nature or status of this first principle. It must effectively resist any assimilation to the class of explicanda; it must thoroughly exempt itself from these entities or states of affairs whose existence is explained in reference to it.

This demand brings us to the second question, which can be in part understood in this light. The remarkable distinctness of the One in this Neopythagorean monotheism may well be conditioned by the requirement that a first principle establish closure to this regress of explanation by its special nature.[126] It must stand apart from its consequents, whose existence it is invoked to explain. We may well see in this claim of the transcendence of 'being' the beginnings of a conceptual strategy to establish that special character for the first principle, setting it apart from all those whose existence it secures.

It is also the case, however, that in order to conclude this hierarchy of principles in a final unity, it was necessary to move beyond the level of the intelligibles, that is, beyond that perfect intelligibility that was associated with forms or numbers. Here is the root of theological paradoxicality: to establish closure to the cosmological regress entailed the postuation of a principle beyond perfect intelligible representation. Negative or apophatic theology is its immediate conceptual result. For the One of this Hellenic monotheism is perforce beyond the principle of intelligibility, beyond the monad. To represent the One, Neopythagoreans were forced to deny that it held any of the predicates appropriate to the second One, or monad. We can see none of this clearly in our sources, except the concrescence of monotheism and apophatic theology. It is in Plotinus that this case will be explicitly agreed; while among the Neopythagoreans we have only fragmentary grounds for conjunction. A full discussion of the conceptual foundations of apophatic theology must be postponed until we examine Plotinian theology.

While our evidence is constraining, it is possible to discern in Neopythagoreanism the emergence of philosophical monotheism within the Greco-Roman religious world. This Hellenic monotheism grew out of earlier forms of dualistic theology and explicitly postulated a final unity that included but transcended these opposites. Distinct from its consequents, the One stood alone as the ultimate and preeminent divine power. It was not to be identified with the cosmos or any of its parts, neither did it require any additional power for the production of the cosmos. From it both matter and intelligence emerged. As such it was not an active causal agent, an active intellect, or a personal deity. Such functions or attributes were eschewed and, with them, the sharp individuation they entail. For the One was certainly unique as the ultimate principle, but it seems not to have been imagined as a distinct person or a divine mind; numerical delineation under such concepts seems to have been avoided. Indeed, a program of proscription of most divine predicates was developed, although the full dimensions of this apophatic theology are difficult to determine. However, we can identify among Neopythagoreans a cluster of related theological themes, which begins to establish an identifiable conception of deity whose trajectory will lead to Plotinus. It is Plotinus who will construct the definitive statement of Hellenic philosophical monotheism for late antiquity.

4. The Demiurgic Theology of Plutarch

Contemporary philosophers of religion conventionally refer to "classical theism," by which is meant the most common conception of deity in Western philosophical theology.[127] Included are notions such as divine transcendence, eternality, omnipotence, and creative efficacy. This conceptual construct can be seen to develop with increasing clarity in late antiquity, due to the efforts of thinkers such as Augustine, Boethius, and John Philoponus. It was finalized by Jewish, Christian, and Islamic scholastics in the High Middle Ages. But classical theism was not classical, for it was never clearly and fully articulated in philosophical theology prior to the late third or fourth century A.D. Neither was it an indigenous product of the Greco-Roman tradition. Many of its prominent features, especially the concept of creation,[128] were the result of prolonged reflection on the Hebrew Bible, the New Testament, and ultimately the Koran by theologians schooled in Greco-Roman philosophy. It was then an intellectual alloy whose formula was subject to some modification over time.

In contrast, we find in Greco-Roman theology a distinctive monotheism developing within Neopythagoreanism, while in Middle Platonic theology the theological models that prevailed were variations upon the *Timaeus*. As we have seen, this was at best a "finite" or "qualified"[129] theism, in which the cosmogonic power of divinity was arrayed over against some primordial but disorderly force, recalcitrant to rational structure. However significant the active principle may have been, in this qualified theism divinity was always limited in some obscure fashion by the exigency of the receptacle. This is no monotheism; it is at best a dualistic theism. Its portrait of divinity was thus thematically tied to the presentation of this primal relation between the divine and its cosmological other. Yet throughout the history of philosophical theology, this limited theism has remained influential both for its own merits and for its representation of a cosmologically active deity, even when the constraints of an opposite, materiate principle had ceased to exercise any normative hold upon the theological imagination.

Plutarch of Chaeroneia provides an excellent example of the development of this finite theism within early Middle Platonic theology. Its central religious postulate was a demiurgic intellect. While Eudorus and Moderatus represent a more monotheistic version of Pythagorean–Platonic theology, Plutarch is closer to the *Timaeus*: admitting a latitudinal and hierarchical treatment of the notion of divinity but retaining a disorderly cosmic power in opposition to the divine demiurge. Plutarch's theology is based on the triadic scheme of the *Timaeus*: forms and demiurge are allied and contrasted with matter. Matter was held by him to be a principle of disorder and evil and was identified with an irrational aspect of the world soul.[130] While this was a two-opposite-principles type of cosmology, the theological focus rested upon the demiurgic intellect, which was clearly the primary divine principle, the seat of order and value. Plutarch's theology thus constitutes a clear-cut instance of "finite theism": an ultimate divine principal is limited in its efficacy by the need for a separate power whose nature is distinctly different and whose causal impact is contrary to that of the divine.[131] The basic structure of this theism can be discerned with some specificity by reading a theological system out of the extant tractates of the *Moralia*, though this may be somewhat hazardous. It should be noted that modern assessments are built upon a range of extant works, which, while considerable, do not include some of Plutarch's more technical philosophical treatises.[132]

It might be said that Plutarch establishes his transcendent divine intellect by a transferral of many of the attributes that had belonged in Plato's dialogues to forms. This move seems a polemically attractive one for a self-declared Platonist engaged in an anti-Stoic theological program, but it may well have been conditioned by an interest in theological economy. I suspect that for Plutarch both factors strongly influenced his approach to theology, resulting in a type of Platonic theology in which the forms are identified and subordinated to the demiurgic element, with a seeming rule of *communicatio idiomatum* applied to sanction the transferal of formal characteristics to the demiurge.

Plutarch's attitude toward true 'being' remains that of Plato's middle dialogues and can be seen in Ammonius' speech in *De E Apud Delphos*, 392e ff.: "What, then, really is Being? It is that which is eternal, without beginning and without end, to which no length of time brings change."[133] 'Being' is, therefore, firmly contrasted with temporality, change, and destruction, along the same lines as Plato's stricter interpretations of this contrast.[134] All temporal language must be excluded of 'being,' since all such language implies a context of alteration or relation, and so would be unfitting: "Wherefore it is irreverent in the case of that which is to say even that it was or shall be; for these are certain deviation, transitions, and alteration, belonging to that which by its nature has no permanence in Being."

Based on this analysis of 'being,' Plutarch then articulates the fundamental principle of his realist theology: the identification of 'being' and divinity. This important theme is accompanied by a series of related claims, most significantly the attribution of a general paradigmatic role to the deity as such so that it functions as a composite for the whole world of the forms. In addition, we should note that 'being' is also identified with the One, a statement that is closely joined to the analysis of being as fundamentally eternal. The passage reads as follows (393a–b):

But God is [if there be need to say so], and He exists for no fixed time, but for the everlasting ages which are immovable, timeless, and undeviating, in which there is no earlier nor later, no future nor past, no older nor younger; but He, being One, has with only one 'Now' completely filled 'For ever,' and only when Being is after His pattern is it in reality Being, not having been nor about to be, nor has it had a beginning nor is it destined to come to an end.

Before taking up the issue of unity, we should perhaps reiterate that the evidence of this passage indicates that Plutarch considered the supreme deity to be 'really real' and, further, that he accorded it as a whole a paradigmatic function with respect to 'becoming.' Both of these doctrines place Plutarch within the realist theological tradition, so questions naturally follow regarding the status, location, and role of the forms. It must be admitted that Plutarch is not extremely clear or specific on these issues, though, as noted, this may well be due to the state of our evidence.[135] Nonetheless, we can discern a general pattern in his thought on these problems.

Plutarch's treatment of the supreme deity as the paradigm of 'becoming' seems to rely upon two related doctrines: (a) that the forms are divine thoughts or ideas of God and thus are intradeical principles, and (b) that these ideas exhibit a fundamental unity so that they constitute an integrated model, which can function as the paradigm for cosmological production.[136] It might be said that the latter appears to be the more prominent doctrine for Plutarch and, as such, helps to give us his thought on this issue a strongly realist aspect. The tendency to equate the cosmic paradigm with the demiurge can, as we have indicated, have varying thematic results, but in Plutarch this development seems to enforce the view that the world of 'becoming' is dependent upon a fixed and stable foundation, one not subject to divine alteration. Besides treating forms as paradigms on some occasions in a way that clearly follows the *Timaeus* (e.g., *Platonicae Quaestiones* 1001eff.), Plutarch also treats forms as constituting a composite model, which is identified with the deity itself. An example of this approach is found at *De Sera* 550dff., where Plutarch himself is the speaker: "Consider first that God, as Plato says, offers himself to all as a pattern of every excellence, thus rendering human virtue, which is in some sort an assimilation to himself, accessible to all who can 'follow God.' Indeed this was the origin of the change whereby universal nature, disordered before, became a 'cosmos': it came to resemble after a fashion and participate in the form and excellence of God."

This passage indicates clearly that the forms are viewed by Plutarch as a composite paradigm and are to be identified as such with the deity. The Platonic language of participation and resemblance accentuates the exemplarist theme so that the identification here of paradigm with deity in no way detracts from this central function nor indicates that the formal principle is radically dependent for its nature or existence upon any activity of the deity. What we have, then, is a controlled identification of two elements from the *Timaeus* theology, such that the fundamental exemplarist function of the forms is retained while the transcendent character of both deity and form is enhanced by the alliance.

A natural outcome of this identification of deity and paradigm would be the treatment of forms as divine ideas or thoughts. In Plutarch's theology the doctrine takes on the overall meaning that it subsequently retained throughout the Middle Platonic tradition, indicating that the forms and demiurge are merged as the preeminent instance of transcendent divinity. For this reason, the earlier Stoicizing Platonists who held superficially similar doctrines should not be assimilated to Plutarch,[137] given their very different metaphysical assumptions. This intent is quite clear in the passage just quoted, as well as in *Platonicae Quaestiones* 1001cff., where Plutarch makes the transcendent Ideas doctrine explicit. Forms had a transcendent character and in this respect constituted intradeical ideas.[138] From this position it is easy to see why Plutarch could have treated deity itself as a composite of the forms and a paradigm in its own right, even though we lack any explicit philosophical articulation for this move. In any case, it is certain that for Plutarch the primary divine principle could be alternatively described either as the unified conjunction of forms, which serves as the real model for 'becoming,' or as an intellective principle, whose intellection is the divine ideas.

Plutarch's deity is, therefore, established along Platonist lines as that which is really real and distinct from 'becoming,' and also as a paradigmatic cause for this subordinate level of reality. We can find in Plutarch as well a number of further causal descriptions of the first principle that follow from its ontological status. In *De E Apud Delphos* (393b–c) this deity is treated as being the One, on the grounds that this follows from its position as true 'being': "But being must be the One, even as the One must be being." This is treated as a firm law so that divergence from unity entails deviation into 'non-being.' This description of deity as One seems to serve two functions in Plutarch. It certainly enforces further the realist aspect of the theology and connects the notion of degrees of reality with that of levels of unity. In addition, there is a strong two-opposite-principle[139] doctrine underlying Plutarch's treatment of unity, and this helps to motivate a causal interpretation for the deity as One. Generally, Plutarch tends to see the One in terms both of simplicity and purity.[140] These themes indicate that the One constitutes a polar opposite to the principle of matter and plurality, by which it is uniquely untainted. Here Plutarch is following more traditional

Pythagorean and Old Academic theology in, as his language indicates, *De Defectu Oraculorum* 428f–429a, for example, where the One and the indefinite dyad are clearly contrasted. Later, at 429b, the indeterminate principle becomes the foundation of the even; while the better principle, that of finitude and order, is the basis of oddness. It is clear, then, from Plutarch's account that the One is to be treated as a cosmologically fundamental element of reality, though, of course, its causal efficacy is coordinated with that of the dyad.

Plutarch's conception of divine causality seems thus to be a complex one, no doubt because of his traditionalist approach to earlier authorities and views. We might, for example, expect that the deity should be seen against the account of final causality from *Republic* 507ff., and Plutarch in fact utilizes this theme. We find sun imagery used to express the basic notion of a supreme object of yearning by the soul and all nature on many occasions, based on a composite rendering of themes from this dialogue, as well as the *Symposium*, *Phaedrus*, and *Metaphysics* Lambda.[141] But we find in addition a tendency in Plutarch to treat the deity as a demiurgic cause, which exercises efficient causal agency with respect to the lower levels of reality for which it is responsible. This element establishes Plutarch's theology as demiurgic, since it explicitly treats the first divine principle as an efficient causal agent. Such a notion entails that the deity be intellective, but this hardly is at issue, as the opening of *De Iside* (351d–e) makes clear, for, as far as Plutarch is concerned, *epistēmē*, *phronēsis*, and *sophia* are terms central, indeed necessary, to the meaning of divinity. Plutarch's description of these attributes entails that the deity be an intellective principle whose thought encompasses not only the formal principles of all reality but the contingencies of their instantiation in 'becoming.' Divine happiness, in fact, consists in knowing the course of events in this lower world: "I think also that a source of happiness in the eternal life, which is the lot of God, is that events which come to pass do not escape His prescience. But if His Knowledge and meditation on the nature of Existence should be taken away, then, to my mind, His immortality is not living, but a mere lapse of time."[142]

This is the initial step necessary to develop demiurgic theology: the deity must be viewed as not merely a self-oriented mind but one that has at least an epistemic interest in lower levels of reality. The second condition for a demiurgic theology is the extension of this claim to include active direction or fashioning of the constituents of 'becoming.' Once again it seems that Plutarch endorsed such a view; he frequently refers to the deity as the divine orderer of all things, in the context of elaborating a general doctrine of providence, *pronoia* (e.g., *De Iside*, 382b–c). In arguing against the Stoics—specifically their immanentist analyses of fate—Plutarch maintains that the transcendent deity exercises the role of a demiurgic craftsman (*De Facie*, 927b–d). So strong is Plutarch's approach that he maintains what amounts to a doctrine of 'special providence,' such that God brings about events that are not naturally conditioned to occur (*De Facie* 927b–d). A similar account of direct demiurgic ordering is found in *De Defectu* (435eff.), where the continued involvement of deity in the world is defended despite possible physicalist interpretations of oracles. All of this no doubt connects up not only with the *Timaeus* (48eff.) but also with *Laws* IV, 709b. What is important is not Plutarch's acceptance of such Platonic sentiments but his apparent systematic localization of demiurgic agency in the primary deity. In doing so, Plutarch is certainly extending the *Timaeus* doctrine: in addition to connecting up the demiurge with the forms and so presenting a unified principle of deity, he is also altering the sort of virtues and excellences that can be attributed to the demiurgic principle. For Plutarch, the deity can now be said to be lacking none of the virtues, for he is inclusive of all of the formal principles of excellence, especially virtues like justice and beneficence. As the unitive principle for being, order, and value, the deity's manifestation of excellence can no longer be restricted to the virtues of a craftsman, as in the *Timaeus*. It is now the case that the deity represents the summation of value, so his theological role is thereby revised; there are grounds for aesthetic and moral attributions of excellence to him, not just attributions of functional excellence restricted to his demiurgic role. Hence, when described as "good," the deity, for Plutarch, is not merely to be thought of as being an effective craftsman, nor only as the formal principle of disinterested value, but as a morally good, providential agent.[143] As Plutarch states in *De Defectu* (423d) with respect to deity: "For He, being consummately good, is lacking in none of the virtues, and least of all in those which concern justice and friendliness; for these are the fairest and are fitting for gods.

Nor is it in the nature of God to possess anything to no purpose or end. Therefore there exist other gods and other worlds outside, in relation with which He exercises the social virtues."

Plutarch's religious thought might be summarized then as a system of Platonic theology that includes a central depiction of deity as a demiurgic agent. There is, however, no evidence that this demiurgic element of divinity was treated as so fundamental that the divine ideas were actually subordinated in content and existence to the demiurge's intellection. Rather, we have here the alliance of two elements in Hellenic theology, joined for the purpose of defending divine transcendence and divine providence. What limited thematic subordination of ideas to divine mind can be found in Plutarch seems to be the resultant effect of this alliance and follows as a product of the imagery as well as of the need to give the theology a sense of unity and coherence. But one does not find in Plutarch an emphasis on the subordinate dependence of the ideas upon the demiurgic mind.

This conjunction of so many theological aspects in a single principle can be problematical, and it must be recognized that Plutarch's theology shows evidence of such tensions. In effect we have in this early demiurgic theology a hybrid construct, meant to answer questions of cosmology, ontology, and value theory; it was this complexity of purpose that was the source of many difficulties. Plutarch, as a theist who accepted a principle of disvalue, had less difficulty than he might have had as a stricter monotheist, but there were problems nonetheless. For example, why should the wholly real deity be engaged in the production of order in the lower world and engaged in this messy struggle with recalcitrant matter and a malevolent world soul, given its exalted ontological status? Why are its intrinsic value characteristics (e.g., goodness) construed as relational virtues (e.g., justice, friendliness, beneficence) that entail the existence of extradeical entities if they are indeed the essential and absolute perfections of this supreme deity? Problems of this sort can, of course, be multiplied to produce a range of theological paradoxes. It seems to be at this point in the Platonic tradition, with the developing coalescence of theological elements, that these issues began to be more acute, though the theistic dualism of Plutarch, with its coordinate principles of divinity and chaos, seems to have mitigated these endemic tensions. Even so we can see in Plutarch the developing resources that the tradition will use to address these difficulties, and we might conclude our analysis with a brief examination of these features.

The chief means by which early Middle Platonic philosophers diffused the tensions inherent within their accounts of the divine principle was to adopt a degree-of-divinity approach to theology. Put in this way, the notion seems a conscious device constructed to a specific end, but this would be a misrepresentation. It seems rather that the broad latitudinal attitude toward 'divinity' traditional in Hellenic religious thought was a resource to which Middle Platonic theologians could resort in their formal systematic constructs.[144] It might be said that the continued significance of the Homeric or Hesiodic pantheons motivated a broad cultural recognition of a hierarchical notion of divinity. Nonetheless, this is certainly not the same notion as a philosophical system of levels of divine principles corresponding to the scale of reality. Middle Platonists, as philosophical theologians, were engaged in a process of transference of certain general concepts and values from a religious or cultural context into a more philosophical one, where these religious views are replaced by more formal concepts that function analogously to their religious prototypes. And so we find in Middle Platonism a philosophical doctrine of degrees of divinity built upon more traditional Hellenic modes of religious reflection but by no means reducible to these. It was this hierarchical notion of divinity, correlated to the levels of reality, that served as the central theological image for Middle Platonism.

In general, degree-of-divinity theology presents the elements of divinity as located on a gradated hierarchy so that each aspect of that which is 'divine' is arranged at a different level of reality. The key to such a representation of divinity rests with the underlying degree-of-reality system of metaphysics itself. Above all, such a theology can neither attenuate this chain of divine principles so that they cease to be significantly related, nor connect these levels so that they appear to collapse into a single principle or be merely descriptive modes of one ultimate principle. Between these two extremes, degree-of-divinity systems of theology seems to have been an effective means by which ancient Platonists addressed their complex philosophical heritage and the multiple religious questions of their time. As a result we find a pronounced tendency for these theologies to gradate the divine characteristics so that some aspect, whether the ontological, the valuational, or the cosmological, is given primacy, with other features then subordinated. This avoids the admixture of attributes and functions that might have attended the development of a more integrated version of Platonic theology. For the moment we can only note in this sketchy way the importance of this theological feature; our continued analysis of Middle Platonism will clarify and substantiate its significance. Whether it actually solves any conceptual problems is another matter.

In Plutarch's case we can see some elements of this degree of divinity theology, though once again we must be careful in our assessment. Degrees of divinity, even in a fairly technical sense, is a notion that certainly could be traced to the *Timaeus* and the Old Academy, especially Xenocrates. For this reason, its existence in later authors like Plutarch may merely be evidence of a strong traditionalism. However, the retention of a certain theological theme, and in this case its growing centrality, is itself a conscious and selective process, so it is of significance to inquire into the conceptual basis for the continued utilization of a given idea. In the case of degree-of-divinity theology, it is neither mere conservatism nor simply an endemic feature of Hellenic religiosity but an instance of traditionalism put to a specific end in philosophical theology.

In Plutarch's theology, one finds a hierarchical structure that has at its apex the divine mind containing the ideas. These constitute an intradeical pattern for the order and structure of 'becoming'; that is, they are the divine forms in a transcendent mode unified with the demiurge.[145] But these ideas can also be found as a subordinate divine aspect at a lower level of reality, for they constitute the inherent principles of order within 'becoming.' As Plutarch's discussion at *De Iside* 373a–b indicates, the forms are the order that inheres in matter, and this is an aspect distinct from and subordinate to the transcendent forms, since the immanent form is subject to eventual dissolution. These immanent forms are no doubt meant by Plutarch to provide a basis of agreement with Stoicism, especially its *logoi spermatikoi* doctrine, and with the theory of forms as understood by some earlier Middle Platonists such as Antiochus. We cannot, however, neglect the fact that this provides a rudimentary foundation for a degree-of-divinity system, since the immanent aspects of the forms are manifestations of order and divinity at the level of 'becoming.'

This hierarchical approach to theology and its important results may also be discerned dimly in a very difficult passage from *De Genio Socratis* (591b) to which both Krämer and Dillon have drawn attention.[146] The passage comes from a context in which daemonic revelations regarding the character of the underworld, the structure of reality, and the types of souls, are being presented. The key section reads as follows: "Four principles there are of all things: the first is of life, the second of motion, the third of birth, and the last of decay; the first is linked to the second by Unity at the invisible, the second to the third by Mind at the sun, and the third to the fourth by Nature at the moon." The four principles of all things are life, motion, birth, and decay. Life is linked to motion by the monad, motion to birth by mind, and birth to decay by nature. The doctrine and its presentation are very obscure. Dillon and Krämer both interpret the scheme as implying a hierarchy of principles, one that may have been derived from Neopythagoreanism. This would involve a primary monad that, though not said to be a mind, would presumably include that quality, as distinct from the second mind, which might be a demiurgic mind. Nature, perhaps equivalent to some aspects of soul, completes the progression. Now, it seems to me that we must be very cautious here in interpreting this material, since it does not appear to have been adopted significantly into the general structure of Plutarch's theology. While one can get some sense of a subordination of metaphysical principles and their functions, it is difficult to discern with exactitude their nature or valence. Above all, it should be said that, while we can discern a suggestion of a system similar perhaps to Moderatus and Numenius,[147] there is no real explicit indication that the scheme includes the location of the demiurge in the second rank. While this passage provides witness to degree-of-divinity theology in Plutarch, it does not seem sufficient to conclude that Plutarch went so far as to endorse a system such as that of Moderatus, where the demiurgic intellect was displaced from primacy in a forced migration to a secondary status. Such a concerted effort to establish the direct cosmological function

of divinity at a separate and lower level of reality will loom large, as
we shall see, in the Platonisms of the second century.

5. Early Platonic Theism

I might perhaps bring this discussion of early Platonic theism
and its antecedents to a close with a few summary observations.
In Plutarch we have seen the development of one type of Platonic
theism, founded upon degree of reality metaphysics. His theology
represents a distinct approach to the triad of elements from the
Timaeus: forms, demiurge, and space or matter. In particular it asserts a coalescence of the demiurgic intellect and the world of forms.
This acceptance of a *nous* theology and its understanding of forms
as divine thoughts may have been the result of a desire to bring
greater conceptual economy to the *Timaeus*, whose theology seems
to have dominated the religious thought of Platonists in the first
century A.D. But it was as well a piece of a classical transcendentalism: in Plutarch, a restoration of the ancient Academy's separation
of 'being' and divinity from 'becoming.' While Aristotelian resonance is to be heard, still the active cosmological role of this divine
nous has considerable prominence in early Middle Platonism. This
can be seen, once again, as an element endemic to theology in the
Timaeus tradition. This demiurgic theme at once set the deity at some
distance from the world and yet asserted the continued immediacy of its directing presence. Intellect is thus everywhere through
its knowledge and causally efficacious in its direction of a cosmos
distinct from itself.

In this early theism new internal problems began to arise, and
novel strategies soon evolved to meet these as yet largely inchoate dilemmas. Chief among these was the thematic association of
being and divinity. In Plutarch the intelligible world had become
wholly identified with divinity. Structural tensions were inevitable,
derived from the requirement that divinity exhibit characteristics
that would warrant its inclusion among the forms (e.g., immutability, perfection, everlastingness, etc.). It has been claimed that this
identification of 'being' and divinity, signaled by the divine thoughts
doctrine, had very widespread and quite negative implications in
Western philosophical theology,[148] giving rise to a static model of

divinity. We must be very cautious, however, in assessing this connection of 'being' to divinity; the details are as yet incomplete. There is after all a precedent against a uniformly static understanding of 'being' as is indicated by the inclusion of motion among the primary realities at *Sophist* 250aff. While true 'being' in the *Republic* or the 'living creature' of the *Timaeus* might be understood to be static in the sense that in each case paradigmatic entities were required to be qualitatively stable and definable, it is not the case that this entailed that forms include only those that could be construed as immutable and impassible. Those whose definition or *logos* included motion would exemplify this aspect unceasingly and inalterably; indeed, they must do so. In fact, later Platonism was concerned, as we shall see, to work out both the motive character of 'being' and the nature of its productive activity. To label ancient Platonic theology as static because of its identification of 'being' and divinity is to miss the point of that relation and to misrepresent the intelligible world.

While the case for the inherently static character of Platonic theology is therefore dubious, there are nonetheless elements of tension within Middle Platonic theology that can be recognized in an early representative such as Plutarch. It is not so much a tension between two theological poles or aspects within the deity, active and passive, as an endemic complexity of purpose. The deity of Plutarch was an answer of sorts to several different questions. It was a finite theism postulated to multiple ends. By combining most of the disparate elements of the *Timaeus* theology, its deity was a compound of theoretical entities that were not yet wholly resolvable into a completely coherent theory. This became the chief desideratum of later Platonic theology and beyond into medieval scholasticism.

Within the later scope of the present study it is this notion of degrees of divinity, grafted upon a hierarchical conception of reality, that will serve as a key mechanism for sorting out these divergent divine functions. But in the early Middle Platonic theism of Plutarch these questions had not yet assumed centrality, for its focus seems mainly to have been upon the fundamental articulation of divine transcendence. It is to this end that the association of 'being' and divinity, as well as the divine thoughts doctrine, seems directed. Such demiurgic theology appears to have been the dominant model from what we can discern through the haze of history. The mere accident of preservation may well have distorted our understanding. But it was the demiurgic intellect that was of theological primacy in early Middle Platonism. Beyond its implication for the subsequent history of theism as such, this demiurgic model had aspects that were especially important for Platonic theology. With divine intellection thus paramount, the status and independence of forms was called into question. One possible result was the denigration of 'being' itself, now assigned to a subordinate and instrumental role in cosmic generation. The very nature of true reality might thus be a product of the cosmogonic deity, dependent upon the intentions of the demiurge. The intellection of the deity would become the central concept in theology, and so the design of the demiurge, unfettered by external constraints, would become the core principle of reality. But this is to overstate the problem historically. Plutarch certainly avoids instrumentalism in his theology, demiurgic though that may be. Neither does he emphasize the volitional character of his god; his adoption of demiurgic theology and the divine thoughts doctrine was clearly based upon other concerns. We have not seen then a direct effort to deploy this demiurgic concept of deity in a way that is depreciative of realist theology. Nonetheless, these conceptual possibilities remained within the structure of this early theism; they cannot be ignored conceptually nor, indeed, were they neglected historically, especially in medieval nominalism. I propose, therefore, to follow the subsequent development of Middle Platonic theology and to examine those systems that seem to have been constructed both to avoid some of the problems of internal coherence that were latent in earlier demiurgic theology and to help strengthen its realist foundations.

CHAPTER TWO

The Demotion of the Demiurge

The study of the history of ideas is always difficult, more so when the subject of inquiry is far removed in time and conceptual space. If want of evidence sufficient to reconstruct a philosophical context is added besides, then such history is a hazardous business indeed. This is the case with the Middle Platonists of the second century A.D., figures whose intrinsic importance is much compounded by their significance in the historical development of philosophical theology. While the outline of their thought and their doxographical pedigrees are generally available to us, their philosophical motivations largely are not; hence, the risk involved in thinking through their metaphysics, in reconstructing the theoretic force behind the appearance of dogma. All this we must allow, although I think the project is worth its danger because of the abiding significance of later Middle Platonism, crucial as it was to the fabric of ancient theism, Hellenic and Christian. Hence, we must proceed in a spirit of caution, though with an admission of conjecture.

Demiurgic theology is one conceptual alternative for a Platonist, one that was widely adopted in the first century A.D. No doubt such theism seemed a natural development of the less centralized model of the *Timaeus*, and no doubt its thematic clarity seemed conceptually more economical. Doubtless, the conjunction of demiurge and forms was as well a polemical buttress, enhancing the transcendence of divinity against pantheistic criticism. These are the decided advantages of demiurgic theism, and they bespeak both the attractions of such theology in the period of its initial adoption and its continued appeal in subsequent ages. We shall now examine some later types of Platonic theism, theologies that seem to have been revised to mitigate tensions inherent in early Middle Platonism. I propose concentrating attention upon one salient feature of later Middle Platonism, the demotion of the demiurge. What is striking about many of the theologies of this period is their efforts to re-define the nature of the divine intellect, paring off features initially integral to the deity in earlier Platonic theism. This is especially true of the active cosmological agency of the first principle, immediately engaged in providential ordering of the cosmos and directed toward levels of reality outside itself. This reconstruction of *nous* theology required its authors to consider anew the character of divinity in light of their commitment to degree of reality metaphysics. Promi-nence was thereby given to a more modalistic understanding of theism; we shall find the notion of hypostatic levels of divinity be-ginning to be widely adopted as an important theme. Together with these changes, perhaps behind them, was a modified representa-tion of the divine thoughts doctrine and thus a critical alteration in the relation of divinity and 'being.'

These developments are the main story line of this chapter. Of course, not all Platonists in the second century joined in demoting the demiurge; some retained the earlier model.[1] The most influential schools seem, however, to have been involved, and it is the theo-logical character of their systems that is central to my thesis. Since we are approaching the period of Plotinus, there is an inevitable tendency to think about later Middle Platonism from the perspec-tive of his metaphysics. While this is to be resisted to some extent, on the general principle that the thought of any figure or school should be evaluated on its own merits, still we should welcome the help. The very rich Plotinian corpus gives us an invaluable basis for thinking about the conceptual problems that motivated these earlier Platonists. This is, to be sure, a retrojective appraisal, one that might be avoided were our sources on Middle Platonism fuller; under the circumstances that prevail, it seems an anachronistical misdemeanor.

1. Numenius and the Degrees of Divinity

The greatest figure of the Neopythagorean tradition[2] was Numenius of Apamea, and it is to the thought of this second-century figure that we shall now turn in order to clarify the implications of theistic Neopythagoreanism for realist theology. Ancient opinion of the significance of Numenius as a first-order thinker is demonstrated both by the fact that Plotinus was charged with plagiarizing his ideas (Porphyry *Vita Plotini* 17) and by Longinus's treatment of Numenius[3] as a central figure in the Pythagorean school. It is worth noting that Longinus saw the work of this group as lacking the precision or accuracy of Plotinus.[4] On the basis of our evidence this seems a fair assessment. My chief interest is not to reconstruct his thought as a whole but to examine the nature of his contribution to the development of realist theology antecedent to Plotinus.[5] The importance of Numenian theology for the realist tradition can be stated directly enough: Numenius provides us with a clear-cut theology that features the demotion of the demiurge and also provides us with a sufficiently detailed articulation of that view so that we can understand its implications. A good deal of the significance of Numenius may be due to the contingency of historical preservation, and if our sources were more complete, our opinions might be modified. This need not, however, be a concern of the present inquiry; the fact is that Numenius is one of our best sources for Neopythagorean theology, and from his thought we can discern some of its chief concerns and the means by which they were addressed.

Numenian theology is characterized chiefly by a triadic system of divine principles related by a system of derivation and corresponding to a scale of degrees of reality. These formal features it shares with the system of Moderatus already considered, so it is likely that this triadic system marked off at least one point commonly agreed upon by a subtradition among the rather diffuse Neopythagorean movement.[6] The details are somewhat different from Moderatus, though the major feature of a subordinated demiurge remains similar. This can all be seen directly in Fragment 11:[7]

The first god, existing in himself, is simple and since he associates only with himself he can never be divisible. The second and third gods in fact are one;

but by coming together with matter, the dyad, he gives it unity, though he is divided by it, for matter has a nature prone to desire and is in flux. Since he is not directed toward the intelligible [that is to say, directed toward himself] because he is looking toward matter, he is preoccupied with it and forgets himself. He is fixed upon the sensible and tends to it, and yet draws it up to his own nature because of his yearning toward matter.

The basic features of the system are (a) a first god, who is simple, divisible, and self-directed, and (b) a second god, who is initially unified but who divides in the process of coming into contact with preexisting matter[8] and results in (c) a third god, equivalent to the rational world soul. The first god's description is fairly clear: he is primarily a principle of self-intellection that exhibits complete unity and stability, the latter conceptions being expected within Platonic–Pythagorean metaphysics. There is no question that the systematic intent of this theology is to distinguish quite sharply between the principle that actively exercises the function of cosmic production and the ultimate first principle of the system. As Fragment 12 states succinctly: the first is not an active and productive demiurge, but rather the first god must be considered the father of the demiurgic god. This theme is then reiterated, with the first god, the king, treated as a quiescent principle free from extrinsically directed activity; it is the second demiurgic god that is the ruling principle of lower orders, whose intellectual power descends into lower levels of reality to bring about order, structure, and life. This distinction between the respective roles of these two deities is also evident in Fragment 13,[9] where the first god is compared to a farmer, while the second is treated as the actual planter of seeds. Similarly, it is the demiurgic second principle that is described in a passage of extensive imagery in Fragment 18 as a helmsman. Here, as in Fragment 13, the demiurge is treated as gazing upon the first god, which is seen as being equivalent to the forms, the object of his contemplation in his steering of matter into harmony.[10]

From these fragmentary reports, we can begin to construct a reasonably clear picture of Numenian theology. As the evidence just reviewed indicates, this is a system that certainly intended to displace the demiurgic function from the first level of divinity, and in doing so it reserved a more quiescent and self-contemplative condition for this primordial principle. As we have seen, this demotion of the demiurge is in keeping with tendencies within Neopythagorean theology such as Moderatus, although there are important differences of detail. In order to clarify the specifics further and to come to a better understanding of its theoretical bases, we might look at a further selection of passages.

One central feature of Numenius's first principle is its activity of intellection. Does transcendence of 'being' necessarily entail transcendence of all intellection or only those sorts that are directed outside the primal principle? It is difficult to conclude with certainty regarding the doctrinal positions or intentions of earlier figures like Eudorus or Moderatus.[11] But the situation in Numenius, while far from clear in argumentative detail, is at least determinable. For Numenius, the first principle is a *nous*; it engages in intellection, though this is a sort of self-focused contemplation that is different from that of the second principle. The latter, given its specific function, must engage in intellection that is intentionally directed both toward the first principle and toward the lower elements to which it gives order. As we have seen in Fragment 12, the second intellect has therefore a certain extrinsic direction toward what is above and below itself in the hierarchy of 'being.'

This description of both the first and second deities as intellects helps to explain one puzzle in the evidential record on Numenius, the description of his first principle as a demiurge by Proclus: "Numenius proclaims three gods; he calls the first 'father,' the second 'maker,' the third 'product.' For the cosmos is according to him the third god. So according to him the demiurge is double, being both the first and the second god, and the third is that which has been made."[12] This version of the theology is certainly different from that found in other fragments, where the division of an initially united principle applies to the second and third gods, not to the first and second. Despite this apparent variation, it is easy to see why one might consider the 'father' in this theology to be demiurgic too in the sense that it exhibits an intellective character. This, however, neglects the distinction between the type of intellection manifested by the first god and that exercised by the second, and it is not surprising that Proclus, from his later perspective, might have assimilated both of these into one intellective principle of only variant aspects. Nonetheless, Numenius does seem to have distinguished between the nature of intellection in these two deities rather carefully, as can be seen in Fragment 15:

Such are the lives of the first and second gods. It is evident that the first god is at rest, while the second on the contrary is in motion; the first is concerned with the intelligibles, while the second is concerned with both the intelligibles and the sensibles. . . . I maintain that in place of the motion inherent in the second, the stability inherent in the first is an innate motion, from which proceed the order of cosmos and its everlasting fixity, and a safekeeping is poured over all things.[13]

Here again we find the first god treated as being at rest and concerned with the intelligible realm, while the second is in motion and directed toward both the intelligible and the sensible. In this case, however, the primary rest of the first god is understood not as being a lack of motion, which might have suggested deficiency, but as an innate form of motion. The static condition of the primary god is, therefore, a form of inherent motion, presumably one that is not resultant from anything else but constitutive of its own nature or based upon this nature. While we cannot, once more, be absolutely certain of all the details, the pattern that can be found here is unmistakable. The proper activity of the first god is a connatural activity, one that is equivalent to rest, in that it entails no diminution or dispersal of capacity. In an intellective principle, it would be reasonable to say that this is a type of self-intellection, pure contemplation. It is possible, though admittedly not demonstrable, that this fragment on the aspects of divine 'life' was meant to clarify the nature of a first principle that is located beyond demiurgic activity, beyond what we have seen to be the natural locus of 'divinity' in the conceptual taxonomy of many earlier figures.

While the 'demotion of the demiurge' is therefore a central element in Numenian theology, the intellective status of the first god is retained by distinguishing the character of its intellection from that of the second, which is properly called demiurgic since its mental activity includes the extrinsic world of 'becoming.' This raises further questions about the implications of this new type of realist theology: How is true 'being' treated in this theology? What is the location of the forms or numbers? We might attempt to clarify some of these issues, though it must be admitted that the solutions available are not satisfactory in all respects.

It might be said, first of all, that Numenius's theology seems to treat the first god as both an intellective principle and as 'being' itself. Both themes are connected in Fragment 17 with the denial of demiurgic activity to the primary god, a form of activity that by its nature is not wholly related to the intelligible world. Hence, the higher self-directed intellection of the first god is fixed in its character, and so it is properly related to true 'being.'[14] A similar line of thought may be found in the much discussed[15] Fragment 22, from Proclus: "Numenius equates the first god with 'the living creature', and says that he thinks by utilizing the second god. He equates the second god with intellect, and says that intellect produces by utilizing the third god; he equates the third god with the discursive mind." This passage probably reflects a discussion of the living creature of *Timaeus* (39e), which is here located at the level of the first god; the clear implication is the identification of the first god with the intelligible world of 'being.'[16] It would seem, then, that there is nothing exceptional about this theology's treatment of the 'being'–intellect relation.

There is, however, considerable evidence that the same logic that was applied to the levels of intellection also is involved in characterizing the location of the intelligible world. Hence, the location of forms becomes itself a complex question. In Fragment 16, we can see evidence of this; the text begins by subordinating the intelligible world to the intellective first principle: "If being and idea are intelligible, and if intellect is agreed upon as superior and their cause, then it alone is discovered as being the good. And if the demiurgic god is the principle of generation, then it suffices that the good is the cause of being." As this passage makes clear, intelligible 'being' is subordinate to a primary principle, the good, and this is to be identified with intellect. The cause or foundation of the intelligible world is the good-intellect, which will later be represented as the first God. It follows from this that the proper location of the forms in this system is at the second level, that of the active demiurgic intellect proper. Subsequent sections of this fragment make clearer the nature of the relationship between these levels: "If the demiurge of generation is good, then the demiurge of being will be the good itself, connatural with being. For the second god, being double, makes its own idea and also the cosmos, being a demiurge, since the first is wholly contemplative." [17] It would seem, then, that Numenius used demiurgic language to indicate the production of the second god from the first, since the passage countenances both a "demiurge of being, the good-itself" and a "demiurge of creation." Given the fact that the good is also an intellective principle, this use of demiurge language seems apposite. But it in no way suggests that the production of 'being' is the result of the active direction of the first intellect. In fact, the second god is himself 'self-productive' of his own form as well as the cosmos. Hence, the doctrine of Numenius includes an aspect of self-production, which helps to explain the generation of the active second god from the self-directed first. [18] In effect, the production of his own formal principle is the result of his contemplative activity, by imitation of the first god. [19] The structure of the theology suggests then that there are levels of divinity, corresponding to gradations of value (e.g., goodness and beauty), and related in terms of imitation. The use of imitation language is clearly intended to suggest the Pythagorean and Platonic explication of the dependence of lower elements of reality upon forms or numbers. Here this language implies participation or imitation relations within the intelligible world itself, since only the third god is at the level of the sensible cosmos. Hence, the intelligible world itself is now distinguished by a clear-cut distinction between a lower level and a higher level, upon which the former depends. It is important to notice that the very nature of each level is sharply differentiated by virtue of this language. The nature of the first deity is that of absolute goodness, and this is said to be distinct from that of the second deity, which, by contrast, is only termed goodness. The language offers grounds for claiming that the levels are closely and intimately connected in such a way that the higher holds a certain property to a greater degree than the latter, while thereby also suggesting that the higher level is the source for the lower one's having the lesser property that it does possess. This type of thinking is being applied here within the intelligible world, between the first god and the second god, both of which share features of the standard description of world of 'being.' Hence, we have a hierarchical logic applied within 'being' itself, and thus we find degrees of reality within 'being.' While there was a similar suggestion of hierarchical causality in the description of the good of *Republic* 509, in Numenian theology ontological dependence was to be understood as explicit in the architecture of that intelligible and divine world.

The implications of this development are considerable, since it accentuates the status of the first god by emphasizing its distinctness and separateness and by establishing a subordinationism between what might be called the higher and lower elements of the divine world. No doubt this is in keeping with Numenius's dualism, since it serves to insulate the first god from any direct involvement with evil and absolves him to an extent from the disvalue inherent in the material world, which may be said to depend directly on the lower or second demiurgic god. No doubt the theme of the self-production of the second god was also meant to buttress this differentiation and to reinforce further the independence and primacy of the first god. The theoretic intent of these doctrines seems, therefore, to be clear.

At the same time, however, Numenius's thought also evinces a concern for the establishment of some more subtle connections between these degrees of reality so that all ontological levels remain fundamentally related in spite of their manifest differences. Clearly, the traditional resources of the Platonic tradition were of use to Numenius in this regard, for Fragment 16 indicates that he emphasized the apparent qualitative similarity of absolute goodness and sensible goodness, so imitation language was also one mode of explaining the connection between levels of reality. But Numenius seems to have maintained as well two doctrines that extend this notion even further, positions that may have been original to him and that were, in any case, identified with him in the later Neoplatonic tradition. These are the doctrine of *proschrēsis* and the claim that all incorporeal entities are interrelated and co-immanent in a manner appropriate to their natures. These warrant brief examination, since they help to complete the structure of Numenian realist theology.

We have already met the concept of *proschrēsis* in Fragment 22 from Proclus. The language seems to be Proclus's own, and yet there is no reason to doubt that the notion itself is Numenian. The basic idea is that production by higher levels of reality of their subordinates is effected by a process in which these upper principles "utilize" immediately lower ones. As Dodds has noted,[20] the result of the doctrine is a blurring of the distinctions between the levels of the system, since the activities of each are closely related to those of other levels. I must admit, however, that while the effects of the doctrine are evident enough, the specifics are not, though this is again a function of our evidence. Why the first god should require the use of a lower active intellect for the exercise of self-intellection is obscure. Alternatively, it might be thought that the activity of this first god is different in type from the intellective second god and that should this god exercise a mental function, he must do so by utilizing the lower god, and so on for the second and third.[21] This leaves unclear why a higher principle would wish to take on the activity characteristic of its immediate subordinate; it might be said that the second god's role as demiurge would require some such function, but this explanation is not available for the declension of the first god to the level of the second, since there is no obvious reason available to require an abandonment of his self-intellection.

While the *proschrēsis* doctrine is obscure, its systematic implications are not, for it helps to bind these levels of reality and divinity very closely so that the process of production from the first entails utilization of a second principle, and so on for the second and third levels. Even though it is not clear why this is so, the interlinking, even blurring, of levels is obvious.[22] This tendency is further augmented by another feature of Numenian theology, again one given us by a later Neoplatonist, in this case Iamblichus. It is not surprising that Neoplatonists like Iamblichus or Proclus, who were concerned to differentiate firmly between levels of reality, should call critical attention to elements in Numenius that would accentuate the opposite. In spite of this polemical interest, there is no reason to doubt the accuracy of the attribution. The doctrine in question, found in Fragment 41, maintains: "all is in all, but in each appropriately to its nature." This is thought to apply to incorporeals.[23] So interpreted, this position would not only deny any fundamental difference among the metaphysical levels but also virtually 'telescope'[24] them into each other. From the evidential record available, it is simply not possible to determine the final import of this position, though some intention at least to interlink these levels seems unavoidable. Hence, both the *proschrēsis* thesis and this doctrine of the mutual immanence of intelligibles indicate a fundamental feature of Numenian theology, its emphasis upon the interrelatedness of levels of reality.

I would submit, therefore, that one can discern a basic, though tentative, outline to the theology of Numenius; there is in this thought an evident focus of theoretical address and unmistakable signs of careful philosophical development. We might, therefore, summarize the structure of Numenian theology in light of the central issues that we have been examining. The significance of Numenian thought rests in its development of a nondemiurgic system of realist theology. As we have seen, the active demiurgic function is located at the level of the second god, with the first god treated as essentially self-directed. In making this conceptual move, Numenius was doubtless attempting to present a cogent explanation of divine causality in relation to the problem of evil. As can be seen throughout the period, there was a continued concern both within the Platonic–Pythagorean tradition and in Gnostic and proto-orthodox Christian circles to explain the relation of the divine realm to the sensible world in light of the fact of evil. Numenian theology accentuated this distance of divinity in its most primordial sense from the principle of disorder by denying any direct involvement of the first god. This was left to a lesser aspect of divinity, a demiurge, which would engage in the struggle with matter and be split in the process into a third and final deity, the world-soul. It was important that the levels of divinity thus postulated be seen to be fundamentally related in a fixed and intrinsic way, one that precluded any major discontinuity in the system. Hence, the emphasis noted above upon notions like participation between intelligible levels, the utilization of lower levels in the activity of production, and mutual inherence. These doctrines precluded the sense that there was any significant division between lower levels and their sources that might indicate their alienation from value or any capacity for higher levels to sever or depart from their subordinates.

While a strong impetus for the development of a nondemiurgic theology may have lain in theodicy, there were doubtless issues of internal systematic coherence that played an important part. But no matter what the theoretic impetus for the doctrine, its import for realist theology was fundamental, and this might be made clearer if we briefly review this somewhat speculative reconstruction of Numenian theology. The demotion of the demiurge provided a new opportunity within the realist tradition to clarify the relationship of three central theological elements: 'being,' intellection, and divinity. By demoting the demiurge, the first principle could be simplified somewhat, freed as it thereby was from direct cosmological production. This move provided some conceptual relief from the difficulties we noted earlier in demiurgic theism, with its multiplicity of divine functions that were never wholly reconciled. In many respects the theology of Numenius seems to meet this issue, pollarding the active cosmologic function from the first principle in favor of a more cosmologically passive and self-oriented principle. As a result, the first god is not directly responsible for ordering and structuring the lower world and 'becoming'; it is not therefore the immediate cosmological foundation of this lower universe. This means, of course, that the aspects of reality for which it is immediately responsible are more limited in scope, with perhaps a resultant promise of thematic reconciliation within the system.

That is probably the most notable gain in Numenian theology, its sense of cohesion. The first god is not the answer to all questions directly, only to some, and while these questions may have ultimate reference to him, the way in which the theory articulates the bases for such responsibility is sophisticated and complex. The core of that explanation lies in Numenius's use of the notion of hierarchy within the intelligible and divine worlds. What is found in Numenius is a theology fundamentally based on degrees of divinity, taking full advantage of this notion and correlating it both to the concept of degrees of reality and to the hierarchy postulated within the intelligible and divine worlds. The upshot of this conjunction is three levels of reality and divinity, two of which (the first and second) lie within the intelligible world of 'being,' with a relation of participation or resemblance obtaining between them. The first is the paradigmatic foundation of all lower levels, hence its identification with the living creature of the *Timaeus*. It is goodness itself, while the second is simply good. It is also 'being' itself, in contrast to the similar nondemiurgic system of Moderatus.[25] The second deity exercises its own self-production based upon this level of absolute 'being,' producing its own idea and presumably[26] a whole range of archetypes that the demiurge uses in his production. There are then a series of divine levels following closely one upon the other, the first two within the intelligible world, the third the product of contact between the second divinity and materiality.

This hierarchical theology is also indexed to intellection so that each divine level represents a separate degree and type of intellection: the first is self-contemplative and hence, in a sense, passive, while active intellect and discursive intellect are proper to the subsequent levels, respectively. While this may also be a development from the thought of Moderatus, there is no question that it reinforces the essential connection and similarity between the fundamental ranks in the system; in a sense it prevents any claims of radical discontinuity in the theological hierarchy, while the very presence of the levels serves to emphasize both the richness of the divine world and the distance of true 'being,' intellection, and divinity from materiality and its inherent disorder.

We have then a realist theology primarily utilizing the concept of hierarchy in its account of divine activity, rather than the image of the demiurge. As I have already suggested, this simplified the account of the first principle, in effect setting certain questions relating to cosmological structure and production aside, to be accounted for by another theoretical entity, the second divinity. While this produced other questions regarding the relationship between these divine levels and their individuation, there were mechanisms available for addressing these issues, such as participation, the immanence of higher principles within their subordinates, and the concept of the separation of ontological products from their causes. These were features of Plato's account of the relationship of 'being' to 'becoming,' and they seem to have become for Numenius resources for a general account of the levels of reality and divinity.

In our discussion of demiurgic theism, I registered concern regarding its possible ultimate ramifications for realist theology: the autonomy and significance of formal principles could well be undercut by complete dependence upon active divine intellection. By contrast, we can see very clearly in Numenius a theoretical development that has as its intrinsic effect the revision of theological realism. By treating the living creature and the forms generally as the inherent products of divine self-intellection, and as constitutive of this intellect-at-rest, Numenius has begun to remove much of the suggestion of intentional dependence of ideas that demiurgic theology implied. Hence, the forms in their primordial phase are the contents of the self-intellection of the first divinity, the very nature of the first god himself. They cannot be altered according to some instrumental design, as might have been possible on the demiurgic account, for such cosmological intentionality has been displaced to a lower aspect of divinity. This sense of the inherency of the ideas within the first divinity, the sense that they must be construed as the content of the primordial god's own self-intellection, is further reinforced by the fact that a similar relation can be dimly perceived in the second god and his self-production. Once again ideas are generated by intellection, but in the case of second divinity this is not the result of internal self-contemplation but the product of contemplating the first divinity, so the ideas generated are thus imitations of those found within the first divinity.

Admittedly, the structure or nature of the intelligibles in Numenius is a result of divine intellection at various levels of the system. But there is no movement toward subordinating the intelligibles fundamentally to active divine intellection and to its cosmological purposes. The forms are, in their primordial nature, above the level of demiurgic thought. As such, they are the intrinsic products of the first divinity's inherently self-directed 'activity,' not of his intentions with respect to production. As Fragment 16 notes, the first divinity is productive of 'being' and so of the forms, and this activity is inherent in his very nature. It is the first divinity's character, then, that seems to be the grounding of the intelligible world of 'being,' for this god is, after all, 'being' itself. Hence, the forms are systematically situated in Numenian theology in a manner that once again enhances considerably their autonomy, establishing the character of the real world and the nature of the good itself as the central foundations of realist theology, rather than the active intellection of the demiurge.

It must be readily conceded that once again we are hampered by a lack of complete detail, whether due to historical accident or Numenius's own lack of precision of the subject of *archai*.[27] Nonetheless, the importance of this nondemiurgic theology for the realist tradition is quite evident, since it provides a significantly different analysis of the intelligible–intellect relation, and so of the status of 'being,' from that found in Middle Platonists like Plutarch. Numenian theology certainly continues to endorse a *nous* theology, but it further moderates its possible implications by two important departures: (a) by treating the primary sense of divine intellection as a passive sort of self-contemplation, and (b) by analyzing the conceptualist nature of forms in terms of this type of intellection, hence making the ideas innate features of the connatural activity of the primordial deity. It is especially important to note as well that the production of the cosmos by the active, demiurgic intellect is clearly modeled upon the exemplarism of *Timaeus* 39e,[28] so the ideas that the demiurge uses in cosmic production and generates in his own act of self-constitution are clearly grounded in a higher principle, the first divinity.

There is no question that there are problems in interpreting Numenius and many conceptual difficulties with the theology itself, but there can be no doubt of the importance of the nondemiurgic theology that Numenian thought represents for the realist tradition. In order to understand better the specifics of such theology, two central and related problems in the Numenian position should be noted in anticipation of Plotinus. As we saw in Fragment 11, the first divinity is treated by Numenius as being simple; this is part of its central description. However, our discussion has focused upon the exemplarist function of the first god, its identification with the living creature and the forms, and this, of course, is suggestive of multiplicity. It is very possible that Numenius treated the forms as present in the first god in a 'seminal' manner,[29] but even so there remains some difficulty in clarifying the meaning of this claim, in presenting a cogent case for divine simplicity. In addition, there is the fact that Numenius certainly seems at times to locate the first divinity above the intelligible world of 'being,'[30] though it is hard to be certain whether this is in fact to be taken as an absolute claim, thus generating inconsistency in his system, or only as a proscription directed against the level of forms and 'being' that the second god represents. This problem is compounded by the language of negative theology, a legacy of Neopythagorean exegesis of the *Parmenides*, which was becoming a theological convention in the period; this too was an element in Numenian theology.[31] While Numenius does seem to make some connection between his apophatic and kataphatic theology, we cannot be certain how precisely this was handled and whether a cogent account reconciling these conflicting tendencies was forthcoming. As we shall see, these issues will dominate the debate in third-century Platonic theology, setting the agenda for the efforts of Plotinus.

Finally, there is the problem of how best to understand the Numenian concept of deity with its multiple levels of divinity and its residual notion of matter. I think it is a mistake to interpret this divine hierarchy as just a set of separating existing powers gradated according to causal efficacy. On this construal these principles would be gods, each a separate entity but together arranged in a 'vertical' pattern. The first god would be the primary power, but all would constitute a subset of the same divine class. In this respect there would be no difference from a more 'horizontal' polytheistic model, in which the gods were roughly equivalent in power and significance. On either theory, a class of separate and distinct gods would be involved. The vertical stacking of divine beings would presumably be the result of a desire to graft traditional cultic polytheism onto Neopythagorean and Platonic metaphysics. This is a possible reading of Numenism theology, although I do not think it is persuasive. There are several related reasons for this demurral. I suspect, first of all, that this version of Numenius fails to do justice to his notion of divine levels. It seems more consistent with the force of the theory to see each level of divinity in Numenius as a progressive unfolding of the divine along the scale of reality. Each is a mode or aspect of the divine, rather than a separate divine entity. Each is a different degree of divinity, not a distinct god. The first principle represents divinity in its primordial sense, just as it represents reality at its most fundamental. From this first principle the other divine modes are derived, and each one constitutes a manifestation both of 'being' and divinity. A certain priority attaches in such theology to the first principle, although all are levels of divinity itself.

The interpretive grounds have thus been shifted from a hierarchical polytheism, in which separate gods are arrayed by rank, to a modalistic theism that construes divinity as manifesting itself at each rung along reality's great chain. This involves, as I suggested earlier, a qualitative or inclusive understanding of theism in which divinity exhibits the character of a property that can admit degrees. Such a model follows from those tendencies in classical Hellenic religious thought already discussed and its gradual recognition of a divine unity behind the pantheon. Numenius would be developing on this reading that same religious conception and presenting a philosophical theology that attempts to clarify that basic model. The result is a theism of degrees, or if you will, of hypostases.[32] Such modalistic theism has a subtle logic, with considerable emphasis upon a primary first principle articulated over against the lower divine hypostases. Yet this primacy is qualified by two attendant themes that are used to articulate this modalism: the unfolding and potential telescoping of the divine hypostases and negative theology. The former establishes a crucial counterweight to subordinationism, certifying that all levels of divinity are collapsible into the primordial first principle. This has the effect of reminding us that the separation upon which the primacy of the first divinity is based and the subordination of its consequents are only one feature of the divine that must be understood alongside its more fundamental, residual unity. The use of negative theology extends the point, qualifying once again the originative primacy of the first principle with an insistence that this description cannot be left to stand as literal. Such language is only vectoral, directing the attention of the intellective soul to divinity. The result is a theology of divine hypostases, all of which are grounded in the primordial divine fundament. This version seems to me to capture the theological character of Numenian theology better than a polytheistic model does. It suggests also that his hierarchical theology was an integral part of his metaphysics, not just an overlay born of a religious preoccupation with cultic polytheism. While it is a theology that remains vitally dualistic because of its continued endorsement of a principle opposite to the divine, its understanding of the divine does not suggest that the three divinities that it postulates are really distinct and separate from each other. It is because of its productive association with matter that the fracturing of divinity occurs, altering the internal self-articulation of the first principle and producing degrees of divinity. Thus, we have a "finite theism," with divinity in some of its aspects limited and changed by its conflict with an independent opposite principle. And while many of the details of Numenius's thought remain obscure and beyond recovery, its general direction and force are evident: a theology significant enough to have been a major presence in Alexandrian theology for over a century, as its influence on the students of Ammonius, the Christian Origen, and Plotinus attests. For this reason, Numenius helps throw into relief some of the issues that Plotinus will address and establishes an appropriate context for his magisterial treatment of classical Hellenic monotheism in the *Enneads*.

2. The *Didaskalikos* of Alcinous

It is a measure of the state of our evidence on second-century Middle Platonism that the name of the author of one of our best sources is unclear. The *Didaskalikos* is an interesting compendium of Platonic philosophy, and though not a technical treatise, it affords considerable insight into the scholasticism of the age. The minuscule manuscript lists a mysterious philosopher, Alcinous, as author, but modern scholars have considered it to be the work of Albinus, following the nineteenth-century philological analysis of Freudenthal. Albinus was the teacher of Galen in midcentury, and his very brief *Introduction to Plato's Dialogues* (*Eisagōgē*) is preserved. Recently John Whittaker has argued convincingly against this shift in authorship.[33] Since our interest is not in reconstructing the 'school of Gaius' but in analyzing the content of the *Didaskalikos* itself, this question is somewhat peripheral. I will follow Whittaker and use the author's name as we find it on the manuscript, since the burden of proof now lies with those who wish to accept the emendation.

Alcinous, like Numenius, is a representative of nondemiurgic theology; his thought is coherent enough when judged against antecedent Platonism to make that assertion.[34] His was a theology that also sought to revise the centrality of the demiurge and refine the understanding of divine intellection, although there are some important differences in emphasis and technical detail. In defining the ideas at the beginning of chapter 9 (163, 3–4),[35] Alcinous makes his adoption of the divine thoughts doctrine evident. He gives a definition of 'idea' that follows that of Xenocrates: "an everlasting paradigm of natural things" (163, 21–2). As we saw in our previous study of the issue, this definition indicates an effort to restrict the scope of the ideas based upon largely aesthetic and moral criteria, rather than upon logical grounds, which would widen the range considerably. The connection between this limited definition and the theological doctrine of divine thoughts is clearly operative for Alcinous; he makes a decisive claim against forms of disvalue: for the ideas are thoughts of god, eternal and perfect. Because they are divine thoughts, only certain universals can be considered as ideas. We should note as well the explicit emphasis upon eternality in both of these remarks of Alcinous on the ideas; in appropriating the doctrine of divine thoughts, Alcinous is clearly ascribing this status to ideas, so we can see from their very definition that the ideas are not subject to divine revision. By his initial description of the ideas, Alcinous has, therefore, located himself quite precisely in the Middle Platonic tradition: (a) he has adopted a version of the divine thoughts doctrine, (b) he has used that position to argue for a Xenocratean, restricted definition of ideas, and (c) he has treated these ideas as eternal principles.

This last claim is then made a central point in Alcinous's first proof for the existence of the ideas, and we can learn a good deal from it (163, 29–31): "Whether god is mind or a being with mind, he must have thoughts, and these must be everlasting and unchanging; and if so, the ideas exist." First of all, God is treated here as being either mind itself or as being 'intellective.' Presumably, the contrast is between a *nous* theology, which postulates an active mind that both thinks the ideas directly and is identified with them, and a theology that ascribed an intellective function to a god that has other definitional features. The latter position might include a system such as that of Numenius, which would distinguish between higher and lower intellectual principles, so that on such an account the first god's utilization of the second divinity would entail an intellective capability in the first. Presumably Alcinous's use of this initial disjunction in his proof is meant to encompass the major systems that postulated a divine *nous* in any sense, and his statement implies that the options are either as *nous* in itself or a *noeron*, a deity that exercises intellection. It is entailed that such a principle be treated as having thoughts, which could be true in various unspecified senses. The proof then maintains that these ideas are everlasting and unchanging, thus reiterating the fixed status of such entities.

The function of these ideas for cosmology is further clarified in the third proof of their existence (163, 34–164, 1), which is based upon the claim that three *archai* are necessary for cosmic production. The text suggests that if the cosmos has not come about by chance, then certain causal principles must have been involved. These are then articulated in terms of a metaphysics of prepositions scheme, the key notions being

1. "that out of which," the material cause.
2. "that by which," the demiurge.
3. "that toward which," the ideas.

It is argued that the last must be ideas. This indicates quite certainly the importance that Alcinous attached to the paradigmatic function of the ideas in cosmology, and while it is certainly not sufficient for any conclusions, we can see, I submit, a pattern in place here. Alcinous seems to be concerned to establish the independent, cosmological character of the ideas; and this should not be surprising, given both the internal significance of this issue within the tradition of Platonic theology already reviewed and the fact that other opposing versions of Platonism in the period certainly accentuated this theme, especially that of Atticus and the Athenian school. Hence, we find the resonance of the *Timaeus* account with its paradigms toward which the demiurge must attend in production.

Perhaps the best insight into the structure of Alcinous's theology is provided by chapter 10, especially the following statement from 164, 16ff.:

Since mind is better than soul, and mind in actuality which is simultaneously and always thinking all things is better than mind in potentiality, and nobler than this is its cause and whatever would be greater yet than these, and this would be the first god, the cause of the eternal actuality of the mind of the whole heaven. Being motionless in itself it actualizes the latter, just as the sun does to vision when someone looks at it, and as an object of desire while itself remaining motionless sets desire in motion, so will this mind move the mind of the whole heaven. Since the first mind is the noblest, it is necessary that its intelligible object be the noblest; but nothing is nobler than itself. So therefore it is always contemplating itself and its own thoughts, and this actuality is its own idea.

This remarkable passage, with its succinct textbook tone, guises a great degree of theological sophistication that would surely be evident if we had a more extensive record of Alcinous's thought or that of his associates. From the standpoint of our inquiry, it should be clear that we have before us once again a hierarchy of divine principles based upon degrees of 'being' and intellection. As both R. E. Witt and A. H. Armstrong have noted,[36] there is a significant component of Aristotelianism in Albinus, and this is manifest in the argument, where Alcinous is rethinking his hierarchy of Platonic principles with the elements of the theology of *Metaphysics* XII clearly in view, especially the *noēsis noēseōs* doctrine. With these elements agreed upon, we might examine the relevant portions of the system and then assess its overall significance. In considering this passage, we should note the postulation of three principles: the primal divinity, mind in activity, and mind in passivity. There has been some question in the literature as to whether the last two elements are wholly distinct in Alcinous, that is, whether the active, demiurgic mind is disparate from the world soul or whether these amount to aspects of the same principle.[37] We have seen much the same issue earlier in Numenius regarding the relationship of the second and third gods and their common source. Nothing crucial hangs on this issue for our inquiry, and so we might treat these principles as being distinguishable, thus giving us a look at the system, as it were, in its fully extended form. While I agree with Dillon[38] that Alcinous does seem to distinguish these functions of intellect into separate entities, he could very well be taken as treating them as finally collapsible into one principle again. Without access to a developed argument on the case we are again compelled to scholarly agnosticism, though we might make the distinction provisionally for our heuristic purposes.

The first divinity in this system is clearly intended to hold a position very like that in Numenius, and the central distinction lies between it and the subordinate deity, which is cosmologically active in production. The hierarchy is very straightforwardly stated: Mind in activity is better than mind in potentiality, and better than these is their cause. The degree of reality component of this scale is also evident, since the cause of both sorts of intellection is said to be in a fashion superior to these. This first divinity is the cause of the eternally active mind, the mind of the whole heaven. The argument then turns to a clarification of the nature of this first divinity and its mode of production. Now, it should be noted that in these theological chapters, Alcinous, even in contrast to Numenius, is careful not to use demiurgic language in regard to the first deity; and in later sections he uses it in a mode that is clearly intended by him to be mythic or approximative (XII.169,8–14).[39] The mode of cosmic production by the first god is explicated in unambiguously Aristotelian terms, and this theme is used to underscore the nondemiurgic character of this first god. The first god is motionless himself and yet is also active toward the mind of the heavens (164, 20–21), as the sun is toward vision or as an object of desire sets desire in motion while being itself motionless (164, 22–23). As Witt notes, this Aristotelian doctrine of divine activity based on the model of an object of desire was used in various ways by Middle Platonists since the time of Plutarch.[40] What is important in Alcinous, however, is that this description of divine production is now made absolutely central, as the dominant explication of the first divinity's nature.

Alcinous goes on to examine further the nature of this nondemiurgic deity, and it is here that his Aristotelianism is especially helpful in clarifying the intellection of highest principle. The argument presented relies on the perfection of the first divinity and holds that its object of intellection must also be the noblest. Since nothing can be better than the first, it would have to be a self-contemplative principle. This articulation of the position, based on the logic of perfection, is itself a sophisticated move that buttresses the claim of divine self-contemplation and clarifies the hierarchy of intellection. But for our purposes it becomes as well a medium for asserting explicitly an important change in realist theology: that the first divinity's self-contemplation entails his thinking of the ideas (164, 26–27).

In this position we find an intriguing interaction between aspects of Platonic and Aristotelian theology. As Armstrong has noted,[41] there is a critical rethinking of the *noēsis noēseōs* doctrine involved so that the bare notion of self-intellection is being expanded to explain the nature of this internal divine contemplation. Armstrong's summary of the position brings this out quite well: "for God to think himself is to think the Ideas, that is the whole of intelligible reality. God is eternally actual thought and that thought is the Ideas, so in thinking himself, what he really is, it is the Ideas which he thinks."[42]

In a sense, this position serves to explicate the nature of a wholly actual, self-directed intellect by broadening out the implicit content of that intellection, thus developing the Aristotelian deity against possible criticisms of its apparent sterility. But it is also a critical rethinking of the simpler demiurgic theology, in which the character of divine intellection in relation to the ideas was unclear. On Alcinous's theology, the ideas are clearly constitutive features of the highest divinity's own essential nature; and further, they are everlasting principles, the product of his perduring activity. We could infer much the same view in Numenius, but in Alcinous the position is thematically explicit. Divine intellection at its most primordial level is wholly self-absorbed, and this self-contemplation is what is meant by 'idea.' The very nature of 'being' itself is the everlasting, immutable, and inherent intellection of this divinity. As such it is not based upon the thought or intention of the demiurge in his generation of the universe. Formal reality, true 'being' itself, is neither a construct produced for instrumental purposes by the cosmic craftsman nor the dependent result of divine intellection, for the objects of divine intellection mutually entailed one another in this theology. If this is an accurate portrayal, then it is obvious that Alcinous's realist theology has gone to great lengths to establish and safeguard the structure of 'being.' 'Being' and divine intellection are, in effect, correlative concepts, inextricably bound up with each other so that neither can be made subordinate in theological significance to the other. Hence, Alcinous's use of Aristotelian theology has provided a description that links 'being' and divine intellection in such a way that real 'being' is not compromised by reduction to a merely intentional status.

One central theme of this theology, which allows for this 'being'–intellection conjunction, is the demotion of active demiurgic causality to a lower level in the system. As in Numenius, the ideas presumably also appear in another manner at that level, since this second principle actualizes its nature by intellection of all things (164, 17–18). Once again, we have a hierarchy established within 'being' itself, within the intelligible world, the purpose of which may not only be to establish a basis for theodicy but also to ensure that 'being' is not located only at the level of the demiurge. The evident effect of Alcinous's theology is to locate the primordial aspects of both intellection and 'being' above the active intellect. In this case it is possible, I think, to argue that the necessary, inherent, and eternal connection of 'being' and divine intellection was instituted at least in part to avoid the possible subordination of 'being' itself, not only to divine intentionality at the level of the demiurge but also to a stronger notion of dependence upon the divine will. *Boulēsis* is a concept that will have, of course, a long and rich history in theology, and it appears to be beginning to be a significant subject of debate among Platonic theologians in the second century. While the conception has precedents in Plato (e.g., *Timaeus*, 29e–30a, or *Laws* XII.967a), it appears to have become a more prominent issue by the second century A.D. We have, however, only a fragmentary picture of the debate.[43] In Alcinous's theology, however, we can see an effort to avoid the possible effects on realist theology of linking the concept of active demiurgic intellection of the ideas to a divine will doctrine. As we have noted, the nature of the intellect–being relation is the chief innovation, since in this context the operative notion of divine will would be self-will, that is, it would amount to a doctrine of voluntary self-production such as can be found, though with significant modifications, in *Ennead* VI.8.13.[44] Alcinous does not give us such an elaboration, though this may be due once again to the nature of this summary textbook. Nonetheless, his treatment of 'being' and divine intellection has the thematic result of precluding any subordination of the separate structure of 'being' to the activity of a divine will. There can be, on this theology, no significant distinction between the divine intellect and the ideas; so if divine will were to be made functionally critical within the first divinity, this would only mean that he was willing his own nature and the ideas into existence. This would be an everlasting process; it would also be one that in effect equated divine will and 'being,' just as the explicit position of Alcinous conjoins divine intellection and 'being.' While this is admittedly to extend the logic of Alcinous's position somewhat, I do not think that it is unguarded speculation.

That the problem of the divine will was of concern to Alcinous is certain from his introduction of the notion at 164, 35–165, 3: "The first god is father since he is the cause of all things and orders the heavenly mind and the world soul according to himself and his thoughts; by his own will he has filled all things himself, rousing up the world soul and turning her towards himself, since he is the cause of her mind." Once again we have a remarkably condensed passage integrating a host of significant themes. The first sentence gives an explanation of the production of the subordinate levels by first divinity, the father. One must keep in mind the vectorial character of this theology: the first divinity is not producing entities by volitional creation or by emanation but is rather arousing them out of materiate disorder into structured order. Hence, the causality in question in this first sentence is final causality, and the ordering involved is not an instance of efficient causality and demiurgic agency but rather of teleology. Alcinous has, by altering his causal analysis of his first principle, restructured the demiurgic account of primordial divine production. This reorientation in perspective carries over into other elements of the *Timaeus* account as well; in particular, there is in this brief section a reference to the general exemplarism of that dialogue. It should be noted that the double use here of *pros*, "toward," clearly echoes the *Timaeus* (28c–29a, 39e) and, given Alcinous's version of the 'metaphysics prepositions,' is intended to indicate final causality. In addition, the lower principles are said to be ordered in accordance with both the thoughts of this divinity and with himself, which seems again to be a muted recollection of *Timaeus* 29e. What Alcinous is doing is giving a revised analysis of Plato's exemplarism such that the first divinity constitutes the ultimate paradigm on a par with the 'living creature' of the *Timaeus* while also representing a purified version of intellection, free from the extrinsic focus of the demiurge. Lower levels of reality—even those within the intelligible world, like the heavenly mind—are ordered in accordance with the first divinity and his thoughts, which therefore serve a paradigmatic function. The basic structure of the theology is similar to Numenius in this respect as well, although the final causality and teleology of Alcinous's version of exemplarism are far more explicit. Hence, what Alcinous has done is revise exemplarism based upon the teleological theology of Aristotle.

Given the *Timaeus* background just referred to, it should not be surprising that Alcinous brings up the issue of divine *boulēsis*, though once again he revises it considerably. While the divine will was never thrown into clear relief in the *Timaeus*, our discussion indicated that passages like 29e certainly suggest the concept and that the whole image of demiurgic intellection brings with it an element of intention and volition. This passage in Alcinous would seem, therefore, to be addressing this inherent component within the cosmological tradition of Middle Platonism as well as those theologies of the period that emphasized the demiurgic will. The conjunction of divine will with both the theme of divine immanence (164, 37–165, 1) and with final causality through the awakening of the lower mind and soul (165, 1–3) suggest that Alcinous was summarizing a type of Platonism that was concerned to avoid a doctrine of a secondary demiurgic will that might have been the basis of a claim for the extreme removal of the first divinity. One thinks inevitably of a possible target in early second-century Gnosticism, antecedent to those attacked by Plotinus in II.9.10–12.[45] There can be, I think, no question that Alcinous was attempting to integrate the element of volition found in Plato's demiurge into his system in a way that related this notion of will to the first divinity without radically subordinating lower levels in the process. We can see in this passage, then, an attempt to show how the divine will can be understood in terms of final causality, a will, we might say, that not so much directs and orders as rouses and enlivens. Furthermore, this is a form of divine activity that fills the world thereby with order and divinity through its teleological presence, not a will that initiates gaps between levels of 'being' or promotes discontinuity in the cosmic hierarchy.

I would argue, then, that Alcinous's theology represents a sophisticated attempt to revise demiurgic theology. No doubt Alcinous is either himself building upon many other systems that were similarly nondemiurgic in structure or simply providing a précis of one such system, but this does not remove the conceptual importance of the positions presented by him. In the *Didaskalikos* we have a theology that is not only nondemiurgic in its scheme but that has been carefully thought through to provide a more consistent understanding of such a Platonism. As I have indicated, this rejection of active demiurgic intellection is at the very core of the system, and I believe it was initiated because of the implications of demiurgic theology, with its inevitable emphasis upon volition. The first deity could, on that model, be understood as a volitional principle that subordinated 'being' as its derivative product. This was a central problem for realist theology, as we have already noted, usurping as it does the initial basis for postulating these independent paradigms of reality and value. As I have argued, Alcinous's doctrine of the inherence of divine intellect and 'being' avoids this difficulty, and in view of his explicit revisal of the notion of demiurgic volition, this doctrine seems directed at precisely this problem. I might add in anticipation that it would not be surprising if the strong emphasis upon the independence of the paradigm in Atticus and the Athenian tradition was a reaction both against nondemiurgic theologies like that of Alcinous and against demiurgic systems like that of Plutarch. It seems reasonable, then, to hold that Alcinous's doctrine was also informed by this context of discussion. His theology's strategy for defending the importance of 'being' as the fundamental and eternal pattern of order and value was to make it inherent within divine intellection itself and to displace the active intellect, to which volition might be applied, to the second place in the system. Here again this active mind is called into existence by being roused to turn toward the first divinity, whose very self and ideas serve as the paradigmatic foundation for the active mind's production. This system can therefore be seen as addressing the problem of the connection of divine intellection with 'being' in a more thoroughgoing fashion. But even if this question were in fact ancillary to Alcinous's own intent, the theology as it emerged does in fact provide a succinct and powerful answer to this problem and represents a major variant within Platonic theology.

The Platonic theology of Alcinous evinced an additional aspect that is critical to its conceptual character. We find elaborated in the *Didaskalikos* a negative theology, perhaps the best example from Middle Platonism and a valuable witness to this type of thinking prior to Plotinus.[46] Its character is complex; in Alcinous it is treated as compatible with a whole array of descriptive epithets for the supreme god. The first deity is said to be "self-sufficient," "eternally perfect," and "wholly perfect."[47] He is also called "divinity," "substantiality," "truth," "symmetry," "good," and "father."[48] All of these serve to mark off the distinctive cosmological function and theological status of the first god. Alcinous provides an explanation of these epithets with a theory of divine names, suggesting that these epithets are not definitional but are only a way of naming god.[49] He iterates what appears to be a scholastic discussion of divine naming and predication. These modes of discourse include analogy,[50] which is represented in reference to the simile of the sun in the *Republic*, and anagogy, the upward movement of the mind toward intelligibles.[51] Diotima's speech in the *Symposium* seems to be the paradigm for the latter.

It is in this context that negative theology is introduced, not as a novelty, but as an established mode of theology.[52] Alcinous's representation of this approach appears to be fairly limited; attributes that might be thought to limit the significance of the first god are proscribed. Thus, he is said to be neither genus nor species nor subject to accidental predication. Neither good nor evil, he neither moves nor is moved. He has no qualities and is neither a part of something nor a composite whole. The critical question then is, how are these claims to be understood and evaluated? The problem is one of scope: Is Alcinous suggesting that all divine predication should be rejected or only that which might be deemed conceptually inadequate on grounds illustrated but not fully articulated in the *Didaskalikos*? Considerable research has been done on the sources of this theology in an effort to address this problem, and although this evidence is not in itself decisive, it is helpful.[53] The most important fact of note is that Alcinous's discussion is cast in terms of *aphairesis*, abstraction, a notion associated both with Aristotelianism and with Euclidian geometry.[54] This suggests a process of stripping off concepts in order to focus upon an underlying unity. As such it is a fairly focused endeavor. It can be distinguished from a broader, logical notion of negation, *apophasis*. The issue is whether Alcinous understood *aphairesis* strictly in terms of abstraction, based upon some tacit rule regarding what notions should be discarded in the identification of the highest divinity, or in terms of the more general notion of negation. Is his use of *aphairesis* a narrow, technical one, or is this notion doing duty for negation? The latter move would suggest that the first principle has slipped beyond all predication, all divine attribution. The broad interpretation was argued by Wolfson, the narrower by Whittaker. Mortley, in his extensive study of this whole tradition, believes that both notions were closely associated, so "whilst there are some clear differences between abstraction and negation in this period, they dissolve upon reflection." While the philosophical background is thus inconclusive, it seems to me that the *Didaskalikos* suggests the narrower, abstractive understanding. In the text itself the discussion of *aphairesis* is immediately connected with the analogical and anagogical methods. The three are represented as related methods for understanding the first god. There is no sense of conceptual discontinuity or even tension among these approaches. Yet on the broader reading, all such divine predication should be proscribed, and so 'negative' theology would be incompatible with analogy theory. On the narrower reading, abstraction could be taken as the removal of unworthy conceptions and so could be quite compatible with analogy and anagogy. That is the way the *Didaskalikos* represents matters. Hence, it seems to me that this is the most reasonable conceptual reading.

Understood in this fashion, the negative or abstractive theology of Alcinous can be seen as part of an effort to clarify the nature of the first principle. It is one important theological technique for clarifying the absolute character of the first god, the primary power of divinity that exists in contrast to matter. We must remember that in Alcinous, as with other Middle Platonists, theism remains finite, for the deity is constrained by the force of an opposite principle. As such, a special theological burden was separating off the highest god from all sorts of materiality. Lower aspects of divinity would not enjoy that status; their nature was defined by this cosmological association with materiality. Demiurgic activity was clearly one such association. But the highest god was distinct in his august separation from lower powers, especially matter. Negative theology, even if understood in an abstractive sense, was thus a salient method for articulating the transcendence of the first god. Abstraction had thus become a mode of theological portraiture, certifying the special status of the ultimate divinity. Negative theology can thus be seen to be part of the developing logic of Hellenic theism, one that will be systematically advanced by Plotinus.

3. The Exemplarism of the Athenian School

While it is certainly too much to suggest that nondemiurgic theology developed exclusively because of problems of internal consistency in earlier accounts or because of perceived difficulties regarding the intellect–'being' relationship, nevertheless, these issues probably had a bearing on the matter. Evidence for this can be found in the fact that other Platonists of the period seem to have been seriously interested in the question of the location of the forms in relationship to intellect and to have proposed alternative solutions to this central realist problem. Atticus, the late-second-century Athenian Platonist, is a good example. From the available doxography it is possible to discern the contours of his answer, which seems to be a return of sorts to exemplarism.

The discussion of Proclus at various places in his *Timaeus* commentary indicates that Atticus maintained a type of demiurgic theology, which made an effort to distinguish the forms from the demiurge itself so that the exemplarist scheme of the *Timaeus* would be retained. The issue is presented by Proclus at *In Tim.* I.305, 6ff., from what is admittedly a later, more sophisticated perspective, though his reading of Atticus is probably accurate in general outline. The key passage reads as follows:

Atticus, the Platonic successor, held the demiurge to be the same as the good, but surely it is called good by Plato, not the good itself; and he said it is a mind, though we know according to the Republic that the good is the cause of all being and beyond being. What then does he say regarding the paradigm? Is it prior to the demiurge and so more worthy than the good? Or is it in the demiurge, then making the first principle plural? Or is it posterior to the demiurge and the good, which is not proper to say, since he will think by turning towards things posterior to itself?

We can infer from this text that Atticus certainly endorsed some sort of demiurgic theology. The demiurge is clearly identified with intellect and also with the good, though this might violate the letter of the *Timaeus*. This demiurgic intellect is also said to be beyond being, given its identification with the good of the *Republic*, though the exact meaning of this phrase is left open. Proclus then raises the central question of the relation of such a principle to this 'paradigm', that is, to the forms collectively. We should notice the force of his characterization of the problem. The options are (a) that the paradigm be prior (at least conceptually) to the demiurge, in which case it would be more significant than the good (given the assumed identification of demiurge and the good); (b) that the paradigm be within the demiurge, that is, a strict demiurgic system with forms as intramental entities, in which case the problem of a pluralized first principle is raised; or (c) that the paradigm be conceptually anterior to the demiurge and the good. As Dillon has pointed out,[55] Proclus gives us Atticus's evident resolution of the question in favor of the last option, at *In Tim.* I.431, 14ff. Proclus is discussing *Timaeus* (30 D-31 A) and is probably relying on Porphyry for his information of Atticus:

> Atticus expressed doubts on these matters, whether the demiurge is contained by the intelligible living creature. It seems that if it is contained, then it would not be perfect. The parts of the living creature, he says, are not perfect and as a result those things akin to these are not beautiful. If it is not contained then the self living creature would not embrace all the intelligibles; he readily settled the difficulty, holding that the demiurge is superior to the living creature.

Now according to this bit of doxography, Atticus would seem to be arguing that the demiurge must be seen to be prior to the forms. As is stated, if the paradigm or the collection of living creatures (the living creature of the *Timaeus*) were to contain the demiurge, then the demiurge would be imperfect and inferior; but if the paradigm does not include the demiurge, then it becomes incomplete. The evident answer of Atticus seems to be one that simply placed the demiurge above the forms, in a sense avoiding this problem of the latter's scope by establishing what amounts to a distinction of type, setting the demiurge off from the entities that would fall within the scope of the paradigm. The upshot of this move is both to delineate sharply between these two sorts of principle and to make the demiurge the superior entity in his systematic hierarchy.

Nonetheless, it does not seem that Atticus extended this relation of demiurge to paradigm into a radical notion of subordinationism. While he shows evidence of using the standard divine thoughts doctrine,[56] he was also criticized on the grounds that he endorsed separate and disjointed constituents of reality: matter, demiurge, and ideas.[57] Given his fundamental theological dualism, it is likely that there was a cosmological alliance between forms and demiurge over against materiality, as in the *Timaeus*, but that is no reason to conflate these cosmological principles. In fact the discussion of

Porphyry as recounted by Proclus at *In Tim.* I.394, indicates that the forms were treated as existing by themselves in Atticus, which seemed to Porphry to make them into inert models. It seems to me that Atticus was trying to do justice to those elements of the *Timaeus* that indicate the separation of the paradigm and its independence.

It is reasonable to conclude, then, that some elements of the Middle Platonic tradition endorsed a theology that made the demiurge central but nevertheless held that the forms had an independent status. Atticus[58] is the best example of this exemplarism, and his system is evidence of an attempt to meet the same theoretical issues addressed by other realists but to do so by a return to exemplarism. Within the context of the period, this position must have had considerable strength beyond its exegetical utility for analyzing the *Timaeus*. Rather than demoting the demiurge, it retained this principle's preeminence. This has the merit of avoiding an explicit, internal plurality of elements within its first principle. From the perspective we have been considering, it avoids as well any reduction of the structure of 'being' to that of intradeical thoughts or intentions directed toward cosmic production, and this is central to the intent of realist theology. It should not be surprising, then, that this position was strongly adhered to by Athenian Platonists until at least the time of Longinus and Porphyry.

4. Middle Platonic Theology

We might now bring this inquiry into Middle Platonic and Neopythagorean theology to a close by summarizing some of the salient features of their chief varieties. The most important positions for the development of philosophical theology include (a) demiurgic theology, exemplified by Plutarch; (b) exemplarism such as that of Atticus; and (c) nondemiurgic theology, evinced by Numenius or Alcinous. The concept of a demiurgic deity held a place of influence throughout the period. The complexity of the problems addressed by its simple and straightforward imagery occasioned its continual adoption and revision; for our purposes its chief difficulty was accounting for the status of forms. The danger of subordinating the structure of 'being' itself, and also of all order and value, to the intention of an active demiurgic intellect remained a crucial issue.

The problem was not one of theological preference; it was rather a question of internal systematic coherence, since the core of this theology's articulation of the transcendent and divine realm rested upon the existence of forms. To make these hostage in nature or function to the demiurge is to undercut the very basis of realist theology, which would require a wholly different account of transcendence to buttress it. At the same time, it must be admitted that this theological issue was only partly recognized in antiquity and that no figure within the ancient Platonic tradition seems to have fully pressed the implications of demiurgic thought.

Nonetheless, the exemplarist elements of realist theology were reasserted in an important modification of demiurgic theology, that of Atticus. While not denying that divinity is primordially an intellect, Atticus treated the ideas as a separate and independent type of reality, to which the demiurge looks in production. This is perhaps no more than an articulation of themes long part of Platonic theology since the *Timaeus*, but their significance in Atticus indicates some measure of attention to the independence of paradigmatic forms. Even though treated as subordinate in the scale of divinity to the demiurge, the forms for Atticus and the Athenian school seemed to have reacquired an independent, exemplarist status and function, and this represents a subtle though important alteration within the structure of Middle Platonic theism.

Finally, there is the nondemiurgic theology of Numenius, Alcinous, and others, which marks off the most important departure from earlier Middle Platonic theism. While still holding that the primordial deity is intellective, this system revises that ascription by denying that it implies active cosmological production, and so, active intellection. The intellect of the first god is a mind engaged in self-contemplation and so is passive or at rest. In Numenius this revision produced a degree-of-divinity system such that the active demiurgic intellect occupied a second rank. This could imply, as in Alcinous, a complete revision of the causality of the first god, whose role is more properly that of a final cause. Two points emerge as particularly salient in such a theology. First, an important element of exemplarism is retained in this account, since the active intellect must now refer to the nature of the first god and to the forms inherent in its self-contemplative intellect. This certifies that the production and the structure of lower levels of reality are grounded in forms whose independence and status are assured because of their ontological and theological priority as intrinsic aspects of the first god. Second, their character is part of the very nature of divinity in its most primordial character. This comes out especially well in Alcinous, where the 'being'–intellect relation becomes one of virtual mutual entailment: intellect necessarily entailing by its self-contemplative nature the ideas, and 'being', by its character, entailing the value of awareness represented by intellect. Such an analysis provides no basis for treating 'being' as dependent upon active divine intentionality, since the primordial nature of divinity seems now to have two correlative and necessary aspects: 'being' and intellection. 'Being' has been made central to the hierarchy of divinity, and the significance of these immutable foundations of order and value has become theologically secure.

None of this was, however, to the satisfaction of Plotinus, who became a trenchant critic of the insufficiency of all *nous* theology, demiurgic or otherwise. It is on this rich and variegated tradition of Middle Platonic and Neopythagorean theology that his thought was founded and against which it was meant to be sharply distinguished. As such, Plotinian thought established a distinct school of Platonic theology. And so we shall turn now to the theology of Plotinus, with a view toward establishing how it differed from the theologies just examined, why Plotinus found these systems deficient, and what the implications of this new departure were for philosophical theology.

The Mystical Monotheism
of Plotinus

For contemporary philosophy of religion, the hypostases of Plotinus seem an enigmatic polyphony, forgotten dogmas of the distant past outside the canon of modern intuitions. The tentacular reach of the *Enneads* down through medieval, renaissance, and romantic thought may indeed warrant interest from historians of ideas, but the Plotinian theory of divine hypostases appears nonetheless as a confusing enjambment of archaic notions, lacking contemporary resonance. It is not my intention in this final chapter to refurbish Neoplatonism for a new age.[1] But I do intend to clarify the Plotinian concept of deity so that current appraisal of early Neoplatonic theology can be set into a different relief than is customary.

The thesis I shall argue can be straightforwardly stated: the theology of Plotinus ought to be understood as a type of 'inclusive' monotheism consistent with antecedent developments within Greco-Roman thought. This is a critical perspective, which has been not so much denied as it has escaped formulation.[2] This is particularly true of philosophers of religion; studies that survey different concepts of deity have been perplexed by Plotinius, treating him as an "emanationist" in a category by himself.[3] A lingering suspicion of pantheism or monism also attaches to his thought, especially among comparative students of mysticism.[4] My purpose here is not to refute these analyses but to propose a different model, which is, I believe, more adequate to Plotinus's thought when understood in relation to its historical context. On this reading, a type of Hellenic theism emerged with considerable clarity and force in the *Enneads*. This is not to suggest that Plotinus's thought is entirely consistent or conceptually adequate; as with so many figures of the period, there remain lingering difficulties in working out this thesis, particularly with respect to the notion of matter. However, the main outlines of a type of theism are apparent in Plotinus. The present chapter will focus on several aspects of Plotinus's thought that are of special salience to this thesis. Because any form of monotheism is faced with the necessary task of articulating the distinct nature of the first principle, close scrutiny will be accorded to Plotinus's novel account of the character of the One and the particular methods he employed to secure both its ultimacy and its distinctiveness. We will begin with Plotinus's critical revision of Middle Platonic theology and then turn to his development of Hellenic monotheism.

It must be admitted that nothing in the history of Middle Platonism and Neopythagoreanism can really prepare one for Plotinus; there is an incommensurability of philosophical stature involved. Nonetheless, we are now in a better position to study Plotinian theology against the backdrop of its endemic tradition. For all of his claims to being a traditionalist, Plotinus's views on the divine *archai* were controversial and were judged by some of his contemporaries to be in fact innovative. While I shall be interested to some extent in this historical question, I shall again concentrate in this chapter on a conceptual assessment, on Plotinus as a proponent of Platonic theology. Plotinus's metaphysics are integrative of ideas drawn from the rich array of Greek philosophical schools, and this makes his philosophical theology difficult to analyze. We are, however, blessed by Porphyry's information on chronology and by his editorial efforts, however unfortunate his zeal for numerology, so we are in the unusual position of knowing that all *Enneads* are genuine and what their order of composition was.[5] I propose taking advantage of our knowledge of the chronology of the writings and concentrating attention upon the earlier works, which clarify the grounds for Plotinus's break with Middle Platonism. It seems generally agreed among Plotinian scholars[6] that there is no dramatic development within the corpus such as one might find in Plato, and this is no doubt due to Plotinus's maturity when he began writing.[7] There is, of course, refinement, internal clarification, and focal variance in the *Enneads*. Within the earlier works, the novelty of his position seems to have required that Plotinus clarify his views over against the Middle Platonic school traditions, and it is these treatises that I will be considering in some detail, especially V.9(5), V.4(7), VI.9(9), V.1(10), V.2(11), and III.9(13). I might add as well that this method of analysis of a specific set of related treatises seems best suited to Plotinus's own very tight and compressed mode of philosophical discussion. We will begin, then, with an analysis of Plotinus's theory of the intelligibles and on that basis expand to a more comprehensive account of his theology, especially the doctrine of the One.

1. Divine Simplicity

The novelty of Plotinian Platonism seems to have coalesced, for his contemporaries, around his doctrine "that the intelligibles are not outside the intellect."[8] We can gather from Porphyry that his was the major point of issue between Longinus, the Athenian Platonist with whom Porphyry had studied, and Plotinus. Proclus, in discussing *Timaeus* 29a (*In. Tim.* I.322,24 Diehl) mentions Longinus as placing the ideas posterior to the demiurge, and we can also infer that he placed them somehow outside the demiurgic intellect. It has been suggested that this view may be the result of a serious and diligent attempt at exegesis of Plato, perhaps due to the conjoining of the *Timaeus* cosmology with *Republic* X.597b, where the idea of the bed seems to be a product of the cosmic craftsman.[9] But we should also bear in mind the theology of Atticus, which may very well have continued within the Athenian tradition and which we may take Longinus as representing. Longinus's view would therefore have been a 'conservative' Middle Platonic exegetical position, emphasizing the theological significance of the demiurge but also retaining the exemplarist force of Plato's account of the forms and the 'living creature' by locating the ideas outside the demiurgic intellect.[10]

It can only be wished that we had a better understanding of Plotinus's own education with Ammonius Saccas, for this would doubtless help us to recognize some of the impetus behind the doctrinal line that he ultimately took on this issue. In view of the meager evidence we have on Ammonius, especially solid doxographical evidence,[11] it seems unprofitable to pursue this line of inquiry here.

The same might be said for the school of Ammonius generally, for outside of the view of Longinus on the intelligibles, the evidence on issues of interest to us is rather limited. The pagan Origen provides the only other significant insight. Proclus in the *Platonic Theology*,[12] attributed to him the view that the highest principle is an intellect and a denial that it is beyond *nous* and 'being.' It is possible that he wrote on this subject, but even this is speculation.[13] In any case, there seems to have been no settled opinion within the Ammonian school on the subject of the intellect that accords with what we find in Plotinus's writings. In fact, it seems from our sketchy evidence that the other members we know (e.g., Longinus and the pagan Origen) can be said to have been opposed to this position in favor of a *nous* theology of some sort. Hence, the argument that Porphyry records may go back into discussions of the school itself or else be a product of Plotinus's later development of Ammonian thought after his departure from Alexandria and the probable death of Ammonius in 232–233. It would appear then to be much more profitable to concentrate on the works of Plotinus himself in order to clarify the significance of his position conceptually.

We will begin with a passage, III.9.1(13) listed by Porypyhry as the latest of those we will be considering, although III.9 appears to be a miscellaneous collection, the parts of which might have been produced at different times. Dodds has called attention to III.9.1 as a text indicative of Plotinus's early efforts to come to terms with the *Timaeus* and doing so in a way that is very Numenian.[14] The text begins with a quotation of *Timaeus* 39e 7–9, an exemplarist passage in which *nous* sees the ideas in the 'living creature.' Plotinus then questions whether Plato intends that the forms exist before intellect, which thinks them, as it were, as separate and prior entities. To answer this, Plotinus inquires into the nature of the 'living creature' to discern whether it is an intellect itself. The discussion runs from lines 5 to 15:[15]

First of all, then, we must investigate that reality (I mean the living creature), to see if it is not Intellect, but sometimes other than intellect; for that which contemplates it is Intellect; so we shall say that the living creature is not Intellect, but intelligible, and that Intellect has what it sees outside itself. So, then, it has images and not true realities, if the true realities are there [in the living creature]. For there, Plato says, is truth too, in real being, where each and every thing in itself is. Now, even if the two are different from each other, they are not separate from each other except in so far as they are different. Further, there is nothing in the statement against both being one, but distinguished by thought, though only in the sense that one is intelligible object, the other intelligible subject; for Plato does not say that what it sees is in something absolutely different, but in it, in that it has the intelligible object in itself.

It is initially agreed that the entity that contemplates the 'living creature' is a *nous*, so on this basis it is concluded (a) that the living creature is not an intellect itself but an intelligible (*noēton*) and (b) that the intellect has this object of its attention outside itself. Now, from our discussion of Atticus and Longinus it can be seen that the position under discussion is one that is somewhat like theirs in its exemplarism, though there is no mention of the priority of intellect that they adopted. In fact, priority is accorded here to the intelligibles, at least for the purpose of the discussion. The position under review is closest to the one held by Poryphry upon his arrival in Rome (*Vita Plotini*, 18, 11), in which the separation of intellect and form is maintained but subordination to the demiurge is avoided.[16]

Plotinus then takes up the problem of the nature of the ideas that the demiurgic intellect has if the forms are separate from its mind, a problem that was implicit in exemplarism but that we have not found explicitly considered before this point. Plotinus succinctly notes the difficulty: separation of intellect from form would imply distance between the intellect and 'being,' such that the derivative ideas that *nous* has would simply be secondary images. This would presumably leave the possibility open for the intellect, in its role as demiurge, to be mistaken about the structure of 'being' and hence to be deficient in its production. Plotinus, it should be noted here, is clearly relying upon a realist basis: the *eidē* are truth, they are real 'being,' they exist in themselves. For a Platonist committed to degree of reality ontology, as Plotinus certainly was, the exact status of the intellect's own apprehension of the forms becomes a crucial question. To admit that these intradeical ideas are merely images and not absolute standards would open up a potentially devastating gap, severing the surety of the intellect–'being' relation.

Plotinus then proceeds to review solutions to this problem, and while no conclusion is reached, we can see better than before into the logic of the respective solutions. The first proposal (10–11) is that intellect and forms should not be taken as being wholly separate in this way, though we might accept some differences between them. This notion of difference is certainly obscure, though Plotinus might have 'functional difference' in mind. He then extends the notion further (12ff.) suggesting that *nous* and *noēton* be taken as being the same, distinguishable only conceptually, with one aspect as an intelligible object, the other an intelligible subject. This is an analysis that he often favors, and we will see it in greater detail subsequently.

Another possible solution is then considered, one that seems to be that of Numenius (15–25):

> Or there is nothing against [this solution]; the intelligible object is also an intellect at rest and in unity and quietness, but the nature of the intellect which sees that intellect which remains within itself is an activity proceeding from it, which sees that [static] intellect; and by seeing that intellect it is in a way the intellect of that intellect, because he thinks it; but that thinking intellect itself too is intelligent subject and intelligent object in a different way, by imitation. This, then, is that which "planned" to make in this universe the four kinds of living creatures which it sees in the intelligible. Plato seems, nevertheless, to be making, obscurely, the intending principle something other than those two. But to others it will seem that the three are one, the living creature which exists in itself, the intellect, and the planning principle.

This intelligible object, which is also at rest, in unity, and in quietude, has been convincingly identified by Dodds as the "*nous* at rest," the first principle of Numenius.[17] The entity would be an intellect–ideas compound, from which there proceeds a second intellect. There is no mention here of self-production, only of possession, but the similarity to Numenius is close enough. This second intellect is an *energeia* of the first, and the first may be said to think of itself through this second intellect (19–20). Although *proschrēsis* language is not used by Plotinus, the thought is very close to the Numenian 'utilization' theory, including the suggestion of an imitation relation of the second *nous* to the first (21). The theory would therefore safeguard the passivity of the first principle, itself both intellect and intelligibles, by postulating a second intellect that exercises active intellection on its behalf. To mitigate somewhat the problem of the grounding of this second set of intelligibles located within the second principle, imitation language is used, although this seems to be an unconvincing solution.

The question of the location of the demiurge is then considered, and it is interesting to see how this issue emerges. Plotinus suggests initially (21–22) that the second intellect should be the demiurge, referring to *Timaeus* 39e–40a, but then indicates that Plato may have obscurely intended to treat the demiurge as a separate and lower principle. This would give the following hierarchy: the 'self-existing living creature,' the active intellect, and the 'planning principle.' In suggesting this, Plotinus is proposing to revise the Numenian system and further demote the demiurge to the level of soul. His grounds for doing so seem to center upon his construal of that principle's chief function, which is construction by ordering and division. This third principle is that which planned "to construct and make and divide into parts the things seen by intellect in the living creature."[18] We would thus have a self-directed first principle that exercise active intellection through a second, which then exercises production and the division among entities necessary to this end through a demiurgic soul. Plotinus is relying here upon the fact that Numenius had identified discursive reasoning with the soul. Proclus,[19] as we noted in chapter 2, considered the third principle in Numenius, the 'planning' or 'intending' principle,[20] to be the soul; and as Dodds argued, the implied distinction between intellective functions is therefore between intellective *nous* and discursive *nous*.[21] On this construal the proper function of soul for Numenius would be discursive reasoning. Hence, Plotinus, in developing Numenius's triadic scheme, is here entertaining the view that the characteristic activity of the demiurge is discriminating among or dividing off the various aspects of the intelligible world and on this basis producing the sensible world. As such, the demiurge ought to be located at the level of the soul, the level of *dianoia* (35ff.).

III.9.1 gives us a good insight, therefore, into the way Plotinus viewed two major options in the Platonist tradition that we have been tracing, the exemplarist and the nondemiurgic. In the first case, we can see his concern with the ramifications of this sharp division between intellect and intelligibles, a distinction that we recognized to have merits but which on Plotinus's analysis also had a serious drawback. It lay open to doubt the fundamental connection between real 'being' and the conceptual paradigms within the productive intellect and so also the entire connection between 'being' and the structure of 'becoming' that this intellect produces. Hence, we can uncover here the root of Plotinus's denial of the view of Atticus, Longinus, and Porphyry, that the intelligibles are outside the intellect.[22] We can also discern in III.9.1 how Numenius's system appeared to Plotinus, and one gets a much better sense of the sorts of arguments and concerns that must have surrounded its postulation and acceptance. Clearly, Plotinus was concerned with the implications of nondemiurgic theology; he was willing at least provisionally to consider such a version of *nous* theology, though one that further displaces the demiurge to the third rank. Plotinus, as we shall see in V.9.3 and 5, sometimes identified the demiurge with *nous* (i.e., the second level of reality), although that was in the context of a theology very different from that found here.[23] In his mature thought, he will vigorously reject any theory, such as this version of Numenius, with three minds: one in response, one an active intellect, and one 'planning' and productive intellect. In II.9.[33].1 and 6, he argues against this view and against distinctions within *nous* as such; his target seems to have been Gnostics within his own circle who attenuated these levels of reality in a way similar to Numenian theology.[24] In light of this initial consideration of earlier Platonic theologies, we can begin to examine Plotinus's development toward his own distinctive position.

The short treatise V.4.[7] provides a ready point of access to these same issues, since it continues in some respects Numenian themes and also clarifies the insights that seem to have motivated Plotinus's break with Numenian nondemiurgic theology. The first section begins by announcing a law of ontological derivation: If there is anything after the first, it must necessarily come from the first, whether directly or indirectly through the hierarchy of 'being.' The text then focuses upon what is a central and characteristic theme in Plotinian metaphysics, the simplicity of the first principle and the implications of that total simplicity. The argument in lines 5–17 is as follows:

For there must be something simple before all things, and this must be other than all the things which come after it, existing by itself, not mixed with the things which derive from it, and all the same able to present in a different way to these other things, being really one, and not a different being and then one; it is false even to say of it that it is one, and there is "no concept or knowledge" of it; it is indeed also said to be "beyond being." For if it is not to be simple, outside all coincidence and composition, it could not be a first principle; and it is the most self-sufficient, because it is simple and the first of all: for that which is not the first needs that which is before it, and what is not simple is in need of simple components so that it can come into existence before them. A reality of this kind must be one alone: if there was another of this kind, both would be one.

As we examine this discussion, the Middle Platonic–Neopythagorean background to this reflection must be kept in view. First of all, the initial law of ontological derivation is clarified by the introduction of the notion of the first's simplicity, for it is precisely in virtue of that simplicity that it warrants primacy (10–12). Simplicity connotes for Plotinus lack of mere coincidence of existence and lack of compositeness, both of which would preclude primacy. A composite entity is grounded upon its conceptually prior parts, and an entity that is not self-sufficient has need of that which provides its nature and existence (12–15). This sort of argumentation brings Plotinus close to the medieval notion of necessary being (i.e., of ontological self-sufficiency), and it is the foundation for the primacy of a wholly simple first principle.[25] Most important, Plotinus argues that there can be only one such being (15–16), for uniqueness is in his view an essential property of a truly necessary being, one that is ontologically self-sufficient.

There is, I would argue, nothing within the evidential record of Middle Platonic thought that shows as sophisticated a grasp of this key notion in philosophical theology as this early text from Plotinus. The central criticism being made here is that simplicity is an essential feature of a first principle, from which an implicit corollary can be drawn regarding Middle Platonic first principles that they were lacking in simplicity and so were deficient in their primordial role. This we shall see as we progress; more immediately obvious is the logic upon which Plotinus based his notion of simplicity. Lines 5–10 amount to careful analysis of many of the characteristics associated with the intelligibles by earlier Platonists and now made applicable to the single first principle by Plotinus. We should notice the line of thought: This unity is simple in contrast to those that follow it, as well as being separate from them, and so is capable of presence among them. It is understood to be a fundamental unity, free from composition. All of these concepts, along with the general notion of self-sufficiency, are core components of the theory of forms in the middle-period dialogues. What we have here is an application of this conceptualization to the first principle of all things, the final one above the many. This is the conceptual foundation upon which the Neoplatonic criticisms of Middle Platonic theology will be grounded, and as such they are based not just upon some aesthetic criterion of what counts as '*theoprepēs*' (fitting to the divine) but rather upon the ontological bases that supported ancient Platonic theology. Appeals to the form of the good and to the first hypothesis of the *Parmenides* are explicitly made. Given that the basic argument for transcendent reality relies upon the forms, Plotinus is now using that general mode of argument to clarify the status of the chief principle within that ontological hierarchy, which he thinks must be, by the inherent laws of that system, a primordially simple one.

This passage gives as well some initial clues to Plotinus's understanding of his theism. The One is simple in the sense that it transcends or supersedes any composition; the tacit logic of hierarchy is evident in Plotinus's language of "before." This conception of simplicity assumes that the One is such that it is free from multiple aspects and from the composition that those elements would entail. Otherwise, it would not be an ultimate principle: the principle of sufficient reason might be invoked to inquire further into the bases of the elements and the formula for their conjunction. Thus understood, the One is not represented here by Plotinus as simple in the sense currently under discussion in Anglo-American philosophical theology; that is, because the One is identical with the divine attributes (e.g., goodness, beauty, omnipotence), he has no physical or metaphysical complexity.[26] This approach would suggest that the One is a property, to be identified with these others. But this would be unacceptable to Plotinus because his understanding of properties is based on the Platonic conception of forms as perfect properties; to assume that the One is simple in the sense of being a property identified with other perfect properties would entail its location within the complex, interstital network of self-instantiating forms. This would both broach the specter of self-instantial regress from the *Parmenides*, since the One would be a form, and draw the One into a logic of association with the whole range of formal properties or aspects whose complete or relative identity would have to be argued.[27] This is not the direction in which Plotinus is heading.

The root insight in this discussion of simplicity might be called the "aseity intuition."[28] This would be the conviction that the One must be such that it depends on nothing distinct from itself and that everything distinct from itself is absolutely dependent upon the One.[29] This intuition is central to Plotinian monotheism, and its conceptual corollary is the assertion of the One's simplicity, that is, lack of composition. While it is difficult to pry apart the compressed elements of this discussion, it is clear that for Plotinus there can be no conceptual possibility that the One depends upon or is essentially related to anything distinct from it. The claim of divine simplicity is thought to follow from this aseity intuition: the ontological distinctness and the simplicity of the One are fundamentally related claims. Plotinus understands this as a statement of ontological location: setting the One 'before,' or outside, the realm of formal properties entirely. Behind this claim lie both the hierarchical ontology of the Platonic tradition and the Plotinian determination to establish the first principle outside the boundaries of that understanding of conceptually determinable reality. While there is much here that bears subsequent examination, one point is striking in this line of reflection. The One is fundamentally distinct from all other beings because it is simple, not in the sense that it is a unique property nor because it is a cluster of identical properties nor because it is a unique property instance of divinity but because it stands apart from the level of reality that is betokened by the complexity of predicate attribution, albeit perfect self-predication. As such the One is a radically different conception of deity, sharply distinct from all other beings but also transcendent of all conceptually specifiable representations of reality. In this respect the One is understood by Plotinus to be unique; the simplicity and distinctness of the One are evidence of a developing form of monotheism.

Plotinus initiated a trajectory of discussion on divine simplicity that would not only define later Hellenic monotheism but would also be subsequently absorbed into the Abrahamic tradition.[30] The Plotinian One's ultimacy was grounded in the fact that it was un-

caused; it was "the most self-sufficient." This aseity excluded components, as it would in Abrahamic theology, although the argument
was cast in somewhat different terms. The One is both simple and
thus ultimate because it is free from the composition inherent to
all other realities, both intelligible and sensible. Negative theology
functions in a salient fashion to articulate this distinctiveness: the
One must be said to be beyond 'being' in order to be represented
as simple and ultimate. To treat it as intelligible 'being' would have
suggested the context of essential predication, something that implied logical composition to Plotinus. This may seem an odd way of
reflection, one that we will explore further, but it may initially be
worth recollecting that Plotinus had inherited an intellectual legacy
in which 'being' implied a predicative context. Absolute simplicity
thus required transcendence of that ontological level.

This adoption of a simple or noncomposite first principle by Plotinus was also directly bound up with the deficiency that had become apparent to him in earlier versions of Platonic theology. In
effect, the intellective first principle of such systems was seen as
being too complex, lacking the absolute simplicity that attached, in
Plotinus's view, to perfection itself and so warranting a secondary
position in the hierarchy of theological principles. This tendency in
Plotinus to subordinate the intellective principles of earlier Platonism was itself the result of various shortcomings that he discerned in
Middle Platonic theology, based upon his understanding of the re-
quirements of divine simplicity. We might notice as we progress the
extent to which Plotinus's use of the theme of the divine simplicity
seems an answer to the problems of theological complexity noted
above in relation to Middle Platonic theism. The answer, of course, is
not wholly available within the confines of discursive, philosophical
conceptualization, so we should note the growing emphasis upon
the extent to which recognition of divine simplicity entails acceptance of either apophatic theology or paradox within philosophical
theology. This might become clearer if we continue to examine Plotinus's discussion of the connection between simplicity, perfection,
and production in V.4.

V.4.1, 20–21, indicates what seems a law for such theology of
divine simplicity: that anything that comes after the first cannot be

simple. This is what might be called the law of necessary declension, and we will see it applied repeatedly and extended in scope. At this point it applies to *nous*, which is termed a "one-many," a characteristic description by Plotinus and the basis for its secondary position as a product of simplicity itself. The next question that arises is the basis for this principle's production, and Plotinus takes this up in a rich discussion of the power of perfection (23–26): "Whence, then, does this come? From the First: for it certainly does not come by chance, and if it did the First would no longer be the principle of all things. How then does it come from the First? If the First is perfect, the most perfect of all, and the primal power, it must be the most powerful of all beings and the powers must imitate it as far as they are able."

This passage provides the basis for the doctrine of procession in Plotinus and is founded on the paradox that what is most simple is also the productive source of all lower levels of reality. The key conceptual connection is between divine simplicity and perfection, the latter notion being chiefly operative here in the explication of ontological production. The first principle deserves its status in ways similar to a form: it is logically first because of its special character, for it is uniquely what is wholly simple. The implicit argument sets up and extends Platonic ontology: *archai* must be perfectly real, and whatever is really real is productive. The logic in question now applies not to a qualitative unity ranging over its specific instances but to the unique principle of all entities within the realm of 'being.' We should notice how the logic of perfection works to establish this general law: lower principles, to the extent that they are perfect, are productive, from which one is justified to generalize, according to Plotinus, to a uniquely perfect principle, the most productive of all, and hence the final *archē* for all. This is then made clearer as Plotinus introduces the notion of necessary ontological dependence and floats a suggestion of necessary production (34–42):

How then could the most perfect, the first Good, remain in itself as if it grudged to give of itself or was impotent, when it is the productive power of all things? How would it then still be the Principle? Something must certainly come into being from it, if anything is to exist of the others which derive their being from it: that it is from it that they come is absolutely necessary. That which is generated by it must certainly also be the most honourable, and though it is second to the Principle must be better than all else.

Included here is one of the most important Plotinian cosmological themes regarding the first principle, that it is *dunamis pantōn*, the productive power of all things. It is developed in connection with the theme of divine ungrudgingness from the *Timaeus*. The text stops short of attributing a formal theory of necessary production in the sense that the One is somehow constrained to produce. It is in the nature of the One to be productive by virtue of its ontological status; that is, perfection entails ontological production. Once again, the basis for this law is signaled by the use of realist logic: formal principles are perfect, and for this reason they are productive. This is a conceptual law; one can therefore hold that something must be said to come into existence from a formal principle[31]. Plotinus seems especially strong here on this claim[32] in reference to the One: It is necessary that the One be the source of all. It bears mention that this understanding of perfection and production is one of the features of Plotinian Neoplatonism that remains under contemporary discussion.[33] That perfection is productive, that a principle of objective value separate from all consequent being is generative of reality—these are characteristic notions that Plotinus articulated in these early texts of the *Enneads*. This position is distinct from 'classical' or 'personal theism,' to use J. L. Mackie's term,[34] and operates without a central conception of divine volition; and yet it also relies upon a transcendent principle of value whose evaluative perfection is generative of its consequents. In this case, such perfection is not parsed in reference to the goodness that would pertain to an agent but rather is based upon an abstract notion of value. This Neoplatonic position has been called "extreme axiarchism" by John Leslie:[35] "axiarchism" would be any theory that sees the world as grounded in value; "extreme axiarchism" would be the claim that the universe exists because it ought to, where this requiredness is understood as being based in an ultimate, abstract principle of value.[36] This modern restatement may help to exhibit part of Plotinus's argument. For the One is the ground of value, and this perfection entails for Plotinus that it be productive. As we saw in our discussion, existence and value are deeply interconnected on this degree of reality ontology, so the final principle of value is also the final principle of all being. So understood, the perfect existence of the One cannot be represented as nonproductive of consequent beings. This Plotinian axiarchism establishes the cosmological role of the One as the necessary and sufficient principle of reality. It dovetails with the distinctness of the One, established by the discussion of the One's simplicity and aseity, thereby articulating a monotheistic concept of deity, although one that is not dependent upon personalistic imagery. The axiarchical theism of Plotinus uses a distinct set of notions to establish the uniqueness of the One, and in so doing, settles personalistic and demiurgic aspects of the divine into a secondary or tertiary status.

V.4.2, a very unusual chapter in the *Enneads*, may help us to get a somewhat better purchase on the secondary status of any intellective principle and the extent to which Plotinus was willing in his early thought to use some aspects of Numenian theology to avoid the impression that divine simplicity implies sterility. The chapter begins by reiterating the law of declension: Whatever proceeds from a first principle is less than it, and this would apply both to an intellectual first principle as well as to one that is not. The major question is then raised regarding intellective principles: why can the first not be a *nous*? The answer, relying upon the primacy of simplicity as already articulated, is as follows (1–12):

> If, then, the generator itself is Intellect, what is generated by it must be more defective than Intellect, but fairly close to it and like it; but since the generator is beyond Intellect, it is necessary that what is generated should be Intellect. But why is the generator not Intellect, whose active actuality is thinking? Thinking, which sees the intelligible and turns towards it and is, in a way, being perfected by it, is itself indefinite like seeing, but is defined by the intelligible. This is why it is said: from the Indefinite Dyad and the One derive the Forms and Numbers: that is, Intellect. For this reason Intellect is not simple but many; it manifests a composition, of course an intelligible one, and already sees many things. It is, certainly, also itself an intelligible, but it thinks as well: so it is already two. And it is also a different intelligible by being posterior to the One itself.

Nous is not simple but many; it is complex and intrinsically plural, and it cannot be truly simple in spite of whatever unity it does manifest. This becomes the central argument of Plotinus against all versions of *nous* theology. It is his understanding of a first principle that such an entity must be simple, and all types of intellective first principles are inherently deficient in this very regard. The grounds of this plurality in *nous* are easy to see: First, any intellective principle, even the passive self-contemplative principle of Numenius or Alcinous, is always said to have some intentional content. Every *nous* is both an intellect (which exercises thought, *noōn*) and an intelligible (the passive content, *noēton*), according to Plotinus's analysis, and so each principle is fundamentally dual in nature. By articulating a system of *nous* theology, earlier Platonists intended to clarify the role of intellect in cosmic production. This, as we saw, led to a tendency to adopt a 'divine thoughts' doctrine, but no matter which version of this doctrine was adopted, the same division of aspects would apply according to Plotinus. Second, and perhaps more obvious, is the fact that the forms, on any account, are multiple; so that if treated as the content of an intellect, then this principle would be pluralized to a degree. For these reasons, Plotinus insists that any *nous* would be a 'synthetic' or composite unity, not a wholly simple one, and would therefore be secondary. Because Plotinian theology is founded upon a hierarchy of unities, beginning with the formal unities within sensible things and proceeding through the genus–species relations within the intelligible world up to unity itself, it cannot accept a first principle that is a composite unity; only unity itself, complete simplicity, will suffice. This is the core of Plotinus's critical analysis of antecedent Platonic theology.

It must be admitted that this is an odd passage, in which Plotinus seems to be reviewing options from Middle Platonic theology without discussing these fully. Particularly strange is Plotinus's apparent reference to the One as the intelligible object (*noēton*) for the vague or indefinite vision of the intellect.[37] The uncertain vision of the emergent intellect focuses its as yet unordered or unactualized contemplation upon the One, which it represents not as a unity but as a multiplicity. The passage relies upon the Aristotelian distinction between *opsis* (potential vision) and *horasis* (actualized vision);[38] the indefinite vision of incipient intellect requires the ordering and "actualization" of the One. The extent to which the One is causally central to this process is somewhat unclear in the passage,[39] but there is no certain basis to invest the inchoate intellect with primary causal responsibility, that is, as an autonomous self-generative principle; rather, the One seems to remain as the principal causal force for the emergence of intellect, despite its description as *noēton*.[40]

It is also interesting to note how Plotinus understands the inherent duality of intellect, represented oddly by him in reference to the Old Academic–Pythagorean opposite principle theory. Use of the indefinite dyad is clearly meant to resonate with the indefinite state of the emergent intellect's vision of the One. Yet Plotinus is not committed to a formal dualism of ultimate principles,[41] only to the concept of an indefinite dyad that is the product of the One, along the lines of Neopythagoreans such as Eudorus or Moderatus.[42] Hence, the dyad seems to be used here as an image for indefiniteness, rather than as a separate or ultimate power involved in this emergence of intellect.[43]

Nous theology remains of significance to Plotinus as a critical background for this thought; we can find many aspects of earlier Middle Platonism and Neopythagoreanism integrated into his thought in these early treatises as he engages in the process of differentiating his position. In the passage just quoted, besides the reference to the 'indefinite dyad,' there is a suggestion just considered that the notion of an 'intelligible' might be applicable to the first principle, as that to which intelligence looks. This would suggest a Numenian treatment of the first principle as a paradigm of sorts for the active intellect,[44] and we find Plotinus, in fact, picking up on this general mode of analysis in a very unusual passage, 12–19:

But how does this Intellect come from the Intelligible? The Intelligible remains by itself and is not deficient, like that which sees and thinks—I call that which thinks deficient as compared with the Intelligible, but it is not like something senseless; all things belong to it and are in it and with it. It is completely able to discern itself; it has life in itself and all things in itself, and its thinking of itself is itself, and exists by a kind of immediate self-consciousness, in everlasting rest and in a manner of thinking different from the thinking of the Intellect.

Plotinus is using language here of his perfectly simple first principle which he often proscribes, though his reasons for doing so are clear enough. As I have indicated, he has criticized Numenian theology for its deficiently unitary first principle, though he does not intend to reject all features of this concept, especially its character as the ground of intellection for lower principles. We can well imagine criticisms of Plotinus's early thought on this question: How could the One be productive in its absolute simplicity? Or how it could generate the world of intellect and being? In the above passage we find an answer in Numenian terminology to such questions. The One is certainly not a deficient principle; its perfection is such that it includes all aspects within subsequent levels of reality in such a completely perfect unity that it is complete and simple. This amounts to a varied application of the *dunamis pantōn* theme already noted, and we will see this notion again in later treatises. What is interesting about the present passage is the treatment of the One as both an intelligible and an intellect. The use of 'intelligible' language is probably due to Numenian imagery, which suggests that the first principle plays an exemplarist role in relation to the second principle; we might recall its identification by Numenius with the 'living creature' in Fragment 22. Since Plotinus retains this dimension of intellect's contemplation of the One, it is not surprising that he might use the term 'intelligible' in spite of its possibly confusing overtones. As for terming the One an immediately self-conscious principle, Plotinus is evidently trying to avoid the impression, which must have been produced, that his was a nugatory first principle. The language certainly indicates that whatever might be said of the One, deficiency is not an applicable notion, for its transcendence of description is a positive fact, not a falling short. It would be proper then, though wanting in many respects, to say that the One is not insensate and to declare it to be immediately self-aware in a way that is distinct from intellectual awareness.[45] While this is, of course, to come very close to Numenius's self-contemplative first intellect, there is a sense in the passage that Plotinus is not just violating the rules of his metaphysics by lapsing into a Numenian position. Rather, he can accentuate the fecundity of the One by using these descriptions, as a necessary palliative to misinterpretations of his thought from the direction I have suggested. Hence, I suspect that a proper reading of this passage would put emphasis upon the absolute immediacy of this intellect's self apprehension, probably meant to be greater than that found in the bifurcated first intellect of Numenius. Similarly, its containment of life and all things would again be a sense of undifferentiated, 'intelligible,' and wholly realized unity. Such descriptions are certainly a strain on conceptualization and could well be misunderstood as no more than a restatement of Numenius; this, I suspect, was the basis for Plotinus's general avoidance of his approach. Nevertheless, we can recognize here an effort to forestall what has often been a misinterpretation of Plotinus, that his reified first principle was vacuous in its simplicity.

If this passage were merely a vestige of an early, Middle Platonic stage in Plotinus's intellectual development, then it would be a historical curiosity with little significance to his philosophical theology. Despite its unusual character, this early passage exhibits two important features present in Plotinian theology from his earliest writings: First, the One has a positive nature; while Plotinus is loathe to use descriptive language of the One, for several reasons we will subsequently consider, this indicates only that the One exceeds finite description and that Plotinus thinks that such predication can be misleading. This is a second-order judgment regarding the nature of theological language, not an implicit representation of the One as a primal void. Second, Plotinus's One is an ultimate, inclusive principle. The values, properties, and states that emerge from the One must be understood as in some sense being contained in the One. The One, while transcending its consequents also contains them, not in a collective fashion but in an undivided unity. As we have seen already, the simplicity of the One is not understood as the identity of formal properties. Plotinus represents the One as unified in the sense that it exceeds even the aspectual difference of predicational identity. And yet he is also committed to finding an inclusive foundation for all evaluatively positive qualities in the One. This paradox, for it is surely that, might be called the "unum-plenum" paradox,[46] a fundamental image of inclusive monotheism. The transcendent source is absolute unity and simplicity and yet the comprehensive source for all consequent beings that exist at levels of reality lower and distinct from itself.

It should not be thought, therefore, that this argument is exceptional; indeed, there are later treatises in which Plotinus returns to reconsider the positive content that can be sketched, in a highly qualified fashion, in relation to the One (e.g., VI.8[39]). Plotinus may later shrink from attributing intellective functioning to the One in this fashion,[47] but that tells against the nature of such finite, predicate attribution, not against the inner life of the One. It may be too much to claim, as Rist does,[48] that the notion of self-discernment (*diakritikon hautou*) does not violate divine simplicity but in fact expresses it. But if the One is to be seen an inclusive archē, such that "all things belong to it and are in it and with it,"[49] then intellection of some sort, however unified and immediate, must be found there. Hence, the self-discernment of the One, while an unfortunately bifurcative image, is probably best understood along with immediate self-consciousness (*sunaisthēsis*) and self-thinking (*katanoēsis autou*).[50] Plotinus is deliberately speculating on the One's different type of intellection, distinct in kind from that appropriate to the intellect itself. The critical point is that whatever is to be said of the One in regard to its capacity of self-apperception, this cannot violate two intuitions: (a) that the One is simple and so also distinct from all other beings and (b) that the One is the inclusive source of all beings. While Plotinus will later qualify or reject a notion such as "self-awareness,"[51] this is because of the inadequacy of the imagery, not because the One should properly be understood as lacking such self-discernment. Always with Plotinus there is this tension, exhibited even in this early phase, of finding in the One the foundations of all positive qualities and yet retaining a sense that the One exceeds the conditions of their finite predicate attribution.

We have already had occasion to note the pervasive backdrop in Plotinus of the logic of traditional Platonic argumentation in favor of principles of unity. This is once again evident in the above passage, with its continued emphasis upon self-sameness of intellection and consciousness and of self-remaining. Plotinus develops this theme further in the final sections of V.4.2, pressing out the implications of realist ontology with respect to the One in a way that is much more characteristic of his thought (37–44):

For that Principle is "beyond being." That is the productive power of all things, and its product is already all things. But if this product is all things, that Principle is beyond all things: therefore "beyond being"; and if the product is all things but the One is before all things and not on an equality with all things, in this way too it must be "beyond being." That is, also beyond Intellect; there is, then, something beyond Intellect. For being is not a dead thing, nor is it not life or not thinking; Intellect and being are one and the same thing; for Intellect does not apprehend objects which preexist it—as sense does sense-objects—but Intellect itself is its objects, granted that it does not get their forms from somewhere (for where could it get them from?). But it is here with its objects and the same as and one with them: the knowledge of things without matter is its objects.

Here we have a very clear summary statement of the basis for Plotinus's claim that the first principle must transcend 'being' and intellect, as well as some important points regarding the nature of the latter; careful analysis of this section will help to broaden our approach to these issues. The discussion has just turned to intellect, to its self-abiding and its character as 'being' and substance. Intellect has come to this level out of a principle greater than itself, the greatest of all powers. The product of this principle is the world of 'being;' it is *nous*, which contains all intelligibles and all formal realities. Hence, the principle or foundation of this compound of 'being' and intellect must be beyond both of these aspects; that is, there must be a first principle beyond that postulated by Numenius or Alcinous. The argument clearly rests upon the whole fabric of ancient Platonic realism, especially the description of 'being' and its status as the collection of intelligible archetypes. If the hierarchical logic of such metaphysics is pressed, the ontological foundation of these entities would seem to mark off a type of entity beyond the confines of that class. Given the conjunction of 'being' with intellect, the same logic requires a first principle beyond intellection as well. I will refer to this position as the 'ontological type' thesis, and we will see its implications momentarily. With respect to this text, however, it will suffice to notice that this thesis again represents a conceptually sophisticated modification of earlier Platonic theology. Plotinus's rejection of earlier *nous* theology can be said, once again, to be far more than just a demurral from certain aspects of that thought; it is a searching rejection of the structure of *nous* theology, based upon that theology's conceptual roots in the metaphysics of the middle-period dialogues.

2. Intellect and Ideas

Plotinus's theories of the One and of intellect are closely allied, and the significance of his thought for ancient Platonic theology is a result of his approach to both topics. Having introduced the nature and argumentative foundations of Plotinus's break with earlier Middle Platonic theology, we will now concentrate our attention upon his theory of the divine ideas. To this end, we might examine a series of texts from V.9.[5] and V.1.[10].

The passage from V.4.2 just discussed contained a brief reference to the character of the intellect–intelligible relation within the second principle. Plotinus there denies that the ideas preexist the intellect, for intellect and its objects are the same. It is possible to talk about a source for these intelligibles outside of intellect, but this would be the One itself in its role as an 'intelligible.' This latter suggestion is an attenuated use of terminology, since, as we have seen, the One would thus have to be an intelligible beyond 'being,' beyond intellect, and beyond intelligible content. There is, as it were, an exemplarist source to vouchsafe these formal objects, and that is the One, the ultimate ground of 'being,' itself beyond that level of specifiability and finite determination. For this reason, forms may be located within the intellect without suggesting that they are thereby subordinated to the status of the dependent thoughts of the demiurge. Thus, the intelligibles can be said to be within, not outside, the intellect. The way in which Plotinus works out this argument is complex and is, in many respects, a striking solution to the central problem we have been examining in ancient realist theology.

V.9.[5] is another early treatise that concentrates on intellect and being. While its subject is *nous*, the whole discussion is marked in its structure by recognition that there is a further principle beyond the hypostasis under consideration. V.9.5 makes clearer the doctrinal bases for the internal character of *nous*, especially its self-concentrated aspect and its content (1–13):

But if we are to use the word in its true sense, we must take this intellect to be, not that in potentiality or that which passes from stupidity to intelligence—otherwise we shall have to look for another intellect before it—but that which is actually and always intellect. But if it does not have its thinking from outside, then if it thinks anything it thinks it from itself and if it has anything it has it from itself. But if it thinks from itself and derives the content of its thought from itself, it is itself what it thinks. For if its substance was other [than its thinking] and the things which it thought were other than itself, its substance would itself be unintellectual: and, again, potential, not actual. Therefore one must not be separated from the other. But it is our habit, derived from the things in our world, to separate the things of that higher world in our conceptions of them. What then is its active actuality and its thinking, that we may assume it itself to be what it thinks? It is clear that, being Intellect, it really thinks the real beings and establishes them in existence. It is, then, the real beings.

Many of the elements we have found in the descriptions of the first principles of Numenius and Alcinous are here being revised for application to the second hypostasis. The first sentence applies the logic of formal principles to *nous* as a whole. It must be a fully actual principle, not one that holds its character contingently (e.g., by acquisition or change) but one that necessarily is what it is. Hence, its character as *nous* must be construed to indicate this necessary status. To this end, Plotinus utilizes the theme of internal self-contemplation, which we have seen elaborated in Alcinous. This results in an especially important development for Platonic theology, adumbrated in Alcinous but now theoretically central in Plotinus: the equation of intellect and intelligibles. There are many reasons why Plotinus might have wished to endorse this position, not the least of which is the need to clarify the composite unity that *nous* exhibits as the next principle after the One. But there are other concerns that our particular perspective may help to clarify. We have already indicated in discussing III.9.1 that Plotinus may have wished to deny the extrinsic location of forms with respect to intellect because of the danger that this might have for the process of production. The doctrine of intellect–intelligible identification addresses this problem; there is no danger here of effective displacement of the demiurge from the true intelligibles. As the passage indicates, there can be no separation of these aspects in the second hypostasis: the intelligibles cannot be without the intellect and vice versa.

In thinking itself, the intellect thinks the forms, real 'being,' the *onta*. These are the objects of its intellection; these objects are themselves inseparable from the act of their intellection. For this reason,

Plotinus can hold as he does in 12–13 that the forms are established in existence by the activity of the intellect, without actually accepting a conceptualist version of the divine ideas thesis. To hold that ideas, and 'reality' as such, are the products of intellection is, within the framework of this theory, no concession to conceptualism, since these ideas are being equated with the intellect; they are not its products. Unless there is a greater degree of separation than is here allowed between intellect and intelligibles, the subordinationistic force of conceptualism cannot obtain. As we shall see momentarily, Plotinus will take further theoretic steps in V.9.7 and 8 to forestall any misunderstanding on the point. But it should be clear that according to this thesis of self-productive aspects within the second hypostasis, ontological priority is not an appropriate notion.

The theme of self-contemplation by intellect of intelligibles allows Plotinus, within the argument of V.9.5, to make, therefore, three important points. The first is that what the intellect contemplates are the forms themselves. Second, the forms are not the conceptual products of an active intellect; hence, conceptualism is avoided. Finally, *nous* conforms to the generalized Platonic logic for an intelligible principle: it is what it is 'in itself,' without qualification or alteration. As we find in the language of 15–16: "it thinks itself and is in itself."

The broader implications of this central Plotinian theme of the self-contemplation of *nous* are very rich indeed, and Plotinus elaborates some additional corollaries in V.9.5–9. We might examine a few important doctrines that help to clarify Plotinus's answers to some of the central difficulties that we have pursued in our inquiry into earlier realist theology. Many of these have been touched on in passing in our initial exposition, although their full significance can now be better assayed. We might begin then with an interesting passage on the demiurgic character of *nous* from V.9.5, 19–29:

But also, if there must be a "maker of this All," he will not think what is in the not yet existent universe in order to make it. The objects of his thought must exist before the universe, not impressions from other things but archetypes and primary and the substance of Intellect. But if they are going to say that rational forming principles are enough, they must clearly be eternal; but if they are eternal and not subject to affections, they must be in Intellect, and in an intellect of this kind, one which is prior to condition and nature and soul: for these are potential. Intellect therefore really thinks the real beings, not as if they were somewhere else: for they are neither before it nor after it; but it is like the primary lawgiver, or rather is itself the law of being.

The initial reference to 'the maker of this all' from *Timaeus* 28C sets the context well enough, and it seems clear that Plotinus intends to identify *nous* with the demiurge here, in contrast to III.9.1, where it was located at the level of the soul. The discussion that follows addresses the relations between intellect and intelligibles within *nous*. The argument from 20–24 is most important, since it again gives a striking insight into Plotinian Platonism. Intellect in its production does not, as it were, think up the objects of the universe in order to make them, but rather it looks to the eternally preexistent forms. Two points are immediately clear from our previous discussion: This is an argument for exemplarism within the second hypostatic principle; and it is here underscored by a second important point: the paradigms in question exist as fixed and eternal principles, not as the products of the intentions of the demiurge in his role as cosmic orderer. Forms cannot then be seen merely as instrumental principles, postulated to explain the process of cosmic generation and subordinate to the motive force of production. They have a status that is central to the structure of 'being' and also to intellect itself, for they are underscored as real archetypes, first principles, and the very substance of intellect.

This doctrine thus explicitly denies a demiurgic, cosmologically grounded approach to the ideas and so avoids entirely the concept of forms generated by the intentions of the demiurge. It is interesting to note that Plotinus is thereby denying the concept of divine intellection of possible worlds. As a consequence of his understanding of Platonism, it would not be possible to construe forms as a set of potential entities that the demiurge entertains prior to generating the world. They are eternal and actual, temporally neither before nor after intellect. This is a point of paramount importance in locating the Plotinian position in a general taxonomy of Western philosophical theology, since it would involve an implicit denial of any approach to forms as potential prototypes for the world of 'becoming.' Plotinus's specific concern here is directed toward the implications of this imagery for Platonic theology, since it would suggest that the forms could be revised as necessary according to the planning principle's intentions or be seen as not actually productive. The former claim should now also be seen as unacceptable, since it would imply that real beings are subject to externally based change; we will return to this issue momentarily. While these are Plotinus's explicit concerns here, his position has important ramifications beyond those discussed in this text. To deny that forms can be treated as potentialities is to undercut the foundations of one very influential type of conceptualist theology, grounded in the notion of 'possible worlds.' This position holds that the divine mind can examine a range of possible worlds that exist as articulated archetypes within his mind, among which he may then choose on the basis of some evaluative criteria. This sort of 'possible world' theology, radically conceptualist at basis, has been a pervasive element in Western philosophical theology since the rise of late-medieval nominalism and is now fairly common in contemporary Anglo-American philosophical theology.[52] Plotinian theology would be opposed to this whole approach, since Plotinus would deny the notion of potentiality to the formal principles in the sense necessary to establish a 'possible world' theology. The grounds for this denial are the same as those just reviewed: to understand correctly what real beings are is to recognize them as fully actual, productive, and eternal and thus not merely intentional objects within the divine mind.

In reading V.9.5, I have indicated that the dominant thrust of the argument is to construct a version of Platonism; the ontological criteria for such entities are the same as those we found in Plato, centered upon self-sameness. The discussion in the text sums up Plotinus's realist ontology in relation to his theory of the intellect at 32–36 and 42–46:

32–36:   For no one of the real beings is outside, or in place, but they remain always in themselves and undergo no alteration or destruction: that is why they are truly real. If they come into being and perish, they will have their being from outside themselves, and it will not any more be they, but that being which will be reality.

42–46:   And this All shows by its participation in appearances that the real beings are other than they; the real beings are unchanging, but the appearances change, the real beings are set firm on themselves and need no place:

for they are not magnitudes; they have an intelligent existence sufficient to themselves.

The entities that merit the ascription of "true being" or "really real" are those that are unchanging and without alteration and that remain within themselves. This 'internal remaining' is of a special sort: it is a type of intelligent and self-sufficient existence. Plotinus evidently considered his own doctrine, that the intelligibles are within the intellect, to be the best way to ground these foundational principles and to argue for their self-sufficiency. This he is able to claim because of the identification of 'being' with intellect. Nonetheless, this is hardly a very perspicuous position to hold; and, not surprisingly, the exact status of real beings with this intellect–intelligible hypostasis becomes an immediate topic of analysis in V.9.6, 1–3: "Let it be granted, then, that Intellect is the real beings, possessing them all not as if [they were in it] as in a place, but as possessing itself and being one with them. 'All things are together' there, and nonetheless they are separate." If one accepts the Plotinian intellective status of ideas, it might be natural to revert to the Middle Platonic imagery of forms as spatially within the intellect, but Plotinus is evidently concerned to avoid this suggestion. What is involved here is identification, not inclusion. This is, however, only part of the problem, since the differences among these intelligible objects must also be maintained, or else the intent of realism would again be endangered from another direction. To collapse the formal principles into unity would be to undermine their separate exemplarist function and to remove effectively their status as real predicative unities; hence, Plotinus's reliance upon the view that *nous* is a 'one-many' compound, a collective unity. As he avers at V.9.6, 7–9: "In this way, and much more than this, Intellect is all things together and also not together, because each is a special power." *Nous* is the unity of all things, but each formal principle retains its own particular character and power, by which it is what it is and by virtue of which it warrants its status as a really real entity. In order to support his realism, Plotinus must therefore treat the unity of the realm of 'being' in such a way that its cohesion and connectivity do not undercut the very basis for the postulation of that transcendent level.

One centrally important theme that Plotinus uses to motivate this doctrine of collective unity within *nous,* and also to explain the 'intellect-being' relation more adequately than is found in earlier Middle Platonism, is his doctrine that each form is itself an intellect. The compound character of the second hypostasis is such, as we have seen, that it can be said to be both intellect and intelligible. It is also held that each form is both an intellect and an intelligible. What Plotinus in effect maintains is that the compound character of this whole hypostasis should also apply to each intelligible form as well, producing what is best termed a monadology. V.9.8, 1–4: "If, then, the thought [of intellect] is of what is within it, that which is within it is its immanent form, and this is the Idea. What then is this? Intellect and the intelligent substance; each individual Idea is not other than Intellect, but each is Intellect. And Intellect as a whole is all the Forms, and each individual Form is an individual intellect." This is really the core of Plotinus's doctrine that the intelligibles are not outside the intellect. Not only must the intelligibles collectively be seen as 'within' the divine intellect (i.e., these two notions are to be identified macrocosmically), but also each separate intelligible must be seen to have an intellective aspect to it as well. Both the general and the specific versions of the intellect–intelligible identification are together the basis for the Plotinian understanding of *nous,* and the two aspects of the doctrine are closely allied throughout. Hence, his denial of Longinus's position on extrinsic ideas relies on the identification of the intellect and the intelligible at all levels where intellect or intelligibility are present. This can be seen in the passage above from V.9.8, where the nature of *to eidos* is analyzed. It is found to be intellect and intelligible substance, that is, the specific definitional or formal property of this principle. Each intelligible is a separate and distinct intellect, just as this same duality is recognized on the level of intellect as a whole.

Plotinus's realist theology is therefore at base a monadology, for the world of being exhibits upon examination a collective unity of monadic intellects. As our discussion of V.9.6 indicated, this theory helps Plotinus to buttress his Platonism against the charge that the identification of 'being' with intellect would destroy the character of each separate form, upon which that theory ultimately rests. To this claim Plotinus can reply that the self-sameness of each form is ensured by its individual intellective character. Just as *nous* as a whole thinks itself, and "this thinking is *idea*," so also the intelligible character of each form is a function of its own exercise of intellection. Hence, to identify 'being' with intellect would not be to subordinate the former to the latter, nor to subsume the specific nature of forms in general collectivity based upon intellect as a whole. This position also helps to explain why Plotinus felt that this analysis of *nous* safeguarded the self-sameness of real objects so effectively. Since the intellect–intelligible identification applies at all levels, the intellection of each form is alike in character to the self-reflection of *nous* as a whole; that is, it is self-contemplation. Each form, then, contemplates its own intelligible character.

One apparent result of this analysis of the forms as intellective by Plotinus is that it allays the problem of radical subordination of the nature and character of 'being' to intellect. There is no question that Plotinus intended his doctrine of the intellective nature of the intelligibles to bear upon this subject directly. The passage just quoted from the beginning of V.9.8 follows upon a discussion of this very problem at the end of V.9.7 (14–18). The question is whether the intellect–intelligible identification implies a doctrine of divine thoughts, in the sense that we examined in our discussion of early Middle Platonism. The text reads as follows: "It is, then, incorrect to say that the Forms are thoughts if what is meant by this is that when Intellect thought this particular Form came into existence or is this particular form; for what is thought must be prior to this thinking [of a particular Form]. Otherwise how would it come to thinking it? Certainly not by chance, nor did it happen on it casually." We have here an explicit denial of the conceptualist implications of the divine thoughts thesis that we imputed to some versions of Middle Platonism, and this provides witness to that line of analysis. Plotinus himself is concerned that this doctrine could entail the view that the exercise of divine intellection would be productive of the forms and of 'being.' If forms are to be self-same and so also really real, this must be avoided. Plotinus suggests, therefore, that the intelligible content of the form be treated as primary and logically prior. This would underscore the eternal and real character of each form. But given the context of this claim against the backdrop of the doctrine that each form is an intellect, there are no grounds to hold conversely that intellection is thereby seriously depreciated. Because his commitment to forms was a serious one, and because this problem of the connection between the divine intellect and the forms was so important, Plotinus developed this very complex and nuanced doctrinal response. While it may not solve all questions involved, it is certainly a remarkable revision of Middle Platonic and Neopythagorean theories, one that shows clear evidence of being structured to offer conclusions to the problems we have been tracing. We might conclude our inquiry into this aspect of *nous* by looking at one final text from V.9.8, lines 7–19:

This intellect therefore is in itself, and since it possesses itself in peace is everlasting fullness. If then Intellect was thought of as preceding being, we should have to say that Intellect by coming to active actuality in its thinking perfected and produced the real beings; but since we must think of being as preceding Intellect, we must assume that the real beings have their place in the thinking subject, and that the active actuality of thinking is in the real beings, as the active actuality of fire is in fire already existing, in order that they may have Intellect in its unity in them as their active actuality. But being is active actuality: so both have one active actuality, or rather both are one thing. Being and Intellect are therefore one nature; so therefore are the real beings and the active actuality of being and Intellect of this kind; and the thoughts of this kind are the form and shape of being and its active actuality.

Here are addressed several of the central issues in ancient Platonist theology, along with Plotinus's conclusions. Once again self-sameness and self-directedness are to the fore, as we have come to expect, in order to sanction *nous* in its status. Plotinus then denies that intellect can be said to precede 'being,' no doubt in reference to those like Atticus and Longinus who entertained this view, as well as earlier demiurgic theorists. The implications of this view are then spelled out succinctly: if intellect precedes 'being,' then real beings would be produced or perfected by intellect. He thinks this would be clearly unacceptable, and so we find Plotinus employing two major strategies to preserve the *onta*: (a) he claims that if priority is to be assigned, it must be given to 'being' rather than intellect, revising the subordinationism of *nous* theologies as they had been understood; and (b) he then presses his major theme, that 'being' and intellect are one nature. This latter, of course, is the stronger claim, when understood in the particular way in which we have seen it articulated by Plotinus.

I would argue, therefore, that Plotinus's theory of the intelligibles has a demonstrable foundation in the antecedent discussions of realist theology that we have been tracing in this inquiry. The structure of Plotinus's position shows with surety that he recognized the difficulties that *nous* theology posed for Platonism, and he attempted to establish a theoretical position that avoided these dangers. I shall demur from actually passing judgment on the results, though as just indicated, they are doubtless impressive in their ingenuity and especially for the conceptual detail in which they argued. This, even more perhaps than its content, makes Plotinian theology stand out from the available examples of Middle Platonic thought.

Besides these important themes, there are a number of other features of Plotinus's thought on *nous* and the forms in these early treatises that warrant our attention. Before returning to V.9 we might turn to consider briefly some texts from V.1[10].4, which develops some important internal issues that follow upon the understanding of being and intellect as we have been considering it. Lines 26–33 read:

> But each of them is Intellect and Being, and the whole is universal Intellect and Being, Intellect making Being exist in thinking it, and Being giving Intellect thinking and existence by being thought. But the cause of thinking is something else, which is also cause of being; they both therefore have a cause other than themselves. For they are simultaneous and exist together and one does not abandon the other, but this one is two things, Intellect and Being and thinking and thought, Intellect as thinking and Being as thought.

This is an important explication of the intrinsic nature of *nous*, which explains the theory beyond what we have seen thus far. The correlative character of 'being' and intellection is even more explicit here, and their mutual dependence is clarified. Because of their fundamental identity, Plotinus is willing here to say that intellect is productive of 'being' by thinking it, just as it can be said that 'being' gives intellect its existence and essential function in its capacity for being thought. All this, to use temporal language, is simultaneous; we have once again what might be loosely called mutual entailment between these two features of the intelligible world. There is also in this text one point that will be a feature of increasing significance in our discussion, and that is the causal dependence of both 'being' and intellection upon a higher source, the One. The exact interpretation of the foundation of 'being' is quite obviously an issue of immense importance in Plotinian Platonism; we might note its presence here and return to the issue presently.

One topic that we have routinely discussed in considering each earlier version of Platonism has been the constituency of the realm of forms and the interrelationships among these entities. To complete our analysis of Plotinian realism, we might divert our attention to a few points that bear on this subject of the scope of 'being'. There is an especially interesting passage immediately following that just cited from V.1.4, which may help to explain what sorts of formal objects Plotinus was willing to countenance and how these entities do in fact constitute a composite unity without violating the intrinsic character of each form. Lines 34–41 read as follows:

For there could not be thinking without otherness, and also sameness. These then are primarily, Intellect, Being, Otherness, Sameness; but one must also include Motion and Rest. One must include movement if there is thought, and rest that it may think the same; and otherness, that there may be thinker and thought; or else, if you take away otherness, it will become one and keep silent; and the objects of thought, also, must have otherness in relation to each other. But one must include sameness, because it is one with itself, and all have some common unity; and the distinctive quality of each is otherness.

We have returned to the problem of the 'great kinds' and issue of forms of motion, difference, thought, and so on from the *Sophist*. Plotinus's answer seems to be that such forms must be included within their proper sphere. This is determined, as is the case with all of the *eidē*, by the conceptual interweaving of forms, their interstitial network of implication and impossibility. Here we see Plotinus articulating this theme and admitting motion and thought into the intelligible world. The argument is clear enough: thought entails movement of at least an intellectual sort, while sameness entails rest. Otherness is required for all conceptual differentiation; hence it, like sameness, ranges over all other forms. And so the argument can be extended for these highly generic forms. The interrelations are in principle the explanatory basis for all of the connections among formal objects, and it is therefore on a foundation of this sort that Plotinus would hold all forms as constituting an intelligible collectivity. It must be reiterated that passages of this sort certainly give the lie to the conventional view that realist theology inherently entails the exclusion of all motion from the intelligible or 'real' world and that it is fundamentally static. This is simply a misunderstanding, and as far as intellective movement, life, and other notions of the sort are concerned, it is a misplaced criticism of Plotinian Platonism.[53]

Besides the 'greatest kinds,' Plotinus also is willing to countenance forms based upon the traces of intelligible unity 'naturally' found in the world of sense, as he says in V.9.10, 1–3: "All the things, then, which exist as forms in the world of sense come from that intelligible world; those which do not, do not. Therefore none of the things which are contrary to nature are there." While exactitude in this criterion is certainly wanting, its intent is clear enough. Plotinus is following in the Middle Platonic tradition and is rejecting forms that are 'contrary to nature.' This would accord with the definition of a form that we reviewed in Alcinous and that seems to have come down from Xenocrates and the Old Academy. The force of this restriction is perhaps a bit clearer in Plotinus, although the final chapters of V.9 that address these subjects are a bit sketchy. Nonetheless, it is obvious that in this early treatise Plotinus had already adopted a type of Platonism weighted strongly in favor of an evaluative criterion for forms and away from purely logical grounds. The subsequent discussion of this general subject in V.9.10–14 indicates that the issue for Plotinus is important precisely because he intends forms to be both the productive archetypes and the principles of perfection for the sensible world, not merely a set of logically possible universals. For this reason he eschews the primarily logical approach to realism, based upon predication.[54] Hence, the correlation between examples of 'being' and perfection in this lower world and their sources in the intelligible world is very tightly drawn, for this latter world is not made up of merely speculative or conceptual entities but of real and productive powers.

We might note, though we cannot develop the issue here,[55] that in V.9.11 Plotinus takes a fairly latitudinal view toward artistic production. His attitude is that those sorts of artistic production that have access to the power of the higher world and that contemplate aspects of the intelligibles are clearly grounded in forms (8–11). Again, exactly which artifacts would correspond to forms is somewhat inexactly considered; but for our purposes the point is clear enough: it is the formal principles as powers productive in the world that is the determining concept in his argument, and true art gains us access to these.

One final observation might be made regarding the scope of Plotinus's realism in V.9. Chapter 12 brings up the difficult question of forms of individuals, which in this brief section he treats summarily, focusing largely on differences between human bodies. The later discussion in V.7[18] will focus on human souls and the extent to which these are individually grounded in the intelligible world. I mention this much discussed issue [56] here only in order to indicate how far Plotinus was willing to diverge from a logically based Platonism, which argues primarily in favor of generic universals. Even to bring up the notion of forms of individuals is indicative of an approach to realism grounded in a view of forms that emphasizes their nature as principles of perfection and that sees them mainly as the productive powers that generate all that is ordered and valuable within the lower world. This is a very important point for assessing his realist theology, since it indicates the extent to which forms were viewed by him as principles of perfection and as generative powers rather than as universals. The focus of the Platonist tradition has thereby been shifted away from these logical aspects, in favor of the foundation for the theory of forms in aesthetics, morality, and theology. Whether this more evaluatively grounded Platonism could ever be totally disjoined from the logical features is questionable,[57] but there is no doubt that Plotinus reinforced a tendency, already prevalent in Middle Platonism, to focus largely on the valuational elements of the tradition. As was the case with Alcinous, whose views in this regard were plainly influenced by his integration of realism and theology, Plotinus was doubtless concerned to avoid a theory that would require countenancing 'negative' sorts of forms because of his theology. V.9.14 makes this plain. Forms of putrefaction and the like are denied precisely because of the origin of all intelligibles in the One. The rule at 8–9 states: "All things which Intellect gets from the First are the best." Here the evaluative bases for the exclusion are founded in the nature of One and in the fact that all elements of 'being' are directly grounded in that perfect source. Once again it is the nature and function of the first principle that is determinative of the shape of Plotinus's Platonism.

I should like now to review our inquiry into Plotinus and the ancient realist tradition in theology by summarizing Plotinus's relation to that long trajectory. The core of this theology is its belief in a transcendent world of real beings, which are the foundations of the existence, order, and value that we find in the fluxion of 'becoming'. Plotinus stands firmly in this tradition, countenancing the existence of such principles, which collectively constitute the intelligible world of 'being.' His metaphysics, however, makes every effort to secure and preserve the insights upon which the postulation of such *onta* depended. A central issue in Platonic theology since the time of Plato was, as we have seen, the relation between these formal principles and the principle of intellection and cosmic production. Plotinus was faced in effect with a choice among a number of theories: (1) those that emphasized the independence of the forms as paradigms separate from the demiurgic first principle, (2) those that subordinated the forms construed as ideas to the demiurgic intellect, and (3) those that treated forms as divine ideas within a first intellective principle but demoted the active intellective and cosmological principle to a lower level of divinity. For Plotinus, the second alternative seems to have been unacceptable, too destructive of the force and intent of Platonism as he understood it, and his own position emerges as a very complex rethinking of elements from these two other positions. Plotinus was evidently concerned to maintain that the forms constituted a set of inviolable and immutable paradigms that were effective in the structure of becoming. From his standpoint, the exemplarist position seems to have removed the danger of the forms being produced at the intent of the demiurge, but it pluralized the number of explanatory principles to an unacceptable degree and separated them in a way that was problematical as well. The removal of demiurgic intellection from the forms seems to have suggested to Plotinus the danger that the cosmological activities of the demiurge might have been conducted upon an incomplete or erroneous understanding of the real paradigms so that the forms would cease to be the true principles of the sensible cosmos. Finally, there were difficulties with the last position, largely due to the fact that, although considered to be a self-contemplative *nous* at rest whose self-thinking was the forms, its first principle was nonetheless deficiently united to serve in the role of the ultimate principle. These, then, were inadequacies in earlier realist theology, from Plotinus's standpoint.

The Plotinian theoretical proposals for the revision of Platonic theology prove to be a remarkable set of doctrines directed at these perceived shortcomings in earlier systems. The initial feature we considered was the identification of intelligibles with intellect. The core of this position was his adoption of the view that each form was itself an intellect, which amounts to treating the intelligible world as a collection of monadic intellects, each self-contemplative of its own 'idea' or formal nature. These intellective forms, in the process of their own introspective self-definition, are aware of overall relation between their own formal nature and those of other forms so that they become cognizant of the whole range of other form-intellects to which they are connected dialectically. This mutual interpenetration of a community of living, formal minds produces the unity-in-diversity that is characteristic of the hypostasis of *nous*. The full ramifications of this position are beyond the range of our focus, but the salient point is the new understanding this doctrine brings to the intellect–form relation. The divine intellect as a whole is really the result of its constituency of intellect-forms, and this renders quite benign the relation of mind to form; for intellect is to be understood as that which is directed toward each form's definitional nature, while that definition emerges in its intelligible specificity by its own self-thought. The whole hypostasis becomes the collective product of this intellective activity, and the demiurgic function becomes markedly less significant, being assigned, as we saw in some discussions, to the third level of soul, though also at times to *nous*. This latter association stems in part from the fact that *nous* as a whole exercises contemplation in regard to its own example and source, the One. No matter how this noetic theory is judged, there can be no question that it reinforces the character of forms as independent and eternal foundations for cognitive order and value, free from alteration by the active divine intellect.

This restoration of realism within Platonic philosophical theology was, therefore, of decisive importance for Plotinus and for the new school he initiated. The Plotinian doctrine of the nature of 'being' provided the basis for a revised appraisal of the first principles of earlier Platonists, and it was on this basis that the Neoplatonic One was developed. It is here that the sophisticated recognition of the nature of a wholly simple principle is felt in Plotinus, for his criticism of Middle Platonic theology was mainly based upon its deficiency in this regard. *Nous* theology lacked the absolute unity and utter simplicity that Plotinus held to be necessary for a primal principle because of the inherent duality of the intellect–intelligibles relation within such a principle as well as the agreed upon plurality of the intelligible archetypes. This rejection of *nous* theology in Plotinus is not the result of some aesthetic preference in favor of a wholly simple absolute. Rather, the postulation of the One was due to his understanding of a conceptual need for a primary principle that was entirely free from composition or any limitation. Plotinus recognized a conceptual need for a principle of divinity that was absolute simplicity, and it was from this perspective that Middle Platonic theology was found wanting.

This Plotinian development of the notion of an absolute being as first principle was, as we saw, conditioned by the Platonic treatment of this concept of 'being'. The One, as an absolute first principle, was a projection from Platonic ontology and its treatment of forms as self-same immutable unities. But in the case of forms there is still an odd sense of dependence upon the definitional 'content' of a form, upon its logical relations to other definitional entities within this dialectically arranged world. This was a controversial issue within the Academy, with the early discovery of the dangers of regress stemming from the need for ever more encompassing unities to explain the definitional character of forms. Plotinus intended that his first principle should have an absolute and self-same character, like that of a form, but should also avoid the difficulties that attached to the form's definitional nature, its 'need' for its own resolution in a higher principle. This necessitated a strong incommensurability thesis regarding the One, to establish that it was ontologically different in type from forms, exceeding their metaphysical status. For this reason we find negative theology invoked to pollard those elements of Platonic realism that would detract from the absolute standing of the One. In the end, Plotinus's theology became not so much an argument regarding the proper character of the One as a projection of an absolute *archē*, which, if it is to serve that function, must exceed the bounds of this ontology itself. This was, of course, to move beyond Middle Platonism and its more limited use of negative theology, since we find in the Plotinian One the initiation of a new discussion of the logical character of a divine absolute.

This important development within Platonic metaphysics was clearly conditioned by Plotinus's special appropriation of that tradition. To ignore the dominant theme of the One's positive transcendence of 'being' and the richness of the intelligible world is to denude Plotinian thought of its whole point. The fundamental direction of Plotinian Platonism is from 'becoming' into the deeper level of 'being' and thence to the absolutely simple and wholly unified level of the One. As the principle projected beyond his ontology's highest discursive or theoretical level, it cannot be described by that ontology, but this negative condition should not then be ascribed to the One and made the basis for some supposed inadequacy. To miss the vectorial character and force of Plotinus's Platonism is to mistake the systematic position and nature of the One entirely; this is my excuse in part for this section's inquiry. From the standpoint of Platonic theology, the Plotinian One is more unified than even our finest conceptual insights can grasp and more perfect than our modes of description can represent. While Plotinian Platonism intends that theology should conclude in contemplative vision, understanding the discursive foundations of its philosophical theology remain necessary to that end.

3. Hid Divinity

It could be said that in some respects Plotinus's doctrine of the One amounts to the isolation of certain features of the first principles of figures like Moderatus or Numenius and the reification of these elements into a principle whose role remains similar to these older *archai* but whose description is rigidly restricted by negative theology. This would be, however, to miss much of the theological force of the Plotinian doctrine of the One and to reduce it to the terms of Middle Platonism. While I should like to examine the One from the perspective of the earlier Platonic theology we have considered, I wish to do so as far as possible without any such reductionism. It seems to me, however, that examining Plotinus's initial writings on the One from the perspective of ancient Platonism remains an especially effective vantage point from which to assess its unique character and its special significance for philosophical theology. As in the preceding sections of this chapter, I propose focusing upon some of the early treatises that address the One–intellection relation, particularly VI.9[9], V.1[10], and V.2[11].

We might begin with a passage from V.9.2 (23–27), which gives a striking image of the real and intelligible world's relation to the One: "Should we then stop at Intellect as the First, or must we go beyond Intellect, and does Intellect stand from our point of view in front of the first principle, as if in the porch of the Good, proclaiming to us all that is in it, like an impression of it in greater multiplicity while the Good remains altogether one?" Here we are urged to press on in contemplation beyond the divine intellect because of its intrinsic location in the structure of things. The hypostasis of 'being' and intellect is not the first; it is that which stands "on the porch of the Good,"[58] and its intelligible structure proclaims the nature of the One. This recalls both the status of *nous* as a collective unity as well as the *dunamis pantōn* theme. As the text indicates, the intelligible world in a sense proclaims what is within the absolute simplicity of the One at a greater level of multiplicity. As far as Plotinus's Platonism is concerned, the intelligibles are clearly meant to be manifestations at the level of eternality and self-sufficiency of what is beyond 'being'. This implies that they are also dependent ontologically upon what lies beyond them, within the absolute simplicity of the first hypostasis. This raises two issues that bear examination: (a) the extent to which *onta* can be said to be grounded in the One and (b) why the postulation of a primal One is warranted within this theology.

Two passages, from V.2.1 and V.1.7, provide a clear statement of the emergence of *nous* from the One and so of its bases in that higher hypostasis. V.2.1, 9–13 details the superabundant overflow of the One: "This, when it has come into being, turns back upon the One and is filled, and becomes Intellect by looking towards it. Its halt and turning towards the One constitutes being, its gaze upon the One, Intellect. Since it halts and turns towards the One that it may see, it becomes at once Intellect and being." As we saw, Numenian theology had identified the 'living creature' with the first principle and had assigned an exemplarist function to it (frag. 22). There is in this passage a residual exemplarism, in spite of the ineffability and qualitative transcendence of this absolutely simple first principle. '*Nous* turns back upon the One and is filled' so that it gazes upon the One and turns toward it in order to become what is its nature as the second hypostasis. It is self-constitutive because of this turning, but it is only by virtue of its contemplation of the One that it can establish itself as 'being' and intellect. We should note the emphasis of external contemplation of an independent principle toward which *nous* looks and that is the source of its content. This theme of procession provides the basis for an account both for the separation of hypostatic levels and for the ultimate grounding of the forms themselves. This can be seen in a similar passage from V.1.7, 1–7: "But we say that Intellect is an image of that Good; for we must speak more plainly; first of all we must say that what has come into being must be in a way that Good, and retain much of it and be a likeness of it, as light is of the sun But intellect is not that Good. How then does it generate Intellect? Because by its return to it it sees: and this seeing is Intellect." The imagery of the Good, the sun, and its light from the *Republic* establish the fundamental relation between levels. Here the connection of *nous* and the One is strengthened by the use of image language, with *nous* and its content being termed an image of the One. That which has come into being must be in some sense the One or at least retain much of it and be like it, since it is its first manifestation. But the two cannot be identified, for *nous* is, as we have seen, a multiple representation of absolute unity. Once again the notion operative here is degrees of reality. The second hypostasis is the representative image of the One at the level of reality, but it is the best image available. It is in a sense the One at that level, though that last qualification also establishes their fundamental separateness. This is further enforced by the imagery of the intellect's looking back upon the One.[59] This reversive contemplation by *nous* is understood by Plotinus as central to its taking on of order and structure: values and characteristics that are characteristic of it *qua* 'being.' Its movement from inchoate or potential vision to true or actualized sight is also its act of productive self-awareness. By turning upon the One, *nous* becomes a distinct entity, an image of the One at the next level of being. As such it is also separate from the One. Intellect is not the One; it has come forth from it and constituted itself through reflexive awareness of its source. More clearly than in Numenius, this process of reversive self-constitution by *nous* is free from the notion that the One is employing a lower, intellective aspect of itself for the purpose of self-reflection or cosmic production. In Plotinus, the One is thus sharply distinguished from intellect by this theme of paradigmatic contemplation; they are not assimilated. We have here further indication of the developing language of transcendence by which the One is distinguished in Plotinian theism from its consequents.

There are two conflicting, though partly reconcilable, themes in Plotinus on this issue of the grounding of *nous* and the forms in the One. Clearly, he wants to see the intelligible world as the genuine and best representation of the One available, and to this end passages like those above are employed. The language is traditionally Platonic, with an emphasis upon likeness and fundamental connectivity; hence, Plotinus is once again relying upon the middle-period dialogues' account of the form–particular relation to explain an aspect of the One. But as with forms, there are resources for arguing that this likeness does not connote identification of One and *nous*, only immanence. In the case of forms and particulars, the transcendence of forms is asserted on the basis of their ontological preeminence, that is, by resorting to an ontology of degrees of reality. Plotinus employs this same logic, but he cannot simply invoke this Platonic notion of hierarchy, since the principle upon which he focuses is beyond 'being,' beyond the standard dimensions of this ontology.

Plotinus solves this dilemma by two strategies. The first approach is to base this distinction upon the function of the One, and in this respect the One does become assimilated to an extent with its products. We have seen this approach already, and it is a theme that tends to make Plotinus resemble earlier thinkers, such as Numenius. The second move is more radical and connects with the Plotinian theme of the uniqueness and absolute simplicity of the One.

This is the critical Plotinian departure. The distinction of the One and its subsequents must be said to be one of ontological type; that is, they are simply different in all fundamental respects. The One is not a 'being'; it transcends limitation and qualitative definition. Hence, it cannot be classed among things, cannot be assimilated to its subsequents, cannot be circumscribed in any way that applies to its nature; it is different in type from all beings, even the really real ones of the intelligible world.

These are hard sayings. We should note how both of these strate- gies are conjoined in the discussion: the One is distinguishable both by its distinctly different nature and by its function. These themes are in fact joined to help answer the problem discussed earlier of how such an absolutely simple principle, different from all others to such a complete extent, can be productive. An important pas- sage from V.1.7, 13–24, may help to clarify matters; the discussion is focused upon *nous* and its emergence from the One:

Intellect, certainly, by its own means even defines its being for itself by the power which comes from the One, and because its substance is a kind of single part of what belongs to the One and comes from the One, it is strengthened by the One and made perfect in substantial existence by and from it. But intellect sees, by means of itself, like something divided pro- ceeding from the undivided, that life and thought and all things come from the One, because that God is not one of all things; for this is how all things come from him, because he is not confined by any shape; that One is one alone: if he was all things, he would be numbered among beings. For this reason that One is none of the things in Intellect, but all things come from him. This is why they are substances; for they are already defined and each has a kind of shape.

This passage illustrates the major conflicting aspects of the Plotinian theory of the intellect–One relation.[60] The early portion, down to line 18, emphasizes the strong connectivity of these two hypostases. The initial notion of the self-definition of its own 'being' by intellect is tied carefully to the power of the One. This then becomes the basis for a strong statement of the closeness of *nous* and the One. The substance of *nous* is even termed a "sort of single portion of what is of the One and from the One." Then this proximity is reversed. Characteristically, Plotinus resorts to the image of the actualized perception of *nous* to establish this separation. In this case, *nous* recognizes the One as its source, the source of its own constituent elements such as life and thought. This begins the use of the first strategy we have noted, that of the One's characteristic function in the overall system. We then have the ontological-type thesis introduced as well at 18–19. 'The One is not one of all things.' It lacks any intelligible shape (20); it is alone one; that is, it is uniquely simple. The One cannot be numbered among beings; hence, it is distinct from the class of real beings and from intellect as a whole (21 ff.) This is a very strong claim, one that relies on a firm distinction of type between the class of beings, that is, those entities that can admit of finite definition. The argument mixes this view with the claim that the One is also separate as universal source, for, as noted, these are commonly conjoined themes in Plotinus.

Before attempting further analysis, we might review two further statements of both of these positions, the first from V.2.1, 1–7:

> The One is all things and not a single one of them: it is the principle of all things, not all things, but all things have that other kind of transcendent existence; for in a way they do occur in the One; or rather they are not there yet, but they will be. How then do all things come from the One, which is simple and has in it no diverse variety, or any sort of doubleness? It is because there is nothing in it that all things come from it: in order that being may exist, the One is not being, but the generator of being.

The opening line articulates the ontological-type theme and is based upon the same sort of thought as *Parmenides* 160 d–ere ff. The paradox of the One's nature is very sharp here: it is all things, in virtue of being their *archē*, but it is also not to be assimilated to that class. Because of its simplicity it cannot be described, and in this sense it might be said that 'there is nothing in it.' Because it is a principle of such manifest simplicity and unity, all more limited entities can proceed from it. Once again the connection is made between the function of the One as ontological source and the argument for the separation of One from 'being'.

One final passage on this question of the distinction of One and intellect, which articulates both the functional and the ontological uniqueness of the One, is VI.9.3, 36–45:

> It is not therefore Intellect, but before Intellect. For Intellect is one of the beings, but that is not anything, but before each and every thing, and is not

being: for being has a kind of shape of being, but that has no shape, not even intelligible shape. For since the nature if the One is generative of all things it is not any one of them. It is not therefore something or qualified or quantitative or intellect or soul; it is not in movement or at rest, not in place, not in time, but "itself by itself of single form," or rather formless, being before all form, before movement and before rest: for these pertain to being and are what make it many.

Here the force of what I have called the ontological-type distinction is immediately obvious in its application to the first and second hypostases. Intellect as a whole can be assimilated to the class of 'being', while the One is such that it cannot be so located and circumscribed. It is prior to 'being' and all beings, that is, all forms and all other entities that can be descriptively appropriated. From Plotinus's standpoint this applies to the class of all beings, to the collective intellect itself, since it is amenable to real description and definition as the paragon of all intelligibility. Again we find that the One cannot be given form, even intelligible form unlike all beings that have finite essential descriptions. Now this is a very clear statement of the grounds for maintaining the transcendence of the One, and it rests largely on this fundamental difference between what is finite and limited by description, however perfect, and what is outside that domain entirely. In this passage we also find the ontological priority of the One maintained, as in earlier texts considered, so that the argument of the separation from intellect is again made on the basis of systemic function of the One. Because it produces all beings, it cannot be included within that class. The combination of these two themes provides the philosophical warrant for the rather extraordinary list of negative proscriptions regarding the One found throughout VI.9. As we would expect, the One must be beyond quality, quantity, intelligence, and soul. Since both motion and rest are within the intelligible world, and since they both apply to specific forms and to realm of 'being' generally, the One must be beyond both these qualities. All of these are the characteristics that make *nous* multiple, and what is absolutely simple must transcend this level entirely.

But in what sense does the One transcend the intelligible level? There is a great deal of ambiguity in this notion of "beyond being" and in the negations that are applied in apophatic theology. The ontological-type distinction emphasizes the radical distinctness of the One, a thesis that is established in part by this striking denial of all "intelligible shape." Yet it should be recalled that the nature of the intelligible world is such that it is said to proceed from the One, and as just noted, many passages that feature this doctrine of ontological difference between One and intellect also maintain that the intelligibles are somehow grounded in the One. If *nous* establishes its own nature by reflexive contemplation of its source, what are we to make of this *archē* beyond intelligible description, beyond 'being'? These are especially difficult issues to address in Plotinus, without straying beyond the confines of philosophical theology as such and into contemplative practice.[61] However, we might attempt to consider these issues in order to answer the two related questions that we are concerned to pursue in this section: In what way are *onta* based upon the One, and how is the transcendence of the One beyond 'being' and *nous* accounted for?

While there are many ways to approach Plotinian apophatic theology,[62] I wish to focus on the fundamental Platonic ontology with which Plotinus was working. The doctrine of the One as the transcendent ground of being is postulated largely as an extension of Platonic ontology, or as Aubenque more broadly maintained: "un dépassement de l'ontologie grecque classique."[63] We might recall our earlier discussion of the characteristics of Platonic ontology, especially its emphasis upon entities that hold their essential descriptions necessarily. As we noted, this amounts to a selective focus upon those entities that are predicatively the same, without the possibility of alteration (i.e., upon definitional entities). Ideas, those formal objects that are what they are by definition and that have an absolute status, are accorded metaphysical preeminence in such a system. As we also noted, such an ontology allows for the gradation of entities according to their 'being', according to the extent that they approximate this standard of essential predicative surety. What we find in Plotinus is a generalized employment of this type of conceptualization, based upon a system of degrees of unity. The level of the forms is again made central, as in Plato, because of the definitional unity, the self-sameness, which these *onta* uniquely exhibit. This can be seen quite clearly in VI.9.1. The treatise opens with the annunciation of an ontological law: "It is by the one that all beings are beings." On the view being developed here, this is a richer claim than just a statement of existential dependence, as Plotinus's development shows. "For what could anything be, if it was not one?" Indeed, existence is fundamentally linked to predicative unity, and its removal entails loss of existence but only, presumably, under a given description: "For if things are deprived of the one which is predicated of them they are not those things." Removal of unity thus deprives that which has been marked off under a certain description of its existence as such a thing. The examples that follow clarify the point: existence *qua* house or ship is destroyed with the loss of the qualities in question (7–8). That this is a process that admits of degree is clear from the discussion of the bodies of plants and animals; should they be broken down into multiple parts, they lose the substantial character that they possessed and become other sorts of things, to the extent that they exhibit lesser degrees of unity (11–14). Now, one might not think that there is anything exceptional in this line of argumentation. After all, we also find it very difficult to separate existence from essential description. My point is not to cast suspicion on this tendency itself but to indicate how this alteration of emphasis leads to a position quite different from one that we might find within conventions of modern predicate logic. This disparity of outlook is evident as the threads of the argument are drawn together at 26–28: "For of the things which are said to be one each is one in the way in which it also has what it is, so that the things which are less being have the one less, and those which are more beings, more.' It is only possible to admit the notion of degrees of 'being' where essential prediction is tightly linked to existence, and this seems to be very much the case here, for Plotinus moves from a discussion of levels or degrees of predicative unity to one of degrees of 'being'. At best we would expect that a further step or postulate be included here, to spell out just why degrees of unity entail degrees of 'being' and how this concept functions in relation to our notion of existence. These are logically different issues we might say; but it is clear that for Plotinus they were only implicit points, because he was working with the sort of veridical ontology discussed in Chapter 1. We might pursue the point just a bit further by considering the concept of the One as it emerges in a more recognizable form in the argument at line 30. Plotinus has maintained (17ff.) that while soul confers form and hence unity on entities within this world, it nonetheless is not a complete unity. The conclusion of this line of reasoning gives another clue of its tacit ontological background: "And the soul too, which is other than the one, has its beings more in proportion to its greater and real being. It is certainly the one itself." Again we find the degrees of unity notion linked with that of degrees of reality, but now the apex of the former scale is mentioned and in terminology that is suggestive of the middle-period dialogues' description of forms. The implications of this view, if pressed, would lead to the conclusion that the One is also the summit of the scale of 'being', that is, 'really real' or 'real being.' A further result would presumably be that what is true 'being' must have some property that it possesses to a paramount degree. These implications are not pressed by Plotinus, and we need not insist on them, although we do need to recognize that a recognizable conceptual pattern, based on a veridical ontology that conjoins levels of reality with levels of predicative unity, is operative within the discussion.

I would hold then that the specific character of ancient realist ontology was vital to the doctrine of the One. Both of the major themes into which we have been inquiring in this section—the grounding of the forms in the One and One's transcendence of 'being'—can be thrown into interesting relief with this characterization of Plotinian ontology in mind. We might begin with this latter claim of transcendence of 'being.' For Plotinus to argue that there must be a first principle beyond the level of the *eidē* is to endorse the same conceptual tendency that Plato recognized at *Republic* 509b. If one establishes a hierarchy of unities, into which lower entities can be resolved and upon which these depend ontologically, then there arises the question of the source for the existence and unity of these principles. There is, in short, an explanatory regress created, and as is clear in the *Parmenides*, there is a need to cut off this recursive chain. In effect the argument for the transcendence of the One is an effort to provide a basis for ending the regress. To do this, Plotinus must indicate that this first principle is truly unique, unlike those other entities, which, even if self-same, eternal, and perfect, seem nonetheless to refer to a higher unity. This is surely the reason that Plotinus adopts the very strong ontological-type thesis discussed earlier. By holding that the One is an entirely different type of reality, Plotinus can argue that all lower forms of being are grounded in that distinct and higher principle, which itself requires no such no grounding. We may doubt whether this finally solves the riddle, but it seems to have been Plotinus's answer.

It is to this conceptual end that a good deal of the negative theology of the *Enneads* is marshaled, though by no means all. At least one result of denying many of the predicates that Plotinus proscribed of the One in passages like that discussed from VI.9.3 is that the One's uniqueness is thereby stressed over against the *eidē*. The fundamental claim that the One is not being rests on all that Platonic ontology invests in that term. To accept that the One has 'intelligible form' and can admit of essential predication would be to vitiate the philosophical grounds for its postulation. It would itself now have a unitary character that requires explanation and so would fail to address the implications of hierarchy within the intelligible world and the regress entailed by the Platonic description of that world. Hence, Plotinus argues that his first principle, if it is to merit its status as the final principle of a realist system of metaphysics, must be outside the standard range of that ontology's description. The One is a higher-order entity than those that can be described through the logic of predication, even essential or necessary predication.

Plotinus is, therefore, projecting the existence of a first principle outside the range of his ontology in order to ground his metaphysics and forestall the charge that it is viciously recessive. As the earlier discussion of self-predicational forms indicated, this was a serious problem for ancient Platonists and the doctrine of the One's transcendence, developing as it did out of a long tradition of ancient reflection on the *Parmenides*.[64] The doctrine of the One is a possible answer to this dilemma; this is the salient dimension of Plotinus's One from the standpoint of the history of philosophical theology. It also suggests that negative theology has an important systematic role within this thought in marking off the logical boundaries of the One and hence also its ontological boundaries, given the Platonist conflation of these two domains. It is precisely because Plotinus was a realist that the doctrine of an ultimate unity, unique in status and separate from all sorts of predicative unities, was so important to him. The doctrine of the One is the *dépassement* of Platonic ontology, and it must be understood in terms of this ontology.

This whole discussion of a conceptually transcendent One tot-
ters, as has doubtless been recognized, on the brink of paradox.
Plotinus, in projecting this unique first principle on the basis of his
realist ontology, must nevertheless use certain sorts of theoretical
predications of it. Apophatic theology is, therefore, a denial that certain sorts of predications can be applicable to the One, that is, those
that would imply its assimilation to 'being'. It is in this sense that
Plotinian negative theology is similar to that of Alcinous: it is de-
signed as a process of *aphairesis*, of conceptual deconstruction. This
is a limited procedure, not a rejection of all predication.[65] Plotinus
is concerned to reject "intelligible shape" for the One to the extent
that such predicative specificity would deny its status as ultimate
and simple. Negative ascriptions are of use to establish the central
category difference upon which the doctrine of the One rests, but
they remain ascriptions nonetheless. Affirmations and cosmological
epithets are used as well. There is nothing in principle unacceptable
about such a procedure, though there is invariably some tendency
to draw the One back into the system if the range of such ascriptions is allowed to be extensive. What can be found in Plotinus to
mitigate this is the recognition of certain preferred descriptions of
the One; the range is indeed limited. Examples from the early treatises would include 'self-sufficient,'[66] 'principle of all things,'[67] 'first
principle,'[68] 'simple,'[69] 'the first,'[70] 'the good,'[71] and so on. It must be
noted that all of these terms are actually specific theoretical ascriptions necessary either to distinguish the One from the members of
lower orders of reality or else to maintain some aspect of its cosmological primacy in the system. These constitute, therefore, a kind
of higher theoretical discourse, determined by the type of Platonism Plotinus accepted. These are special ascriptions meant to delineate the ontological position and function of the One, and as such
they are largely regulative or systematic. It might be said that these
ascriptions define the grammar of the One, or better, determine
its theoretical location and systematic import. Since this is a realist
ontology, they are based upon that context, and are understandable
only in its terms. I would argue, therefore, that the nature and domain of both apophatic and kataphatic theology, when applied to
the One in Plotinus, can be understood only in light of ancient realist ontology. Neither is the apophatic theology separable from this
ontology and its understanding of degrees of 'being'. The Plotinian

concept of the One is not portable, capable of relocation absent ancient realist metaphysics. The same concept of deity could not be articulated within a nominalist context; denials of these predicates would require a different conceptual articulation. Finally, it bears recognition that we are not faced with a hopelessly contradictory system that at once rejects what it also asserts regarding the One, mixing assertion into the midst of denial. Rather, both negative and affirmative theology are grounded in the conceptual conventions of ancient realism and limited by it. They are directed to the same systematic end: the projection of a first principle beyond the confines of that same Platonic ontology.

Perhaps one final note on this issue of the One's transcendence of 'being' and its bases in Platonic realism: none of what has been said here is meant to suggest that such is the only basis for this important and complex theological doctrine or that the particular approach adopted here is normative or exclusive. This analysis is conditioned by a general focus upon philosophical theology rather than contemplative theology, and my argument here is simply that this approach to Plotinian apophatic theology is heuristic. It must be admitted that this discussion has assumed throughout that Plotinus took his philosophical theology seriously and that he considered such discourse to be cognitive in nature. Even in the case of the One, our language is not wholly without epistemic significance. As we have already found, Plotinus does insist on certain sorts of special terminology based upon his analysis of the levels of 'being'; so while he may not move quite so far as to adopt an articulated doctrine of analogy regarding the One, he certainly does not hold that no terminology whatever has cognitive import. To say that the One is self-sufficient or the ultimate ontological source, or indeed to say that most sorts of predication are inapplicable to it, may not be to apply predicates literally to the One itself; yet as we have seen, these remarks do allow us to locate it conceptually and to gain some grasp of its function or its relations to other levels of reality based upon our understanding of the intelligible world of 'being.' To claim against this enterprise that Plotinus uses language of the One only in a noncognitive way is to misrepresent his position by overstatement. There is no doubt that there are passages that lend credence to the view that discourse

about the One cannot even locate it cognitively but is only protreptic. Examples from within VI.9 would be section such as 3, 49–54,
where the use of contingency language of the One is said to reflect
our own experiences in relation to it; or 4, 11–16, where discussion
of the One is said to be presented in order to give us direction in the
path toward its vision. There is no question that the ultimate goal in
Plotinus is contemplation of the One, which transcends knowledge;
as 4, 3 states, 'a presence which exceeds knowledge.' And yet we
do hear a lot on the subject of the One from Plotinus, statements
such as those discussed above, including the negative ascriptions,
that serve to locate the One conceptually on the basis of his Platonism. No fundamental incompatibility need be found here, as long
as the statements that are made of the One are recognized to be
theoretically based projections from the level of reality next to the
One, providing us with our best foundation to approximate its position and function. Indeed, there is an interesting passage at VI.9.5,
38–46 that bears on the issue in question:

Whatever is even before these, we give the name of "One" to by necessity,
to indicate its nature to one another, bringing ourselves by the name to an
indivisible idea and wanting to unify our souls; we do not when we call it
one and indivisible mean it in the sense of a point or a unit: for what are one
in this way are principles of quantity, which could not have come to exist
unless substance and that before substance had preceded it: so that is not
where one should direct one's thought: but all the same these correspond
to those higher things in their simplicity and avoidance of multiplicity and
partition.

We find here a balance of the major elements in Plotinus's position.
We must use language of the One, and we do so in order both to
clarify our understanding of the One in relation to what we do know
at the level of 'being' and to provide our souls the proper direction
for ascent. We achieve our clarification of the general metaphysical
status, function, and locus of the One from its consequents and by
analogy from certain aspects suggested by 'being,' for example, that
the One is simplicity. This is not to attribute this notion literally to
the One but to indicate the general way in which the One might
properly be regarded. While it is to be granted that this type of
thinking might not suffice as a formal theory of theological language

in a purely analytic or discursively based system of philosophical theology, it is a coherent view provided that one recognizes that the final point of Plotinian theology is unmediated and undifferentiated contemplation of the One. The philosophical theology we have been examining, and the account given of it, must be understood in that light. But it also follows that philosophical theology can be regarded as an integral part of the contemplative theory of Plotinus and that Plotinus articulated his views in this area in such extensive, sophisticated, and painstaking detail because it was so significant. We can gain sufficient cognitive purchase on the One from the level of 'being' that the soul's contemplative ascent can thereby be successfully pursued. In that sense, there is a certain pragmatism in Plotinus's epistemology with respect to the One, despite his commitment to realism in regard to our knowledge of the forms. Beyond 'being', a contemplative instrumentalism begins to emerge, such that the projective terminology used by concession of the One is instrumental to the end of undifferentiated, unitive apprehension of the One.[72] This 'mystical pragmatism' is a theme embedded in the passage just reviewed, and while it is never understood as a separate theory of theological language regarding the One, it seems to have played a critical role in locating the range and significance of Plotinus's apophatic theology.

This discussion allows us to bring up a further question in our inquiry into the theological earlier treatises of Plotinus, and that is the grounding of the *onta* in the One. Given the cognitive direction that 'being' provides to the contemplative in relation to the One, how are these formal principles related to the first principle, and what does this tell us further about the approximate locus of the One? As we have just suggested, Plotinus is very concerned to rule out many common metaphysical descriptions of the One, (e.g., that it is an intellective principle), and he does so not just because of their protreptic inadequacy but because they do not properly represent the relationship between the first and second hypostases. All of this implies that the hypostasis of 'being' is especially well situated in relationship to the One, by virtue of its own contemplation of the One, to represent the One at a level of description and multiplicity. As I have argued, even in the context of his apophatic theology, Plotinus continues to give us an understanding, however dim, of the

One, based on the structure of 'being'; for example, in the passage from VI.9.3, "itself by itself of single form, or rather formless, being before all form." This use of the traditional epithet for forms, uniformity in itself, should be viewed as regulative in force and as a projection of certain aspects or central values of realist ontology that are thought by Plotinus as being surpassed by the One. However, it does not lack these values; it exceeds them. It is prior to finite form, motion, rest, and all the highest *eidē*. This is a point that is vital for properly understanding Plotinian theology. We might summarize it initially by saying that the One is indeed not identifiable by any descriptive conceptualization; this is not because it is deficient in any respect but because it exceeds the capacity of finite description. Because it is the principle that is infinite in its power[73] and in itself and because it is the source for all subsequents, it cannot be graspable in any way by such limited representations. It could therefore be said that the Plotinian *via negativa* is ultimately grounded in the *via eminentiae*: that the negations stated are made to emphasize that the One positively transcends these descriptions.

It is for this reason that being can be traced by Plotinus as the representation of the One at the next hypostatic level. If the One were a nugatory principle and if negative theological assertions were suggestive of deficiency, then it would hardly make sense to treat the One as the source or principle of that perfectly real collectivity that is true 'being.' If the One were indeed so lacking, it would make still less sense to describe intellect as an image of the One. In this respect, we might recall the language of V.4.1, 23–26, quoted above, where the One is described as "the most perfect of all and the primal power." Again, intellect is said to be the image of the Good at V.1.7, 1ff., an impossible claim if the One were indeed a principle that lacks what its subsequents have. And we saw in discussing this passage that what comes into being must be said "in a way" to be the Good, to retain much of it, and to be most like it.

The whole description that follows in V.1.7 of the intellect's act of perception in relation to the One reinforces this theme of the richness of the One, for it is by its power and in relation to it that intellect establishes itself and 'being' coalesces into the "intelligible shape" it has. None of this imagery would be possible unless the One were the principle of perfection. Similarly, the passage discussed above from V.2.1, 1ff. maintains that the One is all things, in the sense that it is their *archē*, and so all things have a transcendent existence there in this source. In general, Plotinian language that focuses on the One as 'principle,' 'source,' 'power,' and so on tends to underscore the fundamental richness of the One, despite the fact that its perfect simplicity makes it different in type from all beings and hence not predicatively circumscribable. This theme of the One as the transcendental ground of all things, radically present throughout all levels of the system, is especially clear in V.2.2, 24–29, which, like many of these earlier treatises, emphasizes the closeness of the hypostatic levels:[74] "All these things are the One and not the One: they are he because they come from him; they are not he, because it is in abiding by himself that he gives them. It is then like a long life stretched out at length; each part is different from that which comes next in order, but the whole is continuous with itself, but with one part differentiated from another, and the earlier does not perish in the later." Here once more we can see that all things are seen to be from the One and are in a way the One. This claim relies on the radical nature of negative theology: since the One is not any specific thing and because it is not circumscribed, it is capable of real presence in all things, which are its representations or expressions at the levels of reality that proceed from it. In this way it can be seen as stretched out throughout the whole chain of 'being'.

These terms are drawn together in VI.9, which makes this fundamental point of the positive transcendence of 'being' by the One evident. There is also an especially interesting passage at VI.9.3, 1–6, which discusses the fear that the soul has in its accent because of the formless character of the One; this may help our recognition of this difficult notion of positive transcendence:

What then could the One be, and what nature could it have? There is nothing surprising in its being difficult to say, when it is not even easy to say what Being or Form is: but we do have a knowledge based upon the Forms. But in proportion as the soul goes towards the formless, since it is utterly unable to comprehend it because it is not delimited and, so to speak, stamped by a richly varied stamp, it slides away and is afraid that it may have nothing at all.

We again find that we cannot know the nature of the One, though *gnosis* of a sort is available through the forms. This is a common enough claim; what is significant here is the description of the soul's distress as it advances toward the One. From our position below, the One appears to be empty because we cannot grasp it within our normal conceptual limits. For this reason the soul fears that the One is really nothing at all. It is clear from the subsequent discussion that the soul is mistaken in this, that the One is not lacking; and Plotinus employs the theme of the One as the *archē* of all reality to enforce the point (15). A true philosophical study of the One would reveal this to the soul (14), and for this reason the soul should not withdraw from this first principle, the Good. This indicates the basic attitude that Plotinus has regarding the nature of the One's transcendence, and it is underscored in the two passages from VI.9 that focus upon the *via eminentiae*.

The first of these is VI.9.6, 1–20, which lays out, through the use of privileged theoretical terminology, the proper way in which the One is to be construed. We should notice the process of progressive *aphairesis*:

In what sense, then, do we call it one, and how are we to fit it into our thought? "One" must be understood in a larger sense than that which a unity and a point are unified. For there the soul takes away size and multi- plicity of number and comes to a stop at the smallest and rests its thought on something which is partless but was in something divisible and is not part- less either in the same way as the smallest: for it is the greatest of all things, not in size but in power, so that its sizelessness also is a matter of power: since the things after it also are indivisible and undivided in their powers, not in their bulks. And it must be understood as infinite not because its size and number cannot be measured or counted but because its power cannot be comprehended. For when you think of him as Intellect or God he is more: and when you unify him in your thought, here also the degree of unity by which he transcends your thought is more than you imagined it to be: for he is by himself without any incidental attributes. But someone could also think of his oneness in terms of self-sufficiency. For since he is the most sufficient and independent of all things, he must also be the most without need: but everything which is many is also in need unless it becomes one from many. Therefore its substance needs to be one. But the One does not need itself: for it is itself.

Its unity is not numerical or geometrical but something more unified than these. Its indivisibility does not connote smallness but greatness, and not physical magnitude but greatness in power. Its indivisibility and its infinity are both meant to refer not to extension but to power. Its very simplicity is the unification of its power. Plotinus goes on to insist that the One is more than intellect, more than divinity, more unified than conceptual unification can achieve. But we can get some understanding of its positive significance not only from the fact that it is more perfect than these superlative notions but also from its self-sufficiency, that is from its status construed along the lines of a form. In a sense the *via eminentiae*, this path of continued superlatives, leads Plotinus here to postulate a form of all forms. The One is characterized in a way very like the forms, but its self-sufficiency is so superlative that it is even without need of its own nature. Unlike a form, whose self-same character and self-sufficiency rely upon their definitional or essential nature, the One's self-sufficiency exceeds even this notion of essential qualitative possession. Once more we find realist language used to provide a general sense of the One and also to indicate its fundamental difference in type. In the process, though, the fact that the One exceeds the status of the forms is made obvious, for it clearly cannot fall short of its products.

The final passage on this theme of positive transcendence that warrants attention is VI.9.9. An extraordinary series of functional attributions is made in regard to the One in lines 1–2, including "source of life," "source of intellect," "first principle of being," "cause of goodness," "root of the soul." All of these serve to focus attention upon the One as the ontological ground of each of these important principles. Life, intellect, 'being,' goodness, soul—all of these central elements of Platonic theology are said to come forth from this first principle, which is hardly intended to be seen as deficient. Just as the forms are the ontological foundations for their instances and are outside the class of entities of which they are productive, so the One stands outside all 'being'. Although it is therefore beyond conceptual demarcation, it can still be identified on the basis of Platonic ontology as the ground of 'being', and therefore we must infer that it is not a blank slate of nothingness but fecund and simple perfection itself. This whole mode of conceptualization is further developed in VI.9.9, 7–12, where the Platonic notion of degrees of reality is applied to the One: "For we are not cut off from him or separate, even if the nature of body has intruded and drawn us to itself, but we breathe and are preserved because that Good has not given its gifts and then gone away but is always bestowing them as long as it is what it is. But we exist more when we turn to him and our well-being is there, but being far from him is nothing else but existing less."

The theme we noted earlier of the One's presence is evident here, and its role is articulated once again by analogy with a form. It is in virtue of the One that we have our own natures, and it does this in virtue of its own self-remaining, as is the case with a form. As long as the One is the very thing it is, it preserves its consequents, though its nature cannot be characterized as can that of a form. We then find the important claim made that in turning toward the One, the soul has a higher degree of 'being'; while in turning away from it, it has a lesser degree. This theme makes clear that while the One cannot be located on the scale of reality as such, it is nevertheless the hierarchical principle that is just beyond the highest point of that scale, toward which we can extrapolate in our theological discourse and to which we can come in contemplation.

Plotinus's philosophical theology rests, therefore, upon his particular understanding of Platonic realism. The arguments that we have reviewed for the transcendence of 'being' by the One are entirely dependent upon the character of that metaphysical level as it was established by the ancient Platonic tradition. It is also clear that Plotinus's crucial avoidance of the charge that his first principle is one that is largely a negative principle, lacking even the character and richness of its own first product, is also based upon the force of his Platonism. To understand the Plotinian One it is necessary that this realism be kept firmly in view. It might be said that this seems an unexceptional claim, for it is a standard point that Plotinus was a Platonist of some sort. I would suggest, however, that while this is indeed widely stated, lack of recognition of the specific type of Platonism Plotinus endorsed and its implications is all too common. For example, it has been argued that Plotinus was inconsistent on the subject of the One's production,[75] that he was faced with serious incoherence when he endorsed both the claim that the One is transcendent and that 'otherness', defined as movement away from One, is the first product of the One. The problem is thought to center on this emanative vector from the One because this entails a movement away from that which is without form in one sense (the One) toward that which is without form in another (non-being). Furthermore, this movement is described as a loss or declension. It has been suggested that Plotinus should have adopted a *creatio ex nihilo* doctrine and treated 'otherness' as a movement into finitude from the infinite ground of the One.

I would argue that there is no basic inconsistency in these premises, only conceptual variability. Insofar as the One is viewed as largely a privative principle in relation to form or intelligibility, then the whole vector of 'otherness' does indeed seem odd. But we must remember that the One is that which exceeds rather than falls short of intelligibility, and so a movement from it toward the level of intellect is, in fact, a loss. On the basis of his Platonism, Plotinus considers the intelligibles to be the highest sorts of unities that can be known discursively, but they are still lacking in complete integrative unity. The One is that which is so unified that it is all-inclusive in a fashion that is best represented as complete simplicity. This provides it with its positive character in the system; so to move from this level to that of the forms, the point at which finite intelligibility is involved, is indeed a declension. "Otherness" is this separating movement away from that total simplicity that can only be approximately recognized by us through the collective and intelligible unity of forms. Provided that it is recognized that the One's transcendence of 'being' is a superlative one, if the *via eminentiae* is seen behind the *via negativa*, then there is no inconsistency in Plotinus's treatment of motion away from the One as being a lack of form. This apparent *aporia* is an example of the necessity of realizing that such issues are conditioned in Plotinus by the special character of his realist theology, and it is for this reason that I have focused upon its logic so intently. It must always be recognized that the One is presented as the apex of realist ontology, as that which exceeds and completes the values of that system.

Apophatic theology is thus constitutive of the grammar of Plotinian monotheism. It is the principal mechanism by which the One is distinguished from all other beings and its transcendence of its consequents secured. Thereby is the One sharply sundered from the whole emanative chain that Plotinian metaphysics attributes to its causal efficacy; it stands apart from all else, resisting any assimilation, and so in divine obscurity it is perceived to be the ultimate principle. To demand that this line of theistic demarcation, between the first principle and all others, be cast in terms of the doctrine of *creatio ex nihilo* is to force upon Plotinian theology a foreign logic. For Plotinus, the One is ultimate, simple, transcendent, and thus unique. In order to represent this inclusive first principle, Plotinus resorts to the paradoxes of mystical theology, denying that many predicates are applicable to the One but attempting to suggest that this denial is the result of the inadequacy of such predication. This theological strategy is never exclusive of certain preferred forms of kataphatic theology: simplicity, ultimacy, and other such notions are also employed to mark off the One's location and function and to ascertain the positive character of its transcendence. But it is apophatic theology that remains the dominant and most salient element in Plotinian theism: the One is ultimate and alone because it is a hid divinity.

Mystical Monotheism

Some theologies seem conceived in iniquity; Plotinus's is not one of these. There are those who perceive divinity exultant in human perdition, while others find divine goodness constrained by malevolent opposition, bound by an obscure charter to everlasting conflict. In Plotinus we encounter instead the omnipresence of the Good, souls rising to felicity through the exercise of their own purification, the surety of divine procession and recession. There is a certain contemplative lyricism in Plotinus, one that has long lingered in Western mystical theology, in its confidence that, although only shreds of language remain when cognitive theology is subsumed into the unitive apperception of the deity, an abiding divine presence perdures and can somehow still be diffidently maintained. We have not come to terms yet with this theology and its conception of divinity. Many might doubt that one can, seeing in Plotinus only charismatic obscurity. This I would certainly deny, and so I should like in conclusion to draw together some strands of this inquiry and consider anew the Plotinian deity.

Ross once drew attention to what he called the "monarchian" tendency in Hellenic religious thought.[1] Characterized by speculative concentration upon an ultimate divine principle, this trajectory emerged with clarity in Plotinus. One hallmark of this developing approach was the gradual withering of *hyle* as an independent power of disorder and evil; this was an element not yet completely resolved within Plotinian theism, although the grounds for a privative solution were worked through.[2] This residual, conceptual difficulty was one that both Hellenic and Abrahamic theism shared.[3] I have suggested that the concept of deity that emerged in Plotinus should be understood as a type of monotheism, albeit a different approach to divine oneness from that which emphasized numerical exclusivity. Provided that one is willing to countenance a broader conception of monotheism than our conventional, culturally freighted one, then there seems no reason to deny that the Hellenic theology that culminated in Plotinus was monotheistic. It was, as we have seen, a theology of divine ultimacy, focused upon the primordial unity behind the cosmos. Plotinian theology was a theism of ultimate simplicity, of the divine ground that stands as the source of all reality while prescinding assimilation to that reality. It was in this respect that Plotinian thought constituted a coalescence of the theistic elements in Hellenic religious thought; the *Enneads* were a charter for later Hellenic monotheism.

The Plotinian One was not so much numerically unique as distinctive for its position as the foundation of all subsequent entities. Plotinus seems to have been especially concerned to articulate the nature of this primordial divinity rather than to secure its singularity. His was an inclusive understanding of theism; the force of his theology was centered not on establishing a single deity against a plurality of gods but in finding a final divine unity within and behind the cosmos. This effort was qualified, of course, by the particular character of Platonic ontology. Plotinus's portrayal of the One resisted conceptual specification, since this would have located it at the pluralized and differentiated level of intelligibility. Rather, his theology was projective; it centered on the stipulation of ultimacy beyond intellectual definition. Nonetheless, the One had what might be called a functional character: based upon its location in Plotinian metaphysics, it retained certain identifiable, systematic features such as 'source,' 'goal,' etc.. These functional descriptions allowed Plotinus to argue for its uniqueness and hence to confer a resultant exclusivity. The One was unique, and it excluded by its metaphysical locus a plurality of ultimate divinities. Such an approach to divinity, which concentrated upon the special nature of ultimate divinity, also entailed a claim of divine exclusivity. It was articulated by a different logic and arrived at through a different conceptual strategy than in the Abrahamic tradition. In Plotinus the functional character of the One entailed its uniqueness.

Rooted in centuries of reflection on the many gods of cultic polytheism, Hellenic religious thought thus evolved in its philosophical theology a monotheism that remained compatible with the notion of plural theophanies at levels of reality subsequent to the One. In this theology a hierarchical model of reality was vital: the many gods, powers, and spiritual beings of this rich universe were all derivatively real. They were grounded in the One, and in no sense were they competitive with it. As we have seen, Plotinus made clear that nothing could form a class with the One, for it was entirely distinct ontologically from all else. Nor were those major divisions of reality and divinity, the hypostases following upon the One, autonomous divinities. In Plotinus it was a theological mistake to view *nous* or *psychē* as a distinct god, meaning by that an independent entity with autonomy of existence, however self-constitutive they may at times have appeared. These hypostases were degrees of divinity; as such they were modes of the One at lower levels of reality. This was vague language, no doubt, and it may also have drawn the One too closely into the system of intelligible realities to have entirely satisfied Plotinus, as our discussion of III.9 suggested. Still, I think this was in part the reason for the Plotinian use of language that telescoped the hypostases. There must be a balance between collapsing these hypostatic levels and attenuating them lest the One appears so wholly beyond even functional description that it becomes a speculative figment, while *nous, psychē*, and any other hypostases assume virtual autonomy. This would be a strange sort of hierarchical polytheism that I do not think was the intent either of Middle Platonists such as Numenius or Alcinous nor indeed of Plotinus.

Plotinian theology is perhaps best thought of as a mystical monotheism, a theism that countenances the idea that the ultimate, unique, but hidden, divinity may manifest itself at various levels of reality. This seems to have been a characteristic feature of Hellenic monotheism, its admission of many modes of divinity, of the hidden One's theophanies. Again, it is a question of balance; from this interpretive direction the danger is not of hierarchical polytheism but of monism. Use of modalistic language, of telescoping hypostases, invariably suggests a formal monism, where all reality is in fact but an illusory appearance of a single divine principle. But this is not what Plotinus maintained, for to have done so would have been to jettison his fundamental, hierarchical ontology and with it the notion of metaphysical transcendence. There is no place in monism for real divine transcendence, only of its illusion. The modes of divinity are fictive ones and the levels of reality only apparently existent. There was none of this in Plotinus. His modalism was that of a theistic Platonist: intent upon genuine divine transcendence, of modes of divinity not fictive but real. His account of reality remained Platonic, for he was serious about the ontological hierarchy. While its scale implied a gradual diminution of reality, these levels were not mistaken demarcations. They approximated complete and full 'being'; they shared in this 'being,' however deficiently; they existed in their own right even if by derivation. And beyond all of these was the One, the final principle more real than 'being' itself. This was not monism.

The mystical monotheism of Plotinus represented divinity as being centered in an ultimate, unique, but obscure principle that manifested itself at separate levels of reality. All were genuine degrees of reality and divinity; none was a fictive mode. *Nous* was the hidden One's theophany at the level of intellect and true 'being,' *psyche* its mode of self-disclosure at the next degree of reality. All elements within these hypostases were as well the actual manifestations of the One. And while these hypostases manifested the One, and upon analysis could be telescoped back into it, they had an eternal existence and a distinct presence. For the hidden One itself transcended its theophanies, a point that we have seen emphasized by Plotinus. As such, he developed what amounts to a double transcendence theory of divinity: the One transcended not only the cosmos of 'becoming,' space, and time, but it transcended the intelligible cosmos as well. In consequence, it could not be assimilated to any known reality, nor could it be subsumed into its modes. To this end, the apophatic theology, with its complex logic of denial, was vital. This reduplicative logic of transcendence was the foundation of Plotinian mystical monotheism. Because each level of divinity was genuinely charted on the scale of being and because the hidden One further exceeded this system of modes, Plotinus's deity remained distinct and primordial. The One was both unitary and singular, and it was thereby capable of real presence throughout a derivative hierarchy of entities. Each was completely dependent ontologically upon the One, and each was, in this sense, nothing but the One present at a given level of being. Yet the One also stood apart from its consequents, since no conjunction or truncation of the levels could equal the One. As has been suggested, I would judge this complex concept of deity to be a version of theism, one whose structure allowed for a pronounced but coordinated emphasis on both the immanence and transcendence of the One.

Nothing illuminates this understanding of Plotinus better than considering his theology in its historical context. Our analysis of antecedent Platonic theology should help set some parameters for interpreting his difficult religious metaphysics. The theology of the earlier *Enneads* that we have reviewed was stamped with the richness of this long tradition and preoccupied by a concentrated criticism of this precedence. Above all, this revision was founded upon the deficiencies that Plotinus perceived in the Middle Platonic accounts of the primordial divine unity and upon his heightened sense of this deity's role as the ultimate and unique source of all reality. Plotinian theology began as a reconsideration of Middle Platonic *nous* theology, and this fact must be kept in mind in assessing its revisionary structure. My analysis here has concentrated on the earlier treatises, where these origins are most evident, but I think that the *Enneads* as a whole bear the mark of this critical reflection upon Platonic theology and were fundamentally conditioned by that tradition.

Against its Middle Platonic background, many aspects of Plotinian theology that appear aporetic from the perspective of later theism are clarified. It must be admitted that Plotinian thought is removed from our culturally received version of monotheism; the One may seem an impersonal, self-oriented absolute, mottled with flecks of personality but still largely denuded of creative purpose, volition, or thought. On this view, only a few fugitive references in the *Enneads* stand opposed to such a conclusion. But this is to read Plotinian theology from the normative basis of a different theistic grammar. Personality, extrinsic orientation, purposive planning, volition, even self-consciousness and intellection, are all denied the One, not because the One lacks these theologically positive attributes but because they are deemed inadequate to it. The apophatic theology is employed with this critical value[4] in Plotinus, based upon his own concept of deity. The central of the One image for Plotinus seems to be that of the undifferentiated but inclusive source of all reality. As such, it was understood as both subsuming all values and all positive properties into the complete simplicity of its inner life but also exceeding any differentiated predication of these. Because it was the source of all, it was the inclusive foundation of all, and yet it stood apart from all elements that emerged from it. To describe it as intellection was, as we have seen, of significance only to the extent that we are thereby dissuaded from representing it as lacking in its august unity what is known at lower, disparate levels of reality as thought, consciousness, or the like. The same held true of volition, personality, and other common divine attributes.[5] The monotheism of Plotinus emerges, then, as a theology that was critically framed in counterpoint to many aspects of what would become the regnant theism of the West. While it endorsed an ultimate and unique first principle separate from all others, it arrived at this position according to its own distinctive logic, whose grammar is marked by a resolution to oppose many of the theological commonplaces of other sorts of theism in the period. Its singular reliance upon the hidden presence of the first principle was particularly salient; the transcendence of the One was secured because its inclusive simplicity was so obscure. The theology of Plotinus was thus a mystical monotheism, whose indigenous character can be discerned in the early *Enneads*.

The mystical monotheism of Plotinus represents the coalescence of many disparate, theistic elements in Greco-Roman religious thought. As such, the One might be said to have been the culmination of Hellenic theism, the philosophical articulation of an increasingly significant strand in ancient theology. Plotinus thus established a separate tradition in late antique philosophical theology, one that would admit of many variations in its formal metaphysics, while also lending support to a broad cultural movement that attempted somewhat paradoxically to retain classical cultic polytheism with the support of Neoplatonic monotheism. Both the modalistic, contemplative theology of Porphyry and the hierarchical, theurgical thought of Iamblichus and Proclus are, each in its different way, based upon the philosophical theism of Plotinus. The obscure, hidden first principle of Plotinus remained the only real deity throughout Neoplatonic theology, so whatever polytheism was admitted at the level of religious observance never undercut the fundamental, philosophical commitment to the One's unique ultimacy. And because it remained rooted in Platonic, degree-of-reality theology, the modalistic aspects of Plotinian theology could never develop into monism, where only the One was real and all other beings were but its illusory epiphenomena. The theology of Plotinus should thus be understood not as monistic or pantheistic but as a special and distinctive sort of monotheism; Neoplatonism is not an advaitic archipelago into Western thought.

Despite its temporary success in late antiquity, the Hellenic monotheism of the Neoplatonists was a tradition lost but for its subsequent absorption into the Abrahamic theological world. A subtonic element in medieval religious thought, it surfaced in complex ways, often dependent upon the historical accidents of textual transmission, across the Abrahamic spectrum in Jewish, Christian, and Islamic theology. The inclusive monotheism of the Neoplatonists qualified—one might even say tempered—this more exclusive sort of monotheism, providing it with a rich philosophical vocabulary and an account of divine primordiality. This complex story cannot be reviewed here, even in outline, but our understanding of the history of Western philosophical monotheism is critically influenced by how we understand the beginning of the tale.

This study in ancient philosophical theology suggests that we think of the early development of philosophical monotheism neither as its progressive emancipation from pagan philosophical polytheism nor as an initially flawed project fraught by the constraints of an essentially polytheistic metaphysics but rather as the concurrent development of two different types of monotheism, alike in dignity. The Hellenic and the Abrahamic traditions, though clearly distinct in religious origins, culture, and cult, ought to be seen as related both in their accepted sources in classical metaphysics and in their parallel efforts to articulate monotheism philosophically. It is on the basis of this revisionist model and its recognition of the mystical monotheism of Plotinus that the history of ancient philosophical theology should be understood. I hope to have contributed with this essay to this endeavor, one whose completion remains a central desideratum in the study of Western philosophical theology. If so, this will not have been a journey after an ancient but posthumous god.

Introduction

1. The disintegration of the ancient realist tradition in theology was a prolonged process with many steps, each of which is difficult to establish exactly, although the result of this complex transposition seems evident by the fourteenth century. The new nominalist construct, which begins to establish clarity of outline by the period of Ockham, is characterized by its emphasis upon the divine will, on the 'potentia Dei absoluta,' upon the great separation of God and the world, and upon the mediation of both this power and this breach through concepts such as revelation, covenant, and the 'potentia ordinata.' Although it seems generally agreed that nominalist theology marks a crucial juncture in this process of transition, it would be a mistake to attribute to the early nominalists a position of such novelty that this theological change might be ascribed to their efforts alone. Technical notions in logic and ontology, such as existence, necessity, etc., had undergone gradual change within medieval scholasticism with resultant modifications in theology. Besides, many of the specifically theological themes usually associated with the nominalist movement can be found in earlier figures as well. Nonetheless, it is with the nominalists that the new theology began to take full shape, and they themselves seemed to have been aware of the divergence, hence their self-definition as the *via moderna*. While this sort of philosophical theology did not completely dominate the field, nominalism did remove realist metaphysics from its position as the foundational core of philosophical theology. Henceforth, this outlook became a hypothesis to be argued, and while this did occur frequently in subsequent theology, it ceased being a standard assumption.

On fourteenth-century theology and nominalism: P. Boehner, *Collected*

Articles on Ockham, ed. E. M. Buytaert, New York, 1958; M. H. Carré, *Realists and Nominalists*, Oxford, 1946; G. Leff, *Gregory of Rimini*, Manchester, 1961, *William of Ockham*, Manchester, 1975, and *The Dissolution of the Medieval Outlook*, New York, 1976; E. A. Moody, *The Logic of William of Ockham*, London, 1935; P. Vignaux, *Nominalism au 14e siècle*, Montreal and Paris, 1948.

On technical developments in scholasticism: W. and M. Kneale, *The Development of Logic*, Oxford, 1962, chap. 4; N. Kretzmann, A. Kenny, and J. Pinborg, eds., *The Cambridge History of Later Medieval Philosophy*, Cambridge, 1982, chaps. 4 and 5.

2. Of course, not all ancient philosophical theists were Platonists; Tertullian qualifies, for example, as a peculiar Stoic Christian. Nevertheless, the majority of philosophical theists drew upon a common cultural admixture of Platonic-Pythagorean, Aristotelian, and Stoic elements in which the first component was dominant.

3. Cf. Gregory Vlastos, "Degrees of Reality in Plato," in *New Essays on Plato and Aristotle*, ed. R. Bambrough, London, 1965, 1–19.

4. The contemporary use of this term in philosophical theology is exhibited in H. P. Owen, *Concepts of Deity*, New York, 1971, 1–48.

5. On Plato's chronology, cf. the conclusions of David Ross, *Plato's Theory of Ideas*, Oxford, 1951, chap. 10. As with so many issues in Plato scholarship, this remains a subject of dispute.

6. Cf. Gregory Vlastos, "Reasons and Causes in the *Phaedo*," in *Plato*, vol. 1 ed. Gregory Vlastos, Garden City, N.Y., 1971, 132–66.

7. Esp. at V.9–12 and V.7. Cf. J. M. Rist, "Forms of Individuals in Plotinus," *Classical Quarterly*, n.s., 13(2) (1963):223–31, and "Ideas of Individuals in Plotinus: A Reply to Dr. Blumenthal," *Revue Internationale de Philosophie*, no. 92, pt. 2 (1971):298–303; H. J. Blumenthal, "Did Plotinus Believe in Ideas of Individuals?" *Phronesis* 11(2) (1966):61–80; P. S. Mamo, "Forms of Individuals in the *Enneads*," *Phronesis* 14 (1969):77–96; A. H. Armstrong, "Form, Individual and Person in Plotinus," *Dionysius* 1 (1977):49–68.

8. Cf. the discussion of A. H. Armstrong on the dispensability of the logical thesis to Platonic theology in "Platonism," in *The Prospect for Metaphysics*, ed. I. T. Ramsey, London, 1966, 93–109.

9. Recent studies include two general approaches: "common core" theories, which are concerned to establish a typology that identifies the fundamental cross-cultural components of such experience; and "tradition-historical" theories, which emphasize specific religious traditions in the analysis of "mysticism." The latter can include a claim of incommensurability across traditions as well as a constructivist understanding of the origin of the phenomena themselves.

Some common-core theorists are W. T. Stace, *Mysticism and Philoso-*

phy, London, 1960; R. C. Zaehner, *Mysticism: Sacred and Profane*, Oxford, 1957; and William Wainwright, *Mysticism*, Madison, Wis., 1981. Traditional-historical approaches include Steven Katz, ed., *Mysticism and Philosophical Analysis*, Oxford, 1978; and *Mysticism and Religious Traditions*, Oxford, 1983; and John Hick, *An Interpretation of Religion*, New Haven, Conn., 1989.

10. Unqualified use of "polytheism" or "monotheism" is thus meant in reference to positions in religious metaphysics. Should it be necessary to signal discussion of notions of divinity at the level of ritual, I will preface these terms accordingly, e.g., cultic polytheism (the ritual observance of cults honoring multiple gods). The need for terminological clarity and flexibility is probably obvious: the Greco-Roman religious tradition often combined cultic polytheism with a type of monotheism in its philosophical theology.

11. H. P. Owen, 1.

12. Philo Judaeus might be seen as too ambiguous with respect to the Hellenic model of a preexisting matter (which God orders) to qualify as a classical theist on this definition. Cf. the discussion of Henry Chadwick, "Philo and the Beginning of Christian Thought" in *The Cambridge History of Later Greek and Early Medieval Philosophy*, ed. A. H. Armstrong, Cambridge, 1967, 142; H. A. Wolfson, *Philo*, vol. 1, Cambridge, Mass., 1947, 295–316. The same would be true of Clement of Alexandria; cf. *Strom.* V. 89.6. Origen, while affirming the generation of matter at *De Prin.* II.1.4, might still be held to be suspect both because of his theory of the finitude of divine power and the question of the temporal character of creation. As R. M. Berchman has argued in *From Philo to Origen: Middle Platonism in Transition*, Chico, Calif., 1984, 133, "Origen denied the existence of an original matter, but he did not support a theory of *creatio ex nihilo*." The character of divine production was yet not completely settled even in Abrahamic theism.

13. The term was used by Paul Tillich in his discussion of types of monotheism: *Systematic Theology*, vol. 1, Chicago, 1951, 226–29: "Mystical monotheism transcends all realms of being and value, and their divine representatives, in favor of the divine ground and abyss from which they come and in which they disappear." He suggests that this concept of deity does not exclude polytheism: "Mystical monotheism does not exclude divine powers in which the ultimate embodies itself temporally." It is contrasted by Tillich to exclusive monotheism.

14. One might note the following as examples of the problem of representing Plotinian theology among students of Western religious thought: George F. Thomas, *Religious Philosophies of the West*, New York, 1965, 46–69; C. Hartshorne and W. L. Reese, *Philosophers Speak of God*, Chicago, 1935, 211–24; H. P. Owen, 59–65.

Chapter 1. The Foundations of Hellenic Monotheism

1. William Butler Yeats, "Among School Children," 1928.

2. Porphyry *Vita Plotini*, 18.8–19, 20.89–95.

3. Cf. Porphyry *Vita Plotini* 18.11.

4. This is the conventional term for the Platonism of the period 100 B.C.–200 A.D. Cf. the discussion of Stephen Gersh in *Middle Platonism and Neoplatonism: The Latin Tradition*, vol. 1, Notre Dame, Ind., 1986, on the problems of terminology and periodization in the history of Platonism.

5. The most comprehensive study is John Dillon's *The Middle Platonists*, Ithaca, N.Y., 1977.

6. Vlastos, "Degrees," 1–19.

7. Cf. Ross, chap. 2; also R. E. Allen, *Plato's 'Euthyphro' and the Earlier Theory of Forms*, New York, 1970. On the issue of Plato's chronology I will follow Ross's account, chap. 10.

8. *Phaedo* 72e–77a.

9. Ross, 25; also 35–36.

10. *Republic* 477a3–7; cf. *Republic* 515d2–4, 597a; *Philebus* 59a ff.

11. Harold Cherniss, "The Philosophical Economy of the Theory of Ideas," in *Plato*, vol. 1, ed. G. Vlastos, Garden City, N.Y., 1971, 7.

12. Vlastos, "Degrees," 7–8.

13. Aristotle *Metaphysics* I.6, 987b.

14. E.g., *Phaedo* 74d–75c, where the recognition of forms is said to be logically independent of sense experience because at least some forms are often instantiated along with their 'opposites,' and would not be differentiable or recognizable on that basis alone.

15. On forms as standards cf. R. S. Bluck, *Phronesis* 2:21–31, and R. E. Allen, "Participation and Predication in Plato's Middle Dialogues," in *Studies in Plato's Metaphysics*, ed. R. E. Allen, London, 1965, 43–60.

16. Cf. Vlastos, "Degrees," passim.

17. On this vexed issue cf. in particular: G. Vlastos, "The Third Man Argument in the Parmenides" in *Studies in Plato's Metaphysics*, ed. R. E. Allen, London, 1965, 231–64, and "Postscript to The Third Man," ibid., 279–91; Peter Geach, "The Third Man Again," ibid., 265–77; J. M. E. Moravscik, "The 'Third Man' Argument and Plato's Theory of Forms," *Phronesis* 8 (1963): 50–62; Alexander Nehamas, "Self-Predication and Plato's Theory of Forms," *American Philosophical Quarterly* 16(2):93–103; A. L. Peck, "Plato versus Parmenides," *Philosophical Review* 71:159–84; Roger Shiner, "Self-predication and the 'Third Man' Argument," *Journal of the History of Philosophy* 8:371–86.

18. Examples of self-predicational passages are *Phaedo* 74a9–c6, where equality is discussed, and *Symposium* 210e6–211a5, where Diotima expatiates on beauty. For other views, cf. Richard Patterson, *Image and Reality in*

Plato's Metaphysics, Indianapolis, Ind., 1986; and C. D. C. Reeve, *Philosopher Kings*, Princeton, N.J., 1988, 100–110.

19. Vlastos, "Reasons and Causes," 132–66.

20. *Phaedo* 102aff.

21. On the method of division in the *Sophist* cf. J. L. Ackrill, "SYMPLOKE EIDON" in *Studies in Plato's Metaphysics*, ed. R. E. Allen, London, 1965, 199–206; and A. C. Lloyd, "Plato's Description of Division," ibid., 219–30.

22. Charles Kahn, *The Verb 'Be' and Its Synonyms: The Verb 'Be' in Ancient Greek*, Dordrecht, 1973; "The Greek Verb 'To Be' and the Concept of Being," *Foundations of Language* 2:245–65; "Why Existence Does Not Emerge As a Distinct Concept in Greek Philosophy," *Archiv für Geschichte der Philosophie*, 58 Bond, Heft 4. Cf. the thesis developed independently by G. E. L. Owen in "Aristotle on the Snares of Ontology," in *New Essays on Plato and Aristotle*, ed. R. Bambrough, London, 1965, 69–95.

23. Cf. Vlasto's discussion in "Degrees," 8–9, which makes out this case very well.

24. Ibid., 8, n. 5; cf. also Owen, *passim*.

25. Absolute character: *Phaedo* 65d4, 74d6; self-sameness: *Symposium* 211 b 1, *Phaedo* 78d5, 101b6, *Timaeus* 51c1.

26. Kahn makes a case for this ontology; cf. "The Verb 'Be,'" 115–18.

27. Cf. Kahn's discussion of the development of Greek philosophical ontology in late antiquity: "On the Terminology for Copula and Existence," in *Islamic Philosophy and the Classical Tradition*, Oxford, 1972, 154ff.

28. *Republic* 515d2–3.

29. Cf. Vlastos's discussion of the valuational aspect of the theory in "Degrees," 7–8; the classic study of Plato and contemplation remains A. J. Festugière, *Contemplation et vie contemplative selon Platon*, Paris, 1967.

30. Purity language: 66a1–3; wisdom as purgation: 69c2–3; forms as divine: 80b1.

31. Translated by G. M. A. Grube, *Plato's Republic*, Indianapolis, Ind., 1974.

32. *Theatetus* 176b1–2.

33. Translated by R. Hackforth, *Plato's Phaedrus*, Cambridge, 1952.

34. *Republic* 509c5–511e5; 517b8–c4.

35. For a modern discussion of the former option: J. N. Findlay, *Plato: The Written and Unwritten Doctrines*, London, 1974, 41–5, 374–75; and of the latter: A. H. Armstrong, "Platonism."

36. The most catholic list of forms is found in the *Seventh Letter*, 342d3–8. If genuine, it would date from the last period of Plato's life, along with the *Laws*. It recognizes as forms moral and aesthetic qualities, properties like straightness and curvature, colors and forms of natural bodies, artifacts, the

physical elements, animals, characters of souls, actions and passions, etc. On this issue and the question of authenticity cf. Ross, 139; cf. most recently the interesting discussion of Harold Tarrant, "Middle Platonism and the Seventh Epistle," *Phronesis* 28(1) (1983):75–103.

37. This treatment has avoided discussion of the related area of mathematicals in Plato, which are problematic with respect to forms; one could generally consider their postulation as based upon a variation of the logical criterion analyzed here. Because they are not directly significant to our inquiry, I have thought it best to step aside from this problem. Cf. Aristotle *Metaphysics* 987b14–988a15.

38. This connection is not often noted and helps to underscore the importance of this issue in Plato's later metaphysics.

39. I follow Ross and Cherniss on this rather than Owen; see G. E. L. Owen, "The Place of the *Timaeus* in Plato's Dialogues," in *Studies in Plato's Metaphysics*, ed. R. E. Allen, London, 1965, 313–38. Cf. H. Cherniss, "The Relation of the *Timaeus* to Plato's Later Dialogues," ibid., 339–78.

40. Outside the dialogues there seems to be some evidence that might bear on this issue, though it is, as usual, difficult to decipher, conflicting, and much discussed in the scholarly literature. Major treatments are to be found in Harold Cherniss, *Aristotle's Criticism of Plato and the Academy*, vol. 1, Baltimore, 1944, 226–318; L. Robin, *La théorie platonicienne des idées et des nombres d'après Aristote*, Paris, 1908, 173–98; Ross, 165–75. Ross has divided the most significant text from Aristotle's *Metaphysics* 990b8–17 very conveniently, and because of its complexity, I will set out his amended, translated version:

> Of the ways in which we [i.e., we Platonists; for in Book A Aristotle writes as a member, though a recalcitrant member, of the Academy] prove that the Forms exist, none is convincing; for [A] from some no inference necessarily follows, and [B] from some there arise Forms of things of which we think there are no Forms. For [1] according to the argument from the existence of the sciences there will be Forms of all things of which there are sciences; [2] according to the 'one over many' argument there will be Forms even of negations; [3] according to the argument that there is an object for thought even when the thing has perished, there will be Forms of perishable things; for we have an image of them. Further [C], of the more precise arguments, [1] some establish Ideas of relative terms, of which we say there is no independent class, and [2] others introduce the 'third man.'

Section A is simply too vague a reference to be helpful for our purposes. Section C is also of doubtful relevance: part 2 refers to the 'third man' argument, an unfortunate logical consequence of the theory not bearing immediately on membership in the intelligible realm, while part 1 charges that the theory entails the recognition of ideas of relative terms as a separate class. It does not deny that relative terms are recognized as entailing forms, only that they cannot be taken as forming a distinct class. Therefore, the key sections for our analysis are B1, 2, and 3.

Section B features arguments offered for forms that lead to the recognition of entities the Platonists would not wish to recognize. Part 1 indicates that the argument from the existence of the sciences entailed unacceptable forms. Ross has pointed out, based on 990b22–9, that the ideas in question seem to have been ideas of things that are not substances. This suggests that the focus of the argument is against those Platonists who were willing to accept only ideas of substances, a position that, in view of the evidence already adduced from the dialogues, seems unlikely to have been held by Plato. The target is more likely, then, to have been other members of the Academy, and unless further evidence can be found to link Plato to this restrictive position, then this argument of Aristotle cannot be taken to show that Plato accepted only substantival forms.

Section B, part 2, is rather more interesting, since it maintains that the 'one over many' argument, that is, the argument for universals, entails the acceptance of forms for negations, which is presumably an unwelcome class. Once again the key question is whether Plato would have been committed to this position. This seems from the evidence to be doubtful. *Statesman* 262c8–263e1 is concerned with the question of making true divisions in dialectic and especially with the problem of dividing up genera properly. The discussion indicates that certain negative terms do not correspond to forms because they do not properly subdivide a genus. The examples are 'barbarian' and 'not-ten-thousand,' which are subdivisions but not proper species of the genera man and number respectively. The inference to be drawn is that not all negative terms refer to forms, though some that do bear a properly logical relation to a genus term may do so. Of course, much hinges on how one treats negation. An important discussion of the subject occurs at *Sophist* 257–258, though the context indicates that Plato's concern was not to give a general theory of negation but rather to give an illustration of the 'weaving together of forms,' in which not-being, or difference, plays a central role. There seems to be no evidence that the formal status of not-being, or difference, need be universalized to all such negative forms. Certainly, the form of difference applies in all contexts of negation, in reference to individual things, but this is no indication that negation amounts to the assertion of negative predicates, which would thus entail negative forms (according to the rule of *Rep.* 596). In addition, we have already noted that Plato does accept negative forms of a sort, those such as injustice, impiety, and the like, which have an independent meaning. This fact, combined with the suggestion of the *Statesman* that well-grounded negative forms mark off species, indicates that Plato did entertain the existence of negative forms within certain specified limits, although we cannot conclude that he extended this admission to all negative forms. I think that it is fair to conclude, then, that Aristotle's argument does not point convincingly at Plato.

The evidence in Aristotle on forms of artifacts is also rather unclear. On the latitudinal side, versions of the logical criterion can be found at *Metaphysics* 987b8–10 and 1078b32–4. On the other hand, there are a number of passages that imply a more delimited thesis. *Metaphysics* 991b6 seems to rule against artifacts, while 1070a18 says that Plato accepted as many sorts of forms as there are kinds of things which exist "by nature." This could be interpreted as meaning the things that regularly occur or the patterns found in things. While still unclear, this would not contrast "by nature" with "by art." Such a reading would accord with Plato's interest in natural divisions found, for example, at *Statesman* 263a2–11 or *Phaedrus* 265e1–3, etc., and with Xenocrates' understanding of forms as paradigms of regularly occurring phenomena (fr. 30 Heinze). The other alternative, contrasting "by nature" with "by art," seems less preferable, and it would be this reading that would be necessary to produce evidence of a rejection of forms of artifacts by Plato. The evidence, especially of the *Republic*, seems against this reading. Of course, Plato would not have admitted forms of the result of imitative art, which produces objects twice removed from 'being.' As Ross points out, this does not entail a rejection of forms corresponding to products of useful art (i.e., that which is teleological and functional). *Republic* 596b and 597b–598d suggest that a manufactured bed is only once removed from its form, in the same way that a natural object is, while a painting of this bed is twice removed. At 510a, manufactured things, the products of useful arts, occupy the same section of the divided line as living things. It would seem then much more likely, given the other passages from the dialogues that mention forms of artifacts, that Plato was not contrasting 'by nature' with 'by art' but rather with 'contrary to nature.' Therefore, the evidence indicates that Plato probably did accept forms of artifacts, though restricting this acceptance to those that are produced in accordance with nature (i.e., with a natural end in view) rather than being just imitative. While this is a very vague criterion for this class, it is no worse than many of the others given for membership within the realm of forms. In any case, there is no decisive evidence that Plato rejected such forms outright.

I think it likely, then, that Plato restricted the logical force of the common name theory for forms only for (a) products of imitative arts, (b) certain negative predicates (e.g., 'not-Greek', 'not-ten-thousand') that are not the result of natural divisions and that can be better treated as denial of positive predicates for which forms are recognized, and (c) false distinctions generally, which do not correspond to natural discrimination revealed by dialectic. Hence, the scope of the theory of forms remains very wide indeed and the population of the world of being rich and variegated.

41. Cf. *Tim* 28a6–b1, where the imagery is made into a theoretical position. Cf. also *Laws* 965b7–c8.

42. Admittedly, an early dialogue in which the theory of forms may not be fully developed, although cf. Allen, *Plato's 'Euthyphro'*, passim.

43. Cf. Aristotle's criticism of the theory as merely reproducing this world at a transcendent level: *Metaphysics* I.9, 990a33ff.

44. Following John Whittaker's analysis in "The 'Eternity' of the Platonic Forms," in *God Being Time*, Oslo, 1971.

45. Cf. Aristotle *Metaphysics* I.6, 987a29ff.

46. I shall be using "ideas" and "thoughts" interchangeably in the colloquial English sense, which suggests mental activity and its contents.

47. On the problem of the 'mythic' character of the Timaeus; see G. Vlastos, "The Disorderly Motion in the Timaeus" and "Creation in the Timaeus: Is It a Fiction?" in *Studies in Plato's Metaphysics*, ed. R. E. Allen (London, 1965), 379–99, 401–19. Cf. also Cherniss, *Aristotle's Criticism*, 392–457, and "The Sources of Evil According to Plato," *Proceedings of the American Philosophical Society* 98 (1954):23–30; F. M. Cornford, *Plato's Cosmology*, New York, 1937, passim; R. Hackforth, "Plato's Cosmogony," *Classical Quarterly*, n.s., 9:17–22.; A. E. Taylor, *Commentary on the Timaeus* Oxford, 1928, passim.

48. See Taylor, 80–83; Cornford, 41; Ross, 41.

49. But other forms mentioned in the dialogue suggest that Plato's intention remained broad. The contents of the living creature are enumerated at 39e and include "the heavenly race of gods" (stars, planets, earth), "the winged things whose path is in the air," "all that dwells in the water," and "all that goes on foot on dry land." In addition to the contents of the living creature there are others mentioned. At 33b the form of shape is suggested; at 35a being, sameness, and difference seem to be forms involved in the composition of the world soul; while at 51b–e forms of the four elements are mentioned. The realm of intelligible archetypes seems, then, to be greater than the contents suggested by the 'living creature' imagery.

50. Cf. C. J. De Vogel, "Some Controversial Points of Plato Interpretation Reconsidered," *Philosophia*, vol. 1, Assen 1969, 183–209; Cherniss, *Aristotle's Criticism*, 104; R. Hackforth "Plato's Theism," in *Studies in Plato's Metaphysics*, ed. R. E. Allen, London, 1965, 444, n. 1.; Cornford, 37.

51. 37a1–2, my translation.

52. Cf. Taylor, 176; Cherniss, *Aristotle's Criticism*, 605, who argues that

"the reference here to the demiurge as 'the best of the intelligibles' means nothing more than does 'intelligible' as used of soul in *Laws* 898d–e."

53. So also Atticus according to Proclus. Cf. Taylor, 83.

54. Taylor, 83; Cornford, 359; Cherniss, *Aristotle's Criticism*, 604–5.

55. See especially H. Cherniss, "On Plato's Republic X; 597b," *American Journal of Philology* 53:233–42.

56. However, cf. Aristotle *Metaphysics* I.6.987b18ff, where the *archai* of forms are discussed.

57. It should be noted that at *Sophist* 265a–266d Plato analyzes the notion of production, dividing this into human and divine. Both categories are then subdivided into the production of imitations and originals. Production of ideas is never mentioned, only of plants, animals, fire, and things of the sort.

Sophist 248ff. is sometimes read as implying that each form is an intellective entity that is capable of change; cf. De Vogel, 194–209. This can be connected with *Timaeus* 30c–31a, on the living creature containing the intelligible living creatures, to adumbrate a monadology of form-intellects in Plato. This is erroneous. This passage from the *Timaeus* seems meant to stress that the archetypes of the cosmos are not dead, but the *Sophist* passage does not imply that each and every form is intellective, motive, and so on. The interpretive key lies at 249b5ff., where the stranger considers how the possibility of knowledge entails the sort of change that comes with intellection. True knowledge would seem to include and its intellectual motion. It would seem that perfect 'being' must include mind and this motion. This is not to claim that each form must involve intellectual motion, life, soul, and reason, only that the whole realm of 'being' is inclusive of these. Note the final statement of the Stranger: it is the sum of all things, 'being' itself, which must be said to be both changeable and unchangeable. Plato is therefore not endorsing a monadology of intellect-forms, although the possibility is thereby opened for Plotinus.

58. Cf. Hackforth, "Plato's Theism," 439–47.

59. Here I follow Hackforth, ibid., and also Luc Brisson, *Le même et l'autre dans la structure ontologique du Timée de Platon*, Paris, 1974.

60. Ross, 41: "Ideas are not changeable things plastic to the will of a Governor; they are standards to which a Governor of the universe must conform."

61. Volition: 30a,d, 41a; reflection: 30a, 37a, 39e; judgment: 30a; forethought: 34a–b.

62. Cf. esp. A. N. M. Rich, "The Platonic Ideas as the Thought of God," *Mnemosyne*, ser. 4, 7:123–33.

63. On Alkimos: Diogenes Laertius, III.13; cf. A. H. Armstrong, "The Background of the Doctrine 'That the Intelligibles Are Not Outside the Intellect,'" *Sources de Plotin*, Entretiens Hardt, 5, Vandoeuvres/Geneva, 1960,

393–413, reprinted in *Plotinian and Christian Studies*, London, 1979; Rich, 127; R. E. Witt, *Albinos and the History of Middle Platonism*, Cambridge, 1937, 70–72.

64. Cf. Armstrong, "The Background of the Doctrine."

65. So Witt argued (p. 72), but cf. the opposing case of Rich, 123–33, and Cherniss, "Review of R. E. Witt, *Albinus and the History of Middle Platonism*," *American Journal of Philology*, 59 (1938), 351–6.

66. 30a, 39e; cf. Rich, 131. This point was recognized in antiquity: Alcinous, *Didaskalikos* IX, and Proclus *Comm in Tim.* I.320, remark on the fact that the Timaeus refers to both internal and external models.

67. Rich, 127. Forms as "mere thoughts" can be found in Alexander of Aphrodisias *Comm in Arist. Met.* 991a23; Justin Martyr *Cohort. VII*; Proclus, *Comm in Parm.* IV.150.

68. Hence, I tend to an agnosticism that respectfully differs from the most recent treatment by Dillon, 28–30.

69. On Xenocrates: Dillon, 22–39; H. J. Krämer, *Der Ursprung der Geistmetaphysik*, Amsterdam, 1964; P. Merlan, *From Platonism to Neoplatonism*, The Hague, 1960; W. K. C. Guthrie, *History of Greek Philosophy*, vol. 5, Cambridge, 1978.

70. 987a29ff.; on the problem see Findlay, *Plato*; Guthrie, *History of Greek Philosophy*; K. Gaiser, *Platons ungeschriebene Lehre*, Stuttgart, 1963; Ross, *Plato's Theory*.

71. Cf. Guthrie's discussion of Plato's dualism 5:441–42.

72. Aëtius, Heinze, 15.

73. Guthrie, 474.; also H. Dörrie, *R.E.*, 2(18): 1512–28.

74. Fr. 15, Stobaeus following Aëtius. Cf. Pierre Boyancé, "Xenocrate et les Orphiques," *R.E.* 36:218ff.; Dillon, 25. The text may be corrupt. If so, then the identification of the dyad and the world soul is rendered uncertain. It is this identification that suggests this stronger dualism, making the world soul into an ultimate principle of disorder inherent in the universe. Xenocrates might have assimilated the world soul and the receptacle to solve the question of a source for the indefinite precosmic motion in the receptacle. Perhaps most likely is simply a conflation of entities by Aëtius. That Xenocrates was constructing a cosmology with an evil and disorderly power as the immediate ruling principle of the generated cosmos seems doubtful.

75. *De An. Pr.* 1012d–e; Heinze 68.

76. Theophrastus *Metaph.* (Ross and Fobes) 6a23, frag 12 (Wimmer, p. 154); cf. Aristotle *Metaphysics* 1028b24ff. (= Heinze, 34).

77. Heinze 30.

78. H. J. Krämer, *Platon und Hellenistische Philosophie*, Berlin, 1972, 116, n. 40; Guthrie, 473, n. 1; Dillon, 28.

79. Heinze 34 = *Metaphysics* 1028b24ff.; this almost certainly refers to Xenocrates; cf. the commentator Asklepios quoted by Heinze (p. 171).

80. Heinze 60, Aristotle *De An.* 404b27; cf. Heinze (pp. 181–85) for later evidence.

81. Aristotle *De An.* 408b32; Cherniss, *Aristotle's Criticism*, 396ff.; Taylor, 112–15.

82. Plutarch *De An. Pn.* 1013c–d; cf. Guthrie 479–480; cf. also Aristotle *De An.* 404b16–27.

83. Heinze 30.

84. Cf. Witt, 71.

85. Dillon, 29.

86. Ross's translation.

87. Even if the chronological development of Aristotle's thought remains at issue, there seems no reason for thinking that some immediate fissure occurred between Aristotle and the members of the Academy after Plato's death. For example, Aristotle and Xenocrates spent time together at Hermias just after Plato's death. Cf. Guthrie, vols. 5 and 6.

88. Speusippus, frag. 28 Taran; cf. *Timaeus* 30c–31b.

89. Dillon, 5dff.; cf. also John Glucker, *Antiochus and the Late Academy*, Göttingen, 1978; H. Dörrie, *Platonica Minora*, Munich, 1976, passim.

90. Dillon, 82ff.; Witt, 71ff.

91. *Acad. Post.* 30ff.; cf. Dillon, 91ff.

92. *Acad Pr.* 30: *Orator* 8ff.; cf. Dillon 92–94.

93. Antiochus evidently held that only material principles could act or be acted upon; hence, divinity must be material in some sense if it is to exercise cosmological and providential causality; e.g., *Acad. Post* 27ff.; 39; cf. Dillon, 95; Witt, 73: "If . . . Antiochus retained the name Idea, it meant to him exactly what *pronoia* meant to the Stoics, and it meant no more"; also Berchman, 26–30. Berchman gives a detailed treatment of Antiochus' fundamental use of Stoic categorical theory.

94. W. Theiler, *Die Vorbereitung des Neuplatonismus*, Berlin, 1930, 16ff.; Dillon, 136–7; Ernst Bickel, "Senecas Briefe 58 and 65," *Rheinisches Museum*, 103, 1–20; H. Dörrie, "Präpositionen und Metaphysik," *Museum Helviticum* 26 (1969): 217–28.

95. Theiler, 18ff.; Dörrie, "Präpositionen," 217ff.

96. *Epistula* 65, 4–10.

97. Dillon, 136.

98. *Epistula* 65.7.

99. Other examples of the metaphysics of prepositions that indicate a continued exemplarist understanding of ideas are Varro apud Aug. *DCD* VII, 28 (cf. n. 94 above). Jove is that 'a quo,' Juno that "de qua," and Minerva,

the Ideas, "secundum quod."; cf. also Aëtius' scheme (Diels, *Doxogr.*, 288) and Dillon. 139. This interpretation was conjoined with the divine thoughts doctrine.

100. Rich, 125.

101. Cf. E. Bréhier, *Les idées philosophiques de Philon d' Alexandrie*, Paris, 1908, 97; H. A. Wolfson, *Philo* vol. 1, Cambridge, Mass., 1947, passim.; and "Extradeical and Intradeical Interpretations of Platonic Ideas," in *Religious Philosophy*, Cambridge, Mass., 1961, 27–68; Berchman, 31–45; David Winston, *Philo of Alexandria*, New York, 1981, 7–21; and D. T. Runia, *Philo of Alexandria and the Timaeus of Plato*, Leiden, 1986, passim.

102. On Hellenic monotheism: A. H. Armstrong, "Itineraries in Late Antiquity," *Eranos Jahrbuch*, 1987, and J. P. Kenney, "Monotheistic and Polytheistic Elements in Classical Mediterranean Spirituality," in *Classical Mediterranean Spirituality*, New York, 1986, 269–92.

103. E. R. Dodds, "The Parmenides of Plato and the Origin of the Neoplatonic One," *Classical Quarterly*, 22 (1928): 129–43; Phillip Merlan, *From Platonism to Neoplatonism; Monopsychism, Mysticism, and Metaconsciousness*, The Hague, 1963; "Greek Philosophy from Plato to Plotinus," in *The Cambridge History of Later Greek and Early Medieval Philosophy*, ed. A. H. Armstrong, Cambridge, 1967, 84–106; John Whittaker, "EPEKEINA NOU KAI OUSIAS," *Vigiliae Christianae*, 23 (1969): 91–104 "Neopythagoreanism and the Transcendent Absolute," *Symbolae Osloenses*, 48 (1973):47–86; J. M. Rist, "The Neoplatonic One and Plato's Parmenides," *Transactions of the American Philological Association*, 93: 389–401.

104. Cf. Cherniss, *Aristotle's Criticism*, and *The Riddle of the Early Academy*, Berkeley, Calif., 1945; Merlan, *From Platonism to Neoplatonism*; Krämer, *Der Ursprung*; L. Taran, *Speusippus of Athens*, Leiden, 1981.

105. W. D. Ross's translation, Oxford edition, reprinted in *The Basic Works of Aristotle*, ed. Richard McKeon, New York, 1941.

106. Taran, Frag. 48; Glenn Morrow and John M. Dillon, *Proclus' Commentary on Plato's Parmenides*, Princeton, N.J., 1987, 583–4; cf. 485–86.

107. Dillon 24; Heinze, frags. 15,68,28.

108. W. Burkert, *Lore and Science in Ancient Pythagoreanism*, Cambridge, Mass., 1972, and "Hellenistische Pseudopythagorica," *Philologus*, 105, 1961; H. Thesleff, *An Introduction to the Pythagorean Writings of the Hellenistic Period*, Abo, 1961, and *The Pythagorean Writings of the Hellenistic Period*, Abo, 1965; *Entretiens Hardt: Pseudopythagorica I*, 1972.

109. *Peri nou kai dianoias* of Ps-Brotinus is dated tentatively by Thesleff, to III-II century B.C.. Whittaker, 95–6, fn. 3, suggests that this is the probable source of Alexander's and Syrianus's comments. He notes however that Ps-Brotinus "may well have been contemporary with or not much anterior to

Numenius and thus liable to employ similar terminology." Because of the variability of dating this pseudopythagorica, I have focused upon the somewhat more specifiable materials of Eudorus and Moderatus. Cf. Alexander *In Metaph* 821, 33ff. Hayd.

110. Syrianus *In Metaph.* 166, 5ff. Kroll, and 183, 1ff.

111. Stobaeus I.27–9, Wachs = Thesleff 19–20; cf. T. A. Szlezak, *Pseudo-Andrytas über die Kategorien*, Berlin, 1972; Thesleff, *An Introduction to the Pythagorean Writings of the Hellenistic Period*, Abo, 1961, passim; Dillon, 120–35.

112. Alex. Polyhistor apud D.L. Viii. 24–33; cf. Dillon, 342.

113. Sextus Empiricus *Adv. Phys.* II.282.

114. Ibid., 261ff.

115. Cf. Dillon, 115–21, 341–44. Translation of Alexander Polyhistor is that of Dillon, p. 342.

116. Iamblichus attributes this position to the Pythagoreans *Theolog. arithm.* p. 5.2ff., 12ff.; cf. Whittaker, "Neopythagoreanism," 77–78.

117. Dillon's translation, (pp. 126–27); Simplicius *In Phys.* 181.10ff. Diels.

118. Dillon's translation (p. 127, n.1).

119. Dodds, *Elements*, and P. Merlan, "Greek Philosophy from Plato to Plotinus," in *The Cambridge History of Later Greek and Early Medieval Philosophy*, ed. A. H. Armstrong, Cambridge, 1967, 93–94.

120. Merlan, "Greek Philosophy," 91–92.

121. Ibid., 94.

122. Cf. Dillon, 348. "It is not formally described as being 'above nous,' as is the first principle of 'Brotinus; or 'Archytas,' but from the fact that the Second One is explicitly termed *noeton*, it is not unreasonable to assume that the First is to be taken as supranoetic."

123. So Dillon concludes as well (p. 348).

124. On other sorts of Neopythagorean theology, esp. Nicomachus of Gerasa, cf. Dillon, 341ff.

125. W. D. Ross's translation, *The Basic Works of Aristotle*, ed. Richard McKeon, New York, 1941.

126. The problem of explanatory regress was well articulated in the 'third man' arguments of the *Parmenides*, as is a One that transcends predication and so might be represented as resistant to predicative regression. It is interesting to note that the Neopythagorean One emerged from a metaphysical reading of the *Parmenides*, so this problem of establishing explanatory closure was part of the intellectual tradition in which it was initially articulated.

127. H. P. Owen, *Concepts of Deity*.

128. *God and Creation*, ed. D. Burrell and B. McGinn, Notre Dame, Ind., 1990.

129. Cf. Owen, *Concepts of Deity*; C. Hartshorne and W. Reese, *Philosophers Speak of God*, Chicago, 1953.

130. Dillon, 202–08; Gaiser, passim; Merlan, "Greek Philosophy," 58–64; P. Thevenaz, *L'âme du monde, le devenir, et la matière chez Plutarque*, Paris, 1938.

131. Owen, *Concepts of Diety*.

132. E.g., number 67 in the "Catalogue" of Lamprias: "Where are the Forms."

133. Plutarch translations from Loeb edition: Vol. 5, ed. F. C. Babbitt, Cambridge, Mass., 1936; Vol. 7, ed. P. De Lacey and B. Einarson, Cambridge, Mass. 1959; Vol 12, ed. H. Cherniss and W. Helmbold, Cambridge, 1957; Vol. 13, ed. H. Cherniss, Cambridge, 1966.

134. *Cratylus* 439d ff.

135. Cf. esp., R. M. Jones, *The Platonism of Plutarch*, ed. Leonardo Taran, New York, 1980.

136. Cf. discussions of Plutarch and the divine ideas: Jones, 317–26; Rich, 123–33; Krämer, *Der Ursprung*, 93–101; Dillon, 201–3.

137. E.G., Dillon, 201. Regarding the ideas, Dillon states: "In their transcendent aspect, in themselves, Plutarch plainly takes them as the thoughts of God, as did his Middle Platonic predecessors." This is true doxographically, but the theological differentiation warrants a greater demarcation from earlier thought. This is not to say that Plutarch's position is original in this respect—we lack the evidence to make that claim—but it is certainly distinct theologically from earlier Middle Platonic attestations.

138. Cf. the discussion of Salvatore Lilla, *Clement of Alexandria*, Oxford, 1971, 202, n. 2.

139. Cf. Merlan, "Greek Philosophy," 30–32, 58–64.

140. *De E* 393c

141. *De Facie* 944e.

142. Translated by Frank Cole Babbitt, *Plutarch's Moralia V*, Loeb Classical Library, Cambridge, Mass., 1936.

143. In this respect my interpretation differs from that of Dillon, (p. 199), who treats this passage as identifying the deity with the good. I would discern a different notion of moral excellence here, one that is proper to causal agency.

144. Hackforth, "Plato's Theism," 439–47.

145. As Dillon points out (p. 201).

146. Krämer, *Der Ursprung*, 98, n. 250; Dillon, 214–15.

147. On Numenius, cf. below; chap. 2.

148. E.G. Charles Hartshorne, *Man's Vision of God*, New York, 1941; *The Divine Relativity*, New Haven, Conn., 1948; La Salle, Ill., 1967; and *Philosophers Speak of God*, 1953.

Chapter 2. The Demotion of the Demiurge

1. Examples of the latter are Atticus and Longinus, who are discussed briefly in section 3.

2. Following Dillon I have tended to treat Neopythagoreanism as closely related to Middle Platonism under the general rubric of realist theology; it was perhaps distinct historically as a philosophical school but similar conceptually. Hence, my terminology is somewhat elastic.

3. *Vita Plotini* 17, 1ff.; cf. Origen's similar attitude of respect, *Contra Celsum* I.15, and IV.51.

4. *Vita Plotini* 20, 74–7; 21, 5–9.

5. Texts will be quoted in my own translation unless noted.

6. Nicomachus of Gerasa seems to retain a fundamental dichotomy of monad and dyad as primary (*Introd. Arith.* II.18, 4), again with the former producing the latter, by a process of doubling or reduplication (*ap. Theol. Arith.* 4, 6ff., De Falco). This monad is a *nous* (*ap. Theol. Arith.* 4.3ff.) and contains the ideas (*ap. Theol. Arith.* 3.1ff.). While the evidence for Nicomachus's system is complex and difficult to interpret (cf., Festugière, vol. 4, 23), the conclusion of Dillon is that Nicomachus adopted a demiurgic theology. As Dillon states (p. 357): "It would certainly be convenient to establish a distinction between Demiurge and Supreme God in Nicomachus, as is to be found in both Moderatus and Numenius; the evidence presented in connection with the Monad, however, seems against it." Dillon concludes (p. 358): "What I see, then, is not the more elaborate hierarchy of Moderatus, and later of Numenius, but rather the more basic Platonic triad of principles, God, Matter and Form (the Ideas of the Logos).

7. Using the numbering of the edition of É. Des Places, *Numénius*, Paris, 1973.

8. We cannot take up Numenius's views on matter in any detail. He certainly held an ultimately dualistic, 'two opposite principles' doctrine (frag. 52), with the dyad or materiate principle being eternal though unordered. In this state, matter is a positive force of evil (frag. 52, 33ff.), which cannot be fully checked by divinity (frag. 52, 113ff.). This rather conservative 'two opposite principles' stance places Numenius in opposition to those Pythagoreans who derived the dyad from the monad in a system of coordinated principles, e.g., the source of Arius Didymus or Nicomachus, or of Eudorus and Moderatus, who accepted a primary One that is the ground of both monad and dyad. Numenius mentions such Pythagoreans at frag. 52, 15–24:

> Sed non nullos Pythagoreos vim sententiae non recte assecutos putasse dici etiam illam indeterminatam et immensam duitatem ab unica singularitate institutam recedente a natura sua singularitate et in duitatis habitum migrante—non recte, ut quae erat singularitas

esse desineret, quae non erat duitas subsisteret, atque ex deo silva et ex singularitate immensa et indeterminata duitas converteretur; quae opinio ne mediocriter quidem institutis hominibus competit.

9. For a discussion of textual difficulties on this fragment, cf. Dodds, "Numenius and Ammonius," *Entretiens Hardt* V, *Les sources de Plotin*, Vandoeuvres-Geneva, 1960; Dillon, 369; and Whittaker, "Numenius and Alcinous on the First Principle," *Phoenix*, 32 (1978): 144ff.

10. Cf., especially lines 10–13.

11. Cf. discussion at I.3.

12. *In Tim.* I, 303, 57–304, 7 Diehl = frag. 21.

13. Dillon, 366–67.

14. Frag. 17, 3–4.

15. *In Tim.* III.103, 28–32 Diehl.; cf. Dillon, 371–72; Festugière, 123–24; Krämer, *Der Ursprung*, 85–91; Dodds, 13, whose reading I follow here.

16. The *proschrēsis* doctrine will be considered subsequently.

17. Accepting Dodds's emendation ("Numenius and Ammonius," 16) also accepted by Dillon, 369; cf., Des Places, 57, who prints the text as received. Dodds's emendation would make philosophical sense, reserving total contemplative activity to the first intellect.

18. Cf. Dodds, "Numenius and Ammonius," 13–16, Dillon, 371–72, Festugiére, 123–24; Krämer, *Der Ursprung*, 85–91.

19. Cf. frag. 16, 7–8, where imitation language is used.

20. Cf. Dodds, "Numenius and Ammonius," 14.

21. This is Dodds's (ibid.) explanation: "*noein* is the distinctive activity of the Second god, and of the Second only: in virtue of the reflexive consciousness which *noēsis* involves he 'makes his 'own *idea.*' The First can *noein* only by calling in the help of the Second; insofar as he does this, he too is *nous*, but his *distinctive* activity or (passivity) must be something other than *noēsis* proper." This explanation is unclear on the distinctive activity of the First God, and the basis for his taking on a lower form of intellection.

22. Especially between the second and third, which are treated often as one principle with aspectual differences.

23. Plotinus V.8, 4, 6–8; and V.8, 4, 11; also IV.9.5; Porphyry *Sententiae* 10 (2, 17 Mommert). Interestingly enough, Syrianus (*In Met.* 82, 1ff.) ascribes this view to "the Pythagoreans," so it is possible that Numenius is following an antecedent Neopythagorean view here. Cf. Proclus *In Parm.* 930, 26ff., and 948, 12ff; Proclus *Elements of Theology*, Prop. 103: "All things are in all things, but in each according to its proper nature." Cf. Dodds, *Elements*, 254.

24. Adapting A. C. Lloyd's phrase from a related notion in Porphyry "The Later Neoplatonists," in *The Cambridge History of Later Greek and Early Medieval Philosophy*, ed. A. H. Armstrong, Cambridge, 1967, 287–93.

25. 17, 3.

26. Dodds, "Numenius and Ammonius," 15: "To the Second God corresponds a different *ousia* which includes his own *idea* and presumably all the *ideai.*"

27. Longinus, according to Porphyry, *Vita Plotini* 21, 5–9.

28. Fragments 16 and 22.

29. So Wallis (*Neo-Platonism*, London, 1972, 33) suggests.

30. As in frag. 16, 1–3.

31. Parmenides exegesis: frag. 5; Numenian spirituality: frag. 2.

32. H. Dörrie, "Hypostasis," in *Platonica Minora*, Munich, 1976, 13–69.

33. John Whittaker, "*Parisinus gr.* 1962 and the Writings of Albinus," *Phoenix* 28 (1974): 320ff., 450ff.

34. J. H. Loenen, "Albinus' Metaphysics," *Mnemosyne*, ser. 4, 9:296–319; 10:35–56; Armstrong, "The Background," 393–413; reprinted in *Plotinian and Christian Studies*, London, 1979.

35. Alcinous's text is that of C. F. Hermann, vol. 6 of his edition of Plato, Leipzig, 1921–36.

36. Cf. Loenen, passim, and Armstrong, "The Background," 403, though the latter emphasized this Aristotelian element more, while the former, in an effort to avoid the charge of eclecticism against Alcinous, has lessened this aspect. Cf. Witt's more eclecticist interpretation, (*Albinos*, passim).

37. Dillon argues the former position (p. 284); Loenen, the latter (pp. 304–11), since once again a definitive and clear-cut answer of this sort aids his case for the consistency and philosophical significance of Alcinous.

38. Dillon, 284.

39. Loenen, 303.

40. Witt, 125.

41. Armstrong, "The Background," 404–5.

42. Ibid., 404.

43. Emphasis upon the divine will in an explicit form can be found throughout the late second and early third centuries, though it should be noted that in Platonic circles the discussion, as in VI.8, tends to focus on the question of self-production and does not concentrate on the will–Ideas relation as much. On self-production, cf. J. Whittaker, "The Historical Background of Proclus' Doctrine of the *authupostata*," *Entretiens Hardt: De Jamblique à Proclus*, Vandoeuvres-Geneva, 1975, 193–230. Ps-Plutarch *De Facto*, 573 B, certainly places emphasis upon the 'will or intellection or both' of the Father of All. In Christian Platonism the notion is prominent: Clement of Alexandria, frag. 7 (214, 11ff. Koetschau), and Origen *De Princ*. II.9, 1. Also, Calcidius *In Tim*. c. 176. There is, therefore, significant evidence to suggest a context of thought that gave increasing evidence to the divine

will. Cf. Dillon, 284; Albrecht Dihle, *The Theory of Will in Classical Antiquity*, Berkeley and Los Angeles, 1982.

44. Cf. Whittaker, "The Historical Background," 215.

45. The attack in II.9.1 against a double intellect doctrine would hold against Alcinous's position as well.

46. For a collection of this evidence, see Festugière, vol. 4, 92–140. An interesting discussion of the development of negative theology is that of Raoul Mortley, *From Word to Silence*, vols. 1 and 2, Bonn and Frankfurt-am-Main, 1986.

47. 164, 28–29: *autotelēs, aeitelēs, pantelēs*. Dillon, 283, suggests a hymnic background. Only the first of these is attested elsewhere, as a Neopythagorean epithet for the monad: Nichomachus *ap. Theol. Arith.* 3, 18 De Falco.

48. 164, 30–35: *theiotēs, ousiotēs, alētheia, summetria, agathon, patēr*.

49. 164, 31.

50. 165, 17–24: *kat' analogian*.

51. 165, 24ff.

52. 165, 4–17; *kat' aphairesin*.

53. Cf. esp., Festugière, vol. 4, 92–140; H. A. Wolfson, "Albinus and Plotinus on Divine Attributes," *Harvard Theological Review* 45 (1952): 115–130; John Whittaker, "Neopythagoreanism and Negative Theology," *Symbolae Osloenses* 44 (1969): 109–25, "EPEKEINA NOU KAI OUSIAS," 91–104, "Numenius and Alcinous," 144–54; Mortley, vol. 2, passim.

54. *Metaphysics* VII, 1029a17–26, where the abstractive process is used to remove breadth, depth, quantity, particularity, and other categorical notions from the materiate substrate in order to clarify its peculiar character. On the Euclidian background cf. Wolfson, "Albinus and Plotinus"; Festugière, vol. 4, 314–15; and Mortley, vol. 2, 20–21.

55. Dillon, 254–55.

56. J. Baudry, Paris, 1931, frag. 9, 815aff.

57. Proclus *In Tim.* I.391, 7–8ff. recounting Porphyry's criticisms of Atticus.

58. Cf. Festugière, vol. 4, 262, n. 1; Dillon, 254–55; Theiler, *Die Vorbereitung*, 15ff.; Witt, passim.

Chapter 3. The Mystical Monotheism of Plotinus

1. Cf. J. N. Findlay, *The Transcendence of the Cave*, London, 1967; and *Ascent to the Absolute*, London, 1970; Stephen Clark, *From Athens to Jerusalem*, Oxford, 1989.

2. Principal theistic analyses include A. H. Armstrong, "Plotinus," in *The Cambridge History of Later Greek and Early Medieval Philosophy*, Cambridge, 1967, 195ff.; Rist, *Plotinus: The Road to Reality*, Cambridge, 1967; Jean Trouil-

lard, *La Purification Plotinienne*, Paris, 1955; and *La Procession Plotinienne*, Paris, 1955.

3. E.g., Hartshorne and Reese, 211ff., where Plotinian theology is termed "emanationism or exclusive monism."

4. E.g., Stace, 236; and most recently, William Wainwright (*Mysticism*, Madison, Wis., 1981, 32–33, 37), who treats Plotinus as a "monist."

5. Porphyry *Vita Plotini*, 18.8–19; 20.89–95.

6. Cf. Armstrong's discussion: *Plotinus*, vol. 1, trans. and ed. A. H. Armstrong, Cambridge, Mass., 1966, vii.

7. Which was in 253–254, when Plotinus was about forty-nine years old, according to Porphyry, *Vita Plotini* 4.

8. Cf. *Vita Plotini* 18.11; also V.5[32].

9. Cf. Armstrong, "Plotinus," 393–94.

10. Cf. Chapter 2, section 3.

11. Dodds, "Numenius and Ammonias," 24ff.; cf. Dodds's discussion of the work of F. Heinemann, "Ammonius Sakkas und der Ursprung der Neuplatonismus" (*Hermes* 61 [1926]: 1–27; E. Seeberg, "Ammonius Sakkas" (*Zeitschrift für Kirchengeschichte* 61 [1942]: 136–70); H. Dörrie, "Ammonius, der Lehrer Plotins" (*Hermes* 83 [1955]: 439–78); and H. Langenbeck, "The Philosophy of Ammonius Saccas and the Connections of Aristotelian and Christian Elements Therein" (*Journal of Hellenic Studies* 77 [1957]: 67–74). Cf. the recent study by Frederic Shroeder, "Ammonius Saccas," *Aufstieg und Niedergang der Römischen Welt*, II, 36.1, 493–526.

12. Cf. Karl-Otto Weber, *Zetemata* 27, *Origenes der Neuplatoniker*, Munich, 1962, frag. 7.

13. *Vita Plotini* 3.33; cf. Armstrong, *Plotinus* vol. 1, 10–11, n. 1, on this work and on the 'two Origens' question, an issue into which we need not inquire: it now seems settled in favor of two figures, both probable students of Ammonius.

14. Dodds, "Numerius and Ammonius," 19.

15. All quotations of the *Enneads* are taken from the Loeb Classical Library edition of A. H. Armstrong, *Plotinus*.

16. Cf. Proclus *In Tim.* I.322, 22ff.

17. Dodds, "Numenius and Ammonius," 19.

18. A. H. Armstrong's translation, *Plotinus*, vol. 3, 409.

19. Proclus *In Tim.* III.103, 28–32 Diehl = des Places 22.

20. Dodds, "Numenius and Ammonius," 13.

21. Ibid., 14, though cf. Armstrong *Plotinus*, vol. 2, 226, n. 1.

22. This is elaborated in the later treatise V.5 (32).

23. Porphyry evidently held that the demiurge did indeed belong unequivocally to the level of soul, according to Proclus (*In. Tim.* I.306, 32–307, 2).

24. Cf. Dodds, "Numenius and Ammonius," 20; Armstrong, *Plotinus*, vol. 2, 226–27, n. 1, which notes that Plotinus's fellow philosopher Amelius may also have been included since he held a three intellect doctrine as well (Proclus *In. Tim.* III.268A, 103, 18ff., Diehl). That Amelius held such a view need not be surprising, since he was a devoted student of the works of Numenius, as Porphyry notes in the *Vita Plotini* (3, 42ff.).

25. Cf. Anthony Kenny, *The Five Ways*, Oxford, 1977; Richard Swinburne, *The Coherence of Theism*, Oxford, 1978; Charles Hartshorne, *The Logic of Perfection*, La Salle, Ill. 1962. On the problem of necessary beings and uniqueness, cf. Paul Henle, "Uses of the Ontological Argument," in *The Ontological Argument*, ed. Alvin Plantinga, Garden City, N.Y., 1965.

26. A different position is the property instance view in which God (or the One) is identified with his *own* properties, i.e., with those instances of the properties attributed to him. Cf. William E. Mann, "Divine Simplicity," *Religious Studies* 18 (1982): 451–71; "Simplicity and Immutability in God," *International Philosophical Quarterly* 23 (1983): 267–76; "The Divine Attributes," *American Philosophical Quarterly* 12 (1975): 151–59; "Simplicity and Properties: A Reply to Morris," *Religious Studies* 22 (1986): 343–53; also Thomas V. Morris, "On God and Mann: A View of Divine Simplicity," *Religious Studies* 21 (1985): 299–318. A predicate instance view is clearly precluded in Plotinus, given his apophatic theology.

27. On relative identity: P. T. Geach, *Reference and Generality*, Ithaca, N.Y., 1962; David Wiggins, *Identity and Spatio-Temporal Continuity*, Oxford, 1971.

28. Alvin Plantinga, *Does God Have a Nature?* Milwaukee, 1980, 26ff.

29. Modifying Plantinga's remarks, which include the concept of absolute divine control, which is not apposite to the Plotinian notion of the One.

30. On simplicity in Jewish, Christian, and Islamic theology: David B. Burrell, *Knowing the Unknowable God*, Notre Dame, Ind., 1986.

31. This is, of course, where modern and ancient realism part company, the former being a logical and ontological theory but without implications for actual cosmological production.

32. N.B. the use of *anagkē* in 39. I might add that the question of 'necessity' of production in Plotinus is an enormously complex issue, as is clear from VI.8, and to examine it would require tracing a somewhat different though related set of concepts.

33. John Leslie, *Value and Existence*, Oxford, 1979; and "Mackie on Neoplatonism's 'Replacement for God,'" *Religious Studies*, 22 (1986): 325–42; J. L. Mackie, *The Miracle of Theism*, Oxford, 1982, 230ff.

34. Mackie, *Miracle of Theism*.

35. Leslie, 1986.

36. It is interesting to note that Leslie's version of the cosmological argu-

ment for theism includes as an option the possibility that this reasoning may point only to some principle of value, which is responsible for the generation of a divine person, who creates the universe (*Value and Existence*, 79). This amounts to a demiurge as a second-rank cosmological power, similar to the ancient theories we have been reviewing.

37. Cf. Paul Henry, "Une comparaison chez Aristote, Alexandre et Plotin," *Entretiens Hardt* 5 (1960): 429–49; John Bussanich, *The One and Its Relation to Intellect in Plotinus*, Leiden, 1988, 10–14; Kevin Corrigan, "Plotinus, *Enneads* 5.4[7], 2 and Related Passages," *Hermes*, 114 (1986): 195–203; A. C. Lloyd, "Plotinus on the Genesis of Thought and Existence," *Oxford Studies in Ancient Philosophy* 5 (1987): 155–86.

38. Bussanich, *The One*, 11; cf. V.1.5.17–19 and the discussion of Michael Atkinson, *Plotinus: Ennead V.1*, Oxford, 1983, 122; also *De. An.* III.2.426a13–14 and 3.428a6–7 on *opsis* and *horasis*.

39. Corrigan, "Plotinus, Enneads," 196ff. and Lloyd, *Plotinus on the Genesis*, 175, who states: "It is not the One which actualizes the sight (or capacity to think) of Pre-Intellect, but *the One as seen (or thought)* by Pre-Intellect."

40. I agree with Bussanich, *The One*, 14, on the causal centrality of the One. As he states, "Lloyd's argument will not do because, though the potential Intellect does not apprehend the One as it truly is, the One's reality determines Intellect's apprehension of it as object. Thus, there is an indissoluble causal link between the One itself and the One as *noēton*: the incessant activity of the former is necessary to make the latter an intelligible actuality for Intellect."

41. Bussanich (*The One*, 16) is right to see the introduction of the dyad here as a typically Plotinian historical aside meant to underscore indefiniteness, not an endorsement of Academic or Peripatetic dualism. For an opposing view, cf. Krämer, *Der Ursprung*, 308–18; and T. A. Szlezak, *Platon und Aristoteles in der Nuslehre Plotins*, Basel-Stuttgart, 1979, 116–18.

42. V.1.5.6–9: "For number is not primary: the One is prior to the dyad, but the dyad is secondary and, originating from the One, has it as definer, but is itself of its own nature indefinite.

43. Cf. III.8.8; V.3.11.

44. Dodds, "Numenius and Ammonius," (19–20) argued for the connection with the double intellect theory of Numenius. This is accepted by Armstrong (*Plotinus*, vol. 5, 146) and Rist (*Plotinus*, 42); the connection with III.9 is also agreed upon. On this view, Plotinus is treating the One as an intelligible object remaining in itself and capable of a self-intellection that is eternal rest; the quiescient *nous* of Numenius would be the pilot scheme for this approach. Rist summarizes the view as follows:

What can be deduced from this except that in the early period of his life, quite probably under Numenian influence, Plotinus toyed with the idea of a double *nous*, one active and the other static, the static and higher also being a *noēton*, but that he later came to reject such ideas? There is evidence then that at some time Plotinus might speak of a *noēton* which itself, though inactive, had some kind of intellection. This is almost what we have in 5.4.2.

This consensus has been challenged by Bussanich, *The One*, 20, who offers several objections. First, that III.9 should not be used to explicate V.4 on the grounds that Plotinus "does not seem to accept a double intellect in III.9[13].1" and "because the former's 'intelligible object at rest,' in spite of the verbal similarity, bears little relation to the latter's 'intelligible' object remaining in itself' " (12) or its reference to the One's 'intellection existing in eternal rest,' " (18). He also suggests that "the problems explored in the two treatises are quite different: in III.9[13].1 the internal nature of Intellect, in V.4[7].2 how and why the One, which is clearly said to be beyond being and thought, generated Intellect." Second, that in his mature treatises, Plotinus continues to refer to the One as *noēton* and as remaining in itself, e.g., V.6[24].2.7–9 and V.3[49].12.35–36. Third, that Plotinus's use of *Timaeus* 42e 5–6, where the demiurge remains in his own character in production, is more important than Numenius in this and later passages, e.g., V.3[49].12.3–4.

I favor the consensus position that is attacked by Bussanich, and I have followed that here. I agree with Bussanich's second and third points, neither of which refutes the Numenian aspects of these treatises but only qualifies that interpretation. The first point, that III.9 and V.4 should be kept separate because their subject matter is different and their terminology is distinct seems dubious; there is some variation in terminology and a different focus but not enough to debar joint exegesis. Finally, the fact that Plotinus's attitude toward a double intellect also varies does not deny that this Numenian position is behind his discussion.

45. One interesting issue is the extent to which contemporary Aristotelianism influenced Plotinus with respect to the character and types of intellection, particularly Alexander of Aphrodisias. Were this a source-critical study the issue would be important. However, for philosophical purposes the question of influence is secondary, although a few points should be registered. Because we have so little of his work and that of other Aristotelians of the period, it is difficult to specify Alexander's significance for Plotinus. While Merlan (*Monopsychism, Mysticism, Metaconsciousness*, The Hague, 1963) emphasized the importance for Plotinus of Alexander's doctrine that intelligibles are the eternal ideas of the divine intellect (Alexander: *de anima* 87.43–88, *de intellectu* 108.7–9, 16–19, 109.23–110.13, *de anima* 88.24–89.5),

both Armstrong ("The Background") and Krämer (*Der Ursprung*) stressed the significance of Middle Platonism. I have followed their approach here. Some recent studies in this Aristotelian trajectory include Armstrong, "The Background"; Blumenthal, "Plotinus Ennead IV.3.20–21 and its sources— Alexander, Aristotle and others," *Archiv für Geschichte der Philosophie* 50, 1968, 254–261; Krämer, *Der Ursprung*, passim; Merlan, *Monopsychism*; P. Moraux, *Alexandre d'Aphrodise: Exegète de la noétique d'Aristote*, Liège and Paris, 1942; "Alexander von Aphrodisias Quaest. 2.3," *Hermes* 95 (1967): 159–169; and "Aristoteles, der Lehrer Alexanders von Aphrodisias," *Archiv für Geschichte der Philosophie* 49 (1967): 169–82; J. M. Rist, "On tracking Alexander of Aphrodisias," *Archiv für Geschichte der Philosophie*, 48 (1966): 82–90; R. W. Sharples, "Alexander of Aphrodisias: Scholasticism and Innovation," *Aufstieg und Niedergang der Römischen Welt* II, 36.2, 1176–1243.

46. Cf. Stace, *Mysticism and Philosophy*, who uses the term "vacuum-plenum."

47. As Armstrong (*Plotinus*, vol. 5, p. 146, n. 1) has stated: "This passage stands alone in the *Enneads* in the clarity with which it attributes a kind of thinking to the One." Both Corrigan, *Plotinus, Enneads*, and Lloyd, "Plotinus on the Genesis," reject this reading, treating this noetic activity as being predicated of the highest intelligible object, between the One and intellect. This has been convincingly opposed by Bussanich, *The One*, 20–27, who reviews the positions of other scholars on this vexed passage.

48. On the self-discernment of the One, cf. esp., Rist, *Plotinus*, 44, who views this as an affirmation of divine simplicity, and Bussanich, *The One*, 22–23.

49. V.4.2.15–17; V.2.1.1–3.

50. For alternative views, cf. Richard Sorabji, *Time, Creation and the Continuum*, Ithaca, N.Y., 1983; Rist, *Plotinus*, 43; Bussanich, *The One*, 26–27.

51. Cf. Rist, *Plotinus*, 41; Bussanich, *The One*, 24–25.

52. On the use of possible world modality: Alvin Plantinga, *The Nature of Necessity*, Oxford, 1974, chap. 10; Richard Swinburne, *The Coherence of Theism*, and *The Existence of God*, Oxford, 1979.

53. Cf. V.4.2 or VI.9.2.

54. Cf. Findlay's discussion of negative forms: *Plato, The Written and Unwritten Doctrines*, 41–45, 374–75.

55. Cf. V.8.1.

56. Cf. Rist, "Forms of Individuals in Plotinus," 223–31 and "Ideas of individuals in Plotinus," 298–303; Blumenthal, "Did Plotinus Believe in Ideas of Individuals?" 61–80; Mamo, "Forms of Individuals in the Enneads," 77–96, Armstrong, "Form, Individual and Person in Plotinus," 49–68.

57. Cf. Armstrong, "Platonism." It is also interesting to note Porphyry's

well-known ambiguity on universals in *De Interpretatione*, an odd ambivalency from the standpoint of classical Platonism though not from that of
this later period; cf. A. C. Lloyd, "The Later Neoplatonists," in *The Cambridge
History of Later Greek and Early Medieval Philosophy*, ed. A. H. Armstrong,
Cambridge, 1967, 283–93.

58. *Philebus*, 64c.

59. Though it is possible that Plotinus is lapsing into some form of a
prochrēsis doctrine, similar to the Numenian section of V.4.2, in which case
5–6 would read: "By its own self-return, the One sees, and this seeing is
intellect." I take it from Henry and Schwyzer, "Addenda ad Textum"; *Opera
Plotini* vol. 3, Paris and Brussels, 1973, 397, that they would now accept this
reading. Cf. their discussion and the division of opposing authorities and
more recently, Atkinson, *Plotinus: Ennead V.1*, 154–5; Bussanich, *The One*,
35; Szlezak, *Platon und Aristoteles*, 153–63.

60. Cf. Atkinson, *Plotinus: Ennead V.1*; Bussanich, 51–54; Lloyd, 161–62.

61. P. Hadot, *Exercises spirituels et philosophie antique*, Paris, 1981, and
"Neoplatonist Spirituality, Plotinus and Porphyry," in *Classical Mediterranean
Spirituality*, ed. A. H. Armstrong, New York, 1986, 230–49.

62. Cf. esp. Armstrong, *Plotinian and Christian Studies*, London, 1979,
XXIII and XXIV: "The Escape of the One," and "Negative Theology";
Mortley, vol. 2.

63. Pierre Aubenque, "Plotin et le dépassement de l'ontologie grecque
classique," in *Le Néoplatonisme*, ed. P. Schul and P. Hadot, Paris, 1971.

64. J. Fiedler, "A Plotinian View of Self-predication and TMA," *Modern
Schoolman*, 57 (1980): 339–47, and "Plotinus and Self-predication," in *The
Structure of Being*, ed. R. B. Harris, Albany, N.Y., 1982, 83–89.

65. Mortley, vol. 2, 19: "In Athenian Neoplatonism negative theology
had always been constructed around the term *apophasis*, whereas in Rome,
Plotinus understood it in terms of abstraction. These are not mere linguistic differences, since Plotinus's own understanding of the via negativa is
quite restricted. He does little more than abstract, or imaginatively remove
concepts." This analysis suggests a narrow reading of negative theology
in Plotinus and is in contrast to the recent, broader reading of Michael
Sells, "*Apophasis* in Plotinus: A Critical Approach," *Harvard Theological Review*
78 (1985):

66. VI.9.6; V.1.6.

67. VI.9.5 and 6; V.1.7.

68. VI.5 and 9; V.1.5 and 11; V.2.1.

69. V.4.2; VI.9.3, 5 and 6; V.1.5.

70. VI.9.2 and 5; V.1.5.

71. VI.9.6.

72. The question of mystical experience and its interpretation is still under debate and cannot be settled here. For theistic readings, Armstrong, "Plotinus," 258–63; Rist, *Plotinus,* 213–30, and "Back to the Mysticism of Plotinus: Some More Specifics," *Journal of the History of Philosophy* 27: 2; P. Hadot, "L'union de l'âme avec l'intellect divin dans l'experience mystique plotinienne," in *Proclus et son influence,* Zurich, 1987, 17. For recent monistic readings, see P. S. Mamo, "Is Plotinian Mysticism Monistic?" *The Significance of Neoplatonism,* Norfolk, Va., 1976; and J. Bussanich, "Plotinus on the Inner Life of the One," *Ancient Philosophy,* 7:163–89, and "Mystical Elements in the Thought of Plotinus," *Aufstieg und Niedergang der Römischen Welt,* Nachtrag in Bd. II. 36.4.

73. Cf. A. H. Armstrong, "Plotinus' Doctrine of the Infinite and Its Significance for Christian Thought," *Downside Review* 73: 47–58; W. N. Clarke, "The Limitation of Act by Potency," *The New Scholasticism* 26:184–89; "Infinity in Plotinus: A Reply" *Gregorianum* 40: 75–98; Rist, *Plotinus,* chap. 3; L. Sweeney, "Infinity in Plotinus," *Gregorianum* 38:515–35, 713–32, "Plotinus Revisited," *Gregorianum* 40:327–31, and "Another Interpretation of *Ennead* VI, 7, 32," *Modern Schoolman* 38: 289–303.

74. In contrast, e.g., to V.3(49), one of the last treatises written, which strongly distinguishes between the levels.

75. J. M. Rist, "The Problem of 'Otherness' in the *Enneads,*" in *Le Néoplatonisme,* ed. P. Schul and P. Hadot, Paris, 1971, 77–87.

Conclusion: Mystical Monotheism

1. W. D. Ross, *Aristotle's Metaphysics,* vol. 1, Oxford, 1924, cxl.

2. This issue would require a study at least as large as the present one; a few brief remarks might be apposite nonetheless.

Few notions in Plotinus are more confused than matter: vague in conceptual outline, it clings to the margins of philosophical articulation in ways more tenuous even than the many other difficult issues of Plotinian metaphysics. Two different notions of matter are distinguished in the *Enneads:* intelligible matter and sensible matter. Intelligible matter is related to notions like "otherness" and "audacity," *tolma* (II.4[12], 2–5). It seems to be deployed by Plotinus for two reasons: in order to explain the emergence and definition of distinct intelligibles (e.g., V.1[10], 5) and to account within his Hellenic monotheism for the first appearance outside the One of those elements that are the ultimate roots of disorder. As we saw, the Old Academic and Pythagorean cosmologies were rooted in two opposite principles, the Monad and Indefinite Dyad. Plotinus had to show that both can be subsumed under the One and so is faced with explaining the initial movement away from the One. This is a vexed issue, for the immediate product of the

One cannot be evil, although evil will be the *parhypostasis* or by-product of this movement from the One. Yet this movement is the foundation of evil, for it is an act of self-will, *tolma*, which brings about any differentiation, even perfect formation, and thus establishes that vector that will eventuate in manifest forms of evil. Hence, it is the vectorial aspect of matter, even intelligible matter, that is critical. Thus construed, a fall doctrine is central to divine production in Plotinus, and intelligible matter is involved in this initial, volitional motion away from the One. We can never forget that Plotinus suggests the application of *tolma* to Intellect (III.8.[30] 8, 32–36; VI.9.[9] 5, 29); there is the suggestion that it would have been better if this primal differentiation had never happened. The desire for separate existence is therefore central to one notion of materiality in Plotinus; this intelligible matter is bound up with audacious self-assertion, that primordial act of volition that engenders the possibility of evil and of chaos, while itself not evil.

Sensible matter shows up in different ways, depending on the context, in such diverse works as II.4[12]; II.5[25]; III.6[26]; I.8[51]. It has a positive side because it is a necessary condition for the generation of the sensible world. It also sustains, however, a much darker portrayal, since the emergence of this world is itself a fact that betokens ambivalency. Sensible matter, which supports this lower world, is thus viewed as non-being, lacking definition, the foundation of false appearance, etc. Once again Plotinus's degree of reality ontology remains critical: matter is primarily the diremption of the One. It is privative, vectorial, and hence parasitic in fundamental character. Yet Plotinus is also capable of combining this metaphysical analysis with one that retains a strong flavor of lingering dualism. At times matter seems like an independent entity beside the One, an evil power, an antisubstance (e.g., I.8[51], esp. 6, 31–49; 15, 9–12). This tension, with deep roots in Greco-Roman modes of philosophic and religious thought, has generated a lengthy debate in recent Plotinian scholarship that, in my judgment, remains unresolved. While the main line of Plotinian reflection is in the direction of monotheism, there persists a more than vestigial remnant of Old-Academic and Pythagorean dualism.

One additional point might be recorded in reference to the question of the origins of matter (II.5.5). Given its status as non-being, this is an odd issue. O'Brien ("Plotinus on Evil," in *Le Néoplatisme*, Paris, 1971, 113–46) has argued that the soul, in an inchoate state of prodution, generates matter; he concentrates on III.9[13], 3. It bears noting that much depends on whether intelligible or sensible matter is being considered. In a subsequent study, O'Brien examines IV.8[6], 6, 18–23, where Plotinus presents two hypotheses: either matter existed always and it was impossible for it not to participate in the intelligible, or its generation followed necessarily upon the causes before it. O'Brien argues that the first hypothesis refers to intelligible matter, so it would be considered as ungenerated; while the latter refers to sensible matter, which is the product of soul. But as Corrigan has noted, this passage may also be interpreted as referring only to aspects of sensible matter; nonetheless, he also suggests that there are several diverse accounts of the generation of matter as a whole in the *Enneads*. Clearly, we are a long way from sorting out the issue.

My own suggestion is that we recognize that Plotinus was a transitional figure who was attempting to move toward a new monotheistic position against the heavy weight of antecedent traditionalism. Moreover, the notions of existence and nonexistence, as opposed to being and non-being, with their implied predicative background, had not yet fully emerged in Greek philosophy, as Charles Kahn has shown. ("Why Existence Does Not Emerge," 4.) Thus, Plotinian conceptualization was freighted with the archaic notion of a quasi-qualitative substratum that served as the medium for any sort of existence, even that of the intelligibles. It was natural for this conceptual condition to be understood as both necessary and eternal, related as it was to the way individuation and existence were portrayed. Thus, matter was both eternal, in its role as the most neutral condition by which the bare existence of anything could be represented, and generated, in its cosmological role as the recalcitrant and chaotic motion that Plotinus wishes to ascribe to the lower aspects of emanation. It will only be later in the history of metaphysics that existence will emerge as a distinct notion, a development that is closely allied to the conceptual framing of monotheism, especially among the Abrahamic traditions, with their emphasis upon *creatio ex nihilo*. (cf. *God and Creation*, ed. D. Burrell and B. McGinn, Notre Dame, Ind., 1990).

Some relevant studies include A. H. Armstrong, "Dualism Platonic, Gnostic, and Christian," *Plotinus amid Gnostics and Christians*, ed. D. T. Runia, Amsterdam, 1984, 37–41; K. Corrigan, "Is There More Than One Generation of Matter in the *Enneads*?" *Phronesis* 21 (1986): 167–81; F. P. Hager, *Der Geist und das Eine*, Noctes Romanae 12, Bern, 1970; D. O'Brien, "Plotinus on Evil," 113–46; "Le voluntaire et la nécessite," *Revue Philosophique de la France et de l'étranger* 167 (1977): 401–22; "Plotinus and the Gnostics on the Generation of Matter," in *Neoplatonism and Early Christian Thought*, ed. H. J. Blumenthal and R. A. Markus, London, 1981, 108–23; J. M. Rist, *Plotinus: The Road to Reality*, Cambridge, 1967, chap. 9; "The Problem of 'Otherness,'" 71–87; H. R. Schwyzer, "Zu Plotins Deutung der sogenannten platonischen Materie," *Zetesis*, Antwerp-Utrecht, 1973, 266–80; J. M. Simons, "Matter and Time in Plotinus," *Dionysius* 9 (1985): 53–74.

3. In Philo Judaeus the notion of uncreated matter occurs at *Fuga* 9 and *Spec. Leg.* I.328; in Clement of Alexandria it is found at *Strom.* V.89.6. Origen initiates a more clear-cut rejection of an original materiate substrate: *Contra Celsum* 6.44.1; *De Prin.* II.1.4. Despite their positions on matter, both Philo and Clement are represented as monotheists. This seems a reasonable move, given their historical context, although the same contextual courtesy should be accorded to figures like Plotinus in the Hellenic tradition, whose theology is also qualified by inconsistency on this score.

4. Cf. Trouillard, "Valeur critique de la mystique plotinienne," *Revue Philosophique de Louvain* 59 (1961): 431–44, and A. H. Armstrong, "The Escape of the One" and "Negative Theology" in *Plotinian and Christian Studies*, London, 1979, XXIII and XXIV.

5. Cf. the late treatise: VI.8.[39].

Ancient Authors

Alcinous (Albinus). *Didaskalikos*. Edited by C. F. Hermann. Vol. 6 of *Platonis Dialogi*. Leipzig, 1921–36.

Alexander Aphrodisiensis. *In Aristotelis Metaphysica commentaria*. Edited by M. Hayduck. Berlin, 1891.

Aristotle. *Aristotle's Metaphysics*. Edited by W. D. Ross. 2 vols. Oxford, 1924.

———. *De Anima*. Edited by W. D. Ross. Oxford, 1961.

Atticus. *Atticos*. Edited by J. Baudry. Paris, 1931.

Chalcidius. *Commentary on the Timaeus*. Edited by J. H. Waszink. London, 1962.

Cicero. *Opera* (vol. 4, pt. 1). Edited by C. F. W. Mueller. Leipzig, 1908.

Clement of Alexandria. *Stromata*. Edited by O. Stahlin. Leipzig, 1906–1909.

Diogenes Laertius. *Vitae Philosophorum*. Edited by H. S. Lang. 2 vols. Oxford, 1964.

Doxographi Graeci. Edited by H. Diels. Berlin, 1879.

Iamblichus. *In Platonis Dialogos Commentariorum Fragmenta*. Edited by J. Dillon. Leiden, 1973.

Nicomachus. *Introductio Arithmeticae*. Edited by R. Hoche. Leipzig, 1866.

———. *Theologumena Arithmeticae*. Edited by V. De Falco. Leipzig, 1922.

Numenius. *Numénius*. Edited by E. Des Places. Paris, 1973.

Origen. *De Principiis*. GCS 22.

Origen, the Platonist. *Origenes der Neuplatoniker*. Edited by K. O. Weber. *Zetemata* 27, Munich, 1962.

Philo. *Philo* (vols. 1–10). Edited by F. H. Colson and G. H. Whittaker. Cambridge, Mass., 1921.

Plato. *Platonis Opera* (vols. 1–5). Edited by J. Burnet. Oxford, 1900.

Plotinus. *Plotini Opera* (vols. 1–3). Edited by P. Henry and R. Schwyzer. Paris and Brussels, 1951–73.

——. *Plotini Opera* (ed. minor) (vols. 1–3). Edited by P. Henry and R. Schwyzer. Oxford, 1964–1982.

——. *Plotinus*, (Loeb edition, vols. 1–7). Edited by A. H. Armstrong. Cambridge, Mass., 1966–88.

Plutarch. *Plutarch's Moralia*. Loeb Classical Library (vol. 5). Translated by F. C. Babbitt. Cambridge, Mass., 1936.

——. *Moralia*. Loeb Classical Library (vol. 7). Edited by P. De Lacy and B. Einarson. Cambridge, Mass., 1959.

——. (vol. 12). Edited by H. Cherniss and W. Helmbold. Cambridge, Mass., 1957.

——. (vol. 13). Edited by H. Cherniss. Cambridge, Mass., 1966.

——. Teubner edition (vol. 6, pt. 1). Edited by C. Hubert. Leipzig, 1954.

Porphyry. *Sententiae ad intelligibilia ducentes*. Edited by E. Lamberz. Leipzig, 1974.

——. *Vita Plotinia*. In *Plotinus* (vol. 1). Edited by A. H. Armstrong. Cambridge, Mass., 1966.

Proclus, *Elements of Theology*. Edited by E. R. Dodds. Oxford, 1963.

——. *Commentarium in Platonis Parmenidem*. In *Procli Opera Inedita*. Edited by Victor Cousin. 617–1258. Paris, 1864.

——. *In Platonis Rempublicam Commentarii*. Edited by G. Kroll. 2 vols. Leipzig, 1899–1901.

——. *In Platonis Timaeum Commentarii*. Edited by E. Diehl. 3 vols. Leipzig, 1903–1906.

——. *Théologie Platonicienne*. Edited by H. D. Saffrey and L. G. Westerink. Paris, 1968–1981.

Ps.-Aristotle. *De Mundo*. Edited and translated by D. J. Furley. London, 1955.

Seneca. *Epistulae Morales* (vol. 1). Edited by L. D. Reynolds. Oxford, 1965.

Speusippus. *De Speusippi Academici Scriptis*. Edited by P. Lang. Bonn, 1911.

——. *Fragmenta*. Edited by L. Tarán. Leiden, 1981.

Syrianus. *In Aristotelis Metaphysica Commentaria*. Edited by W. Kroll. Berlin, 1902.

Xenocrates. *Fragmenta*. Edited by R. Heinze. Leipzig, 1892.

Modern Authors

Ackrill, J-L. "SYMPLOKE EIDON." In *Studies in Plato's Metaphysics*, edited by R. E. Allen. London, 1965.

Allen, R. E. *Plato's 'Euthyphro' and the Earlier Theory of Forms*. New York, 1970.

——, ed. *Studies in Plato's Metaphysics*. London, 1965.

André, J.-M. "Les écoles philosophiques aux deux premiers siècles de l'Empire." *Aufstieg und Niedergang der Römischen Welt* II, 36.1, 5–77.

Armstrong, A. H. *The Architecture of the Intelligible University in the Philosophy of Plotinus.* Cambridge Classical Studies. Cambridge, 1940.

————. *Plotinian and Christian Studies* (collected papers). London, 1979.

————, ed. *Plotinus: Enneads I–VI.* Loeb Classical Library. 7 vols. Cambridge, Mass., 1966–1988.

————, ed. *The Cambridge History of Later Greek and Early Medieval Philosophy.* Cambridge, 1967.

————, ed. *Classical Mediterranean Spirituality: Egyptian, Greek, Roman.* Vol. 15 of *World Spirituality: An Encyclopedic History of the Religious Quest.* New York, 1986.

————. "Plotinus' doctrine of the infinite and its significance for Christian thought." *Downside Review* 73 (1955): 47–58.

————. "Was Plotinus a Magician?" *Phronesis* 1 (1955–56): 73–79.

————. "Salvation, Plotinian and Christian." *Downside Review* 75 (1957): 126–39.

————. "The Background of the Doctrine 'That the Intelligibles Are Not Outside the Intellect.'" In *Les Sources de Plotin,* Entretiens sur l'Antiquité Classique (Fondation Hardt) 393–413. Vandoeuvres-Geneva, 1960.

————. "Platonic Eros and Christian Agape." *Downside Review* 79 (1961): 105–21.

————. "Platonism." In *The Future of Metaphysics,* edited by Ian Ramsey. London, 1962.

————. "Plotinus." In *The Cambridge History of Later Greek and Early Medieval Philosophy,* edited by A. H. Armstrong, 195–263. Cambridge, 1967.

————. "Eternity, Life and Movement in Plotinus' Accounts of Nous." In *Le Néoplatonisme,* Colloques internationaux du Centre National de la Recherche Scientifique. Royaumont 9.–13.6, 1969; Paris, 1971, 67–76.

————. "Neoplatonic Valuations of Nature, Body and Intellect." *Augustinian Studies* 3 (1972): 35–59.

————. "Man in the Cosmos: A Study of Some Differences Between Pagan Neoplatonism and Christianity." In *Romanitas and Christianitas,* by J. H. Waszink, edited by W. Den Boer, P. G. van der Nat, C. M. Sicking, J. C. M. van Winden, 171–94. Amsterdam, 1973.

————. "Elements in the Thought of Plotinus at Variance with Classical Intellectualism." *Journal of Hellenic Studies* 93 (1973): 13–22.

————. "Tradition, reason and experience in the thought of Plotinus." *Atti del convegno internazionale sul tema (Ottobre 1970). Problemi attuali di scienza e di cultura 198,* 171–94. Rome, 1974.

————. "The Escape of the One." *Studia Patristica,* vol. 13. Berlin, 1975.

————. "Beauty and the Discovery of Divinity in the Thought of Plotinus." In *Kephalaion*, edited by J. Mansfeld and L. M. de Rijk, 155–63. Assen, 1975.

————. "The Apprehension of Divinity in the Self and Cosmos in Plotinus." In *The Significance of Neoplatonism*, edited by R. B. Harris, 187–98. New York, 1976.

————. "Form, Individual and Person in Plotinus." *Dionysius* 1 (1977): 49–68.

————. "Spiritual or Intelligible Matter in Plotinus and St. Augustine." In *Augustinus Magister*. London, 1979.

————. "Some Advantages of Polytheism." *Dionysius* 5 (1981): 181–88.

————. "Two Views of Freedom: A Christian Objection in Plotinus *Enneads* VI, 8 (39), 7, 11–15." *Studia Patristica* 17(1) (1982):397–406.

————. "Negative Theology, Myth and Incarnation." In *Neoplatonism and Christian Thought*, edited by D. O'Meara, 213–22. New York, 1982.

————. "The Negative Theology of Noûs in Later Neoplatinism." In *Platonismus und Christentum*, edited by H.-D. Blume and F. Mann, 31–37. Münster, 1983.

————. "Pagan and Christian Traditionalism in the First Three Centuries AD." *Studia Patristica* 15(1) (1984):414–31.

————. "Dualism Platonic, Gnostic, and Christian." In *Plotinus amid Gnostics and Christians*. Papers presented at the Plotinus Symposium held at Free University, Amsterdam, edited by D. T. Runia, 37–41. Amsterdam, 1984.

————. "The Divine Enhancement of Earthly Beauties: The Hellenic and Platonic Tradition." *Eranos Jahrbuch* 53 (1984) 49–81.

————. "The Ancient and Continuing Pieties of the Greek World." In *Classical Mediterranean Spirituality*, 66–101. New York, 1986.

————, "Itineraries in Late Antiquity." *Eranos Jahrbuch* 56 (1987).

Arnou, R. *Le désir de Dieu dans la philosophie de Plotin*. Paris, 1921.

Atkinson, M. *Ennead V.1: On the Three Principal Hypostases*. Oxford, 1983.

Aubenque, P. "Plotin et le dépassement de l'ontologie grecque classique." In *Le Neoplatonisme*, edited by P. Schuhl and P. Hadot. Paris, 1971.

————. "Plotin philosophe de la temporalité." *Diotima* 4 (1976) 78–86.

————. "Néoplatonisme et analogie de l'être." In *Néoplatonisme*. Mélanges offerts à Jean Trouillard. *Cahiers de Fountenay* (1981): 63–76.

Baladi, N. *La pensée de Plotin*. Paris, 1970.

————. "Origine et signification de l'audace chez Plotin." In *Le Néoplatonisme*, Colloques internationaux du Centre National de la Recherche Scientifique. Royaumont 9.–13.6, 1969; Paris, 1971, 89–90.

Bales, E. F. "Plotinus' Theory of the One." In *The Structure of Being: A Neoplatonic Approach*, edited by R. B. Harris, 40–50. New York, 1982.

Bambrough, R., ed. *New Essays on Plato and Aristotle*. London, 1965.

Barnes, T. D. "The Chronology of Plotinus' Life." *Greek, Roman and Byzantine Studies* 17 (1976): 65–70.

Beierwaltes, W. *Denken des Einen: Studien zur neuplatonischen Philosophie und ihrer Wirkungsgeschichte*. Frankfurt, 1985.

———. "Die Metaphysik des Lichtes in der Philosophie Plotins." *Zeitschrift für Philosophische Forschungs* 15 (1961):334–62.

———. "Plotin über Ewigkeit und Zeit (*Enneade* III.7)." In *Quellen der Philosophie*, vol. 3, Frankfurt/Main, 1967.

———. "Andersheit: Zur neuplatonischen Struktur einer Problemgeschichte." In *Le Néoplatonisme*, Colloques internationaux du Centre National de la Recherche Scientifique. Royaumont 9.–13.6, 1969; Paris, 1971, 365–72.

———. "Negati Affirmatio." *Dionysius* 1 (1977): 127–60.

———. "Plotins Metaphysik des Lichtes." In *Die Philosophie des Neuplatonismus*, edited by C. Zintzen, 75–115. Darmstadt, 1977.

———. "The Love of Beauty and the Love of God." In *Classical Mediterranean Spirituality*, edited by A. H. Armstrong, 293–313. New York, 1986.

Berchman, R. *From Philo to Origen*. Chico, Calif., 1984.

Bianchi, U. "Plutarch und der Dualismus." *Aufstieg und Niedergang der Römischen Welt*, II, 36.1, 350–65.

Bickel, E. "Senecas Briefe 58 und 65." *Rheinisches Museum* 103(1960): 1–20.

Bluck, R. S. "Forms as Standards." *Phronesis* 2: 21–31.

Blumenthal, H. J. *Plotinus' Psychology: His Doctrines of the Embodied Soul*. The Hague, 1971.

———. "Did Plotinus Believe in Ideas of Individuals?" *Phronesis* 11 (1966): 61–80.

———. "Plotinus *Ennead* IV.3.20-1 and Its Sources: Alexander, Aristotle and Others." *Archiv für Geschichte der Philosophie* 50 (1968): 254–61.

———. "Soul, World-Soul and Individual Soul in Plotinus." In *Le Néoplatonisme*, Colloques internationaux du Centre National de la Recherche Scientifique. Royaumont 9.–13.6, 1969; Paris, 1971, 55–66.

———. "Aristotle in the Service of Platonism." *International Philosophical Quarterly* 12 (1972): 340–64.

———. "Plotinus' Psychology: Aristotle in the Service of Platonism." *International Philosophical Quarterly* 12 (1972) 340–64.

———. "Noûs and Soul in Plotinus: Some Problems of Demarcation." In *Accademia nazionale dei Lincei: Problemi attuali di scienza e di cultura* 198, 203–19. Rome, 1974.

———. "Plotinus in Later Platonism." In *Neoplatonism and Early Christian Thought*, edited by H. J. Blumenthal and R. A. Markus, 212–22. London, 1981.

———. "Some Problems about Body and Soul in Later Pagan Neoplatonism: Do They Follow a Pattern?" *Platonismus und Christentum*. Festschrift for H. Dörrie, edited by H.-D. Blume and F. Mann, 75–84. Münster, 1983.

———. "Plotinus' 'Ennead' I, 2, 7, 5: A Different Hapax." *Mnemosyne* 4(37) (1984): 89–93.

———. "Plotinus in the Light of Twenty Years' Scholarship, 1951–1971." *Aufstieg und Niedergang der Römischen Welt*, II, 36.1, 528–570.

Blumenthal, H. J., and A. C. Lloyd, eds. *Soul and the Structure of Being in Late Neoplatonism*. Liverpool, 1982.

Boehner, P. In *Collected Articles on Ockham*, ed. by E. M. Buytaert. New York, 1958.

Bos, A. P. "World-Views in Collision: Plotinus, Gnostics, and Christians." In *Plotinus amid Gnostics and Christians*. Papers presented at the Plotinus Symposium held at Free University, edited by D. T. Runia, 11–28. Amsterdam, 1984.

Boyancé, P. "Xenocrate et les Orphiques." *Revue des Études Anciennes* 36 (1948) 218ff.

Bréhier, É. *Les idées philosophiques de Philon d'Alexandrie*. Paris, 1908.

———. *La philosophie de Plotin*. Paris, 1928.

———. *The Philosophy of Plotinus*, trans. by J. Thomas. Chicago, 1958.

Brentlinger, J. A. "The Divided Line and Plato's Theory of Intermediates." *Phronesis* 8: 146–66.

Brisson, L. *Le même et l'autre dans la structure ontologique du timée de Platon*. Paris, 1974.

Brisson, L., M.-O. Goulet-Cazé, R. Goulet, and D. O'Brien. *Porphyre: La vie de Plotin*. Paris, 1982.

Burkert, W. *Lore and Science in Ancient Pythagoreanism*. Cambridge, Mass., 1972.

Burrell, D. B. *Knowing the Unknowable God*. Notre Dame, Ind., 1986.

Bussanich, J. *The One and Its Relation to Intellect in Plotinus*. Leiden, 1988.

———. "Plotinus on the Inner Life of the One." *Ancient Philosophy* 7: 163–89.

———. "Mystical Elements in Plotinus' Thought." *Aufstieg und Niedergang der Römischen Welt*, Nachtrag in Bd. II, 36.4.

Carré, M. H. *Realists and Nominalists*. Oxford, 1946.

Casey, R. P. "Clement and the Two Divine Logoi." *Journal of Theological Studies*, 25: 43–56.

Chadwick, H. "Philo and the Beginnings of Christian Thought." In *The Cambridge History of Later Greek and Early Medieval Philosophy* (pt. 2), edited by A. H. Armstrong. Cambridge, 1967.

Charles-Saget, A. *L'architecture du divin: Mathématiques et philosophie chez Plotin et Proclus*. Paris, 1982.

Charrue, J. M. *Plotin, lecteur de Platon*. Paris, 1978.

Cherniss, H. *Aristotle's Criticism of Plato and the Academy* (vol. 1). Balti-more, 1944.

———. *The Riddle of the Early Academy*. Berkeley, Calif., 1945.

———. "On Plato's *Republic* X, 597b." *American Journal of Philology* 53 (1932): 233–42.

———. "Review of R. E. Witt, *Albinus and the History of Middle Platonism*," *American Journal of Philology* 59 (1938): 351–56.

———. "The Sources of Evil According to Plato." *Proceedings of the American Philosophical Society* 98 (1954): 23–30.

———. "The Philosophical Economy of the Theory of Ideas." *Plato* (vol. 1), edited by G. Vlastos. Garden City, N.Y., 1971.

Clarke, W. N., "The Limitation of Act by Potency." *The New Scholasticism* 26: 184–89.

———, "Infinity in Plotinus: A Reply." *Gregorianum* 40: 75–98.

Copleston, *History of Philosophy* (vols. 2, 3). New York, 1962–63.

Cornford, F. M. *Plato and Parmenides*. New York, n.d.

———. *Plato's Cosmology*. New York, 1937.

Corrigan, K., "The Internal Dimensions of the Sensible Object in the Thought of Plotinus and Aristotle." *Dionysius* 5 (1981) 98–126.

———. "A Philosophical Precursor to the Theory of Essence and Existence in Thomas Aquinas." *Thomist* 48 (1984): 219–40.

———. "The Irreducible Opposition Between the Platonic and Aristotelian Conceptions of Soul and Body in Some Ancient and Mediaeval Think-ers." *Laval Théologique et Philosophique* 41 (1985): 391–401.

———. "Body and Soul in Ancient Religious Experience." *Classical Mediter-ranean Spirituality*, ed. by A. H. Armstrong, 360–83. New York, 1986.

———. "Is There More Than One Generation of Matter in the Enneads?" *Phronesis* 21 (1986): 167–81.

———. "Plotinus' 'Enneads' 5, 4 (7), 2 and Related Passages: A New Inter-pretation of the Status of the Intelligible Object." *Hermes* 114 (1986) 195–204.

Corrigan, K., and P. O'Cleirigh. "The Course of Plotinian Scholarship from 1971 to 1986." *Aufstieg und Niedergang der Römischen Welt* II, 36.1, 575–78.

Costello, E. B. "Is Plotinus Inconsistent on the Nature of Evil?" *International Philosophical Quarterly* 7 (1967): 483–97.

Daniélou, J. *Origène*. Paris, 1948.

———. *Philon d' Alexandrie*. Paris, 1958.

Deck, J. N. *Nature, Contemplation and the One*. Toronto, 1967.

De Gandillac, M. *La sagesse de Plotin*. Paris, 1966.

Deitz, L. "Bibliographie du platonisme impérial antérieur à Plotin: 1926–1986." *Aufstieg und Niedergang der Römischen Welt*, II, 36.1, 124–82.

Des Places, É. *Études Platoniciennes 1929–1979*. Leiden, 1981.

De Vogel, C. J. *Philosophia* (vol. 1). Assen, 1970.

―――. "On the Neoplatonic Character of Platonism and the Platonic character of Neoplatonism." *Mind* 62 (1953): 43–64.

Dillon, J. *The Middle Platonists.* Ithaca, N.Y., 1977.

―――, ed., with G. Morrow. *Proclus' Commentary on Plato's Parmenides.* Princeton, N.J., 1987.

―――. "Image, Symbol and Analogy: Three Basic Concepts of Neoplatonic Allegorical Exegesis." *The Significance of Neoplatonism*, edited by R. B. Harris, 247–62. New York, 1976.

―――. "The Academy in the Middle Platonic Period." *Dionysius* 3 (1979): 63–77.

―――. "Plotinus, Philo and Origen on the Grades of Virtue." *Platonismus und Christentum.* Festschrift for H. Dörrie, edited by H.-D. Blume and F. Mann, *Jahrbuch für Antike and Christentum* 10 (1983): 92–105.

―――. "Plutarch and Second Century Platonism." In *Classical Mediterranean Spirituality*, edited by A. H. Armstrong, 214–29. New York, 1986.

Dodds, E. R. *Proclus: The Elements of Theology.* Oxford, 1963.

―――. *Pagan and Christian in an Age of Anxiety.* Cambridge, 1965.

―――. "The Parmenides of Plato and the Origins of the Neoplatonic One." *Classical Quarterly*, 22 (): 129–43.

―――. "Numenius and Ammonius." *Entretiens Hardt* 5 (1960) 3–61.

―――. "Tradition and Personal Achievement in the Philosophy of Plotinus." *Journal of Roman Studies* 50 (1960) 1–7.

Donagan, A. "Universals and Metaphysical Realism." In *Universals and Particulars*, edited by M. Loux, 128–58. New York, 1970.

Dörrie, H. *Platonica Minora*, Munich, 1976 (collected articles).

―――. "Ammonius, der Lehrer Plotins." *Hermes* 83 (1955) 439–78.

―――. "Die Frage nach dem Transzendenten im Mittelplatonismus." *Les sources de Plotin*, Entretiens sur l'Antiquité Classique (Fondation Hardt), 1957; Vandoeuvres-Geneva, 1960, 193–223.

―――. "Plotin, Philosoph and Theologe." *Die Welt als Geschichte* 1 (1963): 1–12.

―――. "Emanation, ein unphilosophisches Wort im spätantiken Denken." In *Parusia: Studien zur Philosophie Platons und zur Problemgeschichte des Platonismus*, edited by K. Flasch, 119–41. Frankfurt/Main, 1965.

―――. "Prapositionen und Metaphysik." *Museum Helviticum* 26 (1969): 217–28.

―――. "Der König: Ein platonisches Schlüsselwort, von Plotin mit neuem Sinn erfüllt." In *Platonica Minora*, Munich, 1976, 390–405.

―――. "Die Erneuerung des Platonismus im ersten Jahrhundert vor Christus." *Le Néoplatonisme*, Colloques internationaux du Centre National de la Recherche Scientifique. Royaumont 9.–13.6, 1969; Paris, 1971, 17–28.

————. "Die hauptsächlichen Aspekte des kaiserzeitlichen Platonismus." In *Kephalaion*, edited by J. Mansfeld and L. M. de Rijk, 1–34. Assen 1975.

————. "La doctrine de l'âme dans le néoplatonisme de Plotin à Proclus." *Revue de Théologie et de Philosophie*, sér. 3.23 (1973): 116–32.

————. "Plotino, tradizionalista o inventore?" *Accademia nazionale dei Lincei. Problemi attuali di scienza e di cultura 198*, 195–201. Rome, 1974.

————. "Hypostasis." In *Platonica Minora*, 12–69. Munich, 1976.

————. "Tradition und Erneuerung in Plotins Philosophieren." In *Platonica Minora*, 375–89. Munich, 1976.

————, ed. "De Jamblique à Proclus." In *Entretiens sur l'Antiquité Classique* (vol. 21). Vandoeuvres-Geneva, 1975.

Elsas, C. *Neuplatonische und gnostische Weltablehnung in der Schule Plotins*. Berlin, New York, 1975.

Entretiens Hardt, 3, Recherches sur la tradition platonicienne. Vandoeuvres-Geneva, 1957.

————, 5, *Les sources de Plotin*. Vandoeuvres-Geneva, 1960.

————, 11, *Pseudopythagorica* (vol. 1). Vandoeuvres-Geneva, 1972.

————, 21, *De Jamblique à Proclus*. Vandoeuvres-Geneva, 1975.

Evangeliou, C. C. "The Ontological Basis of Plotinus' Criticism of Aristotle's Theory of Categories." In *The Structure of Being: A Neoplatonic Approach*, edited by R. B. Harris, 73–82. New York, 1982.

Festugière, A. J. *La révélation d'Hermès Trismégiste*. Paris, 1944–54.

————. *Contemplation et vie contemplative selon Platon*. Paris, 1967.

Fielder, J. "Chorismos and Emanation in the Philosophy of Plotinus." In *The Significance of Neoplatonism*, edited by R. B. Harris, 101–20. New York, 1976.

————. "Plotinus' Copy Theory." *Apeiron* 11.2 (1977): 1–11.

————. "Plotinus' Reply to the Arguments of Parmenides 130a–131d." *Apeiron* 12.2 (1978): 1–5.

————. "Plotinus' Response to Two Problems of Immateriality." *Proceedings of the American Catholic Philosophical Association* 52 (1978) 98–101.

————. "A Plotinian View of Self-Predication and TMA." *Modern Schoolman* 57 (1980) 339–47.

————. "Plotinus and Self-Predication." In *The Structure of Being: A Neoplatonic Approach*, edited by R. B. Harris, 83–89. New York, 1982.

Findlay, J. N., *Plato: The Written and Unwritten Doctrines*. New York, 1974.

————. "The Three Hypostases of Plotinism." *Review of Metaphysics* 28 (1975): 660–80.

————. "The Neoplatonism of Plato." In *The Significance of Neoplatonism*, edited by R. B. Harris, 23–40. New York, 1976.

————. "The Logical Peculiarities of Neoplatonism." In *The Structure of Being: A Neoplatonic Approach*, edited by R. B. Harris, 1–10. New York, 1982.

Forrester, J. W. "Plato's Parmenides: The Structure of the First Hypothesis." *Journal of the History of Philosophy* 10 (1972): 1–14.

Froidefond, Ch. "Plutarque et le platonisme", *Aufstieg und Niedergang der Römischen Welt*, II, 36.1, 184–233.

Gaiser, K. *Platons ungeschriebene Lehre*. Stuttgart, 1963.

Geach, P. *Reference and Generality*. Ithaca, N.Y., 1962.

———. "The Third Man Again." In *Studies in Plato's Metaphysics*, edited by R. E. Allen, 265–78. London, 1965.

Gersh, S. E. *Kinesis Akinetos: A Study of Spiritual Motion in the Philosophy of Proclus*. Leiden, 1973.

———. *From Iamblichus to Eriugena: An Investigation of the Prehistory and Evolution of the Pseudo-Dionysian Tradition*. Leiden, 1978.

———. *Middle Platonism and Neoplatonism: The Latin Tradition*. 2 vols. Notre Dame, Ind., 1986.

Gilson, E. *Being and Some Philosophers*. Toronto, 1944.

———. *A History of Christian Philosophy in the Middle Ages*. New York, 1955.

Glucker, J. *Antiochus and the Late Academy*. Göttingen, 1978.

Goodenough, E. *By Light, Light*. New Haven, Conn., 1935.

———. *Introduction to Philo Judaeus*. Oxford, 1962.

Graeser, A. "Plotinus and the Stoics: A Preliminary Study." *Philosophia Antiqua* (vol. 22). Leiden, 1972.

Grant, R. M. *Gods and the One God*. Philadelphia, 1986.

Gurtler, G. M. "Sympathy in Plotinus." *International Philosophical Quarterly* 24 (1984): 395–406.

Guthrie, W. K. C. *History of Greek Philosophy* (vol. 4 and 5). Cambridge, 1975 and 1978.

Hackforth, R. *Plato's Phaedo*. Cambridge, 1955.

———. "Plato's Cosmogony." *Classical Quarterly*, n.s. 9, (1959): 17–22.

———. "Plato's Theism," in *Studies in Plato's Metaphysics*, edited by R. E. Allen. London, 1965, 439–47.

Hadot, P. *Plotin ou la simplicité du regard*. Paris, 1963.

———. *Porphyre et Victorinus*. Paris, 1968.

———. *Exercices spirituels et philosophie antique*. Paris, 1981.

———. "Etre, vie, pensée chez Plotin et avant Plotin." In *Les sources de Plotin*, Entretiens sur l'Antiquité Classique (Fondation Hardt) 5: 107–41. Vandoeuvres-Geneva, 1960.

———. "Fragments d'un commentaire de Porphyre sur le Parménide de Platon." *Revue des Études Grecques* 74 (1961): 410–38.

———. "L'être et l'étant dans le néoplatonisme." *Revue de Théologie et de Philosophie*, sér. 3.23 (1973): 101–13.

———. "L'harmonie des philosophies de Plotin et d'Aristote selon Porphyre." *Atti del Convegno internazionale sul tema (Ottobre 1970): Problemi attuali di scienza e di cultura 198*, 31–47. Rome, 1974.

———. "Théologies et mystiques de la Grèce hellénistique et de la fin de l'antiquité." *Annuaire de l'école pratique des hautes études* 80–81.3 (1972–73, 1973–74): 277–87; 82.3 (1973–74): 165–69; 84 (1975–76): 285–86.

———. "Les niveaux de conscience dans les états mystiques selon Plotin." *Journal de Psychologie* 77 (1980): 243–66.

———. "Images mythiques et thèmes mystiques dans un passage de Plotin (V, 8, 10–13)." *Néoplatonisme: Mélanges offerts Jean Trouillard. Cahiers de Fontenay* (1981): 205–14.

———. "Ouranos, Kronos, and Zeus in Plotinus' Treatise Against the Gnostics." In *Neoplatonism and Early Christian Thought: Essays in Honour of A. H. Armstrong*, edited by H. J. Blumenthal and R. A. Markus, 124–37. London 1981.

———. "Neoplatonist Spirituality, Plotinus and Porphyry." In *Classical Mediterranean Spirituality*, edited by A. H. Armstrong, 230–49. New York, 1986.

———. "Structure et thèmes du traité 38 (VI, 7) de Plotin." *Aufstieg und Niedergang der Römischen Welt*, II, 36.1, 624–76.

———. "L'union de l'âme avec l'intellect divin dans l'experience mystique plotinienne." *Proclus et son influence*, 17. Zurich, 1987.

Hager, F. P. *Der Geist und das Eine, Noctes Romanae* (vol. 12, pt. 3) Bern/Stuttgart, 1970.

———. "Zum Problem der Originalität Plotins: Drei Probleme der 'neuplatonischen' Interpretation Platons." *Archiv für Geschichte des Philosophie* 58 (1976): 10–22.

Harris, R. B., ed. *The Significance of Neoplatonism*. New York, 1976.

———, ed. *The Structure of Being: A Neoplatonic Approach*. New York, 1982.

———, ed. *Neoplatonism and Indian Thought*. New York, 1982.

Hartshorne, C. *Man's Vision of God*. New York, 1941.

———. *The Divine Relativity*. New Haven, Conn., 1948.

———. *Philosophers Speak of God*. Chicago, 1953.

———. *Reality As Social Process*. Glencoe, Ill., 1953.

———. *The Logic of Perfection*. La Salle, Ill., 1962.

———. *A Natural Theology for Our Time*. La Salle, Ill., 1967.

Hathaway, R. "The Anatomy of a Neoplatonist Metaphysical Proof." In *The Structure of Being: A Neoplatonic Approach*, edited by R. B. Harris, 122–37. New York, 1982.

Heinemann, E. "Ammonius Sakkas und der Ursprung des Neuplatonismus." *Hermes* 61 (1926): 1–27.

Henle, P. "Uses of the Ontological Argument." In *The Ontological Argument*, edited by A. Plantinga. New York, 1965.

Henle, R. J. *St. Thomas and Platonism.* The Hague, 1956.

Henry, P. *Plotin et l'occident.* Louvain, 1934.

———. *Études Plotiniennes: 1. Les états du texte de Plotin.* Museum Lessianum, Section Philol. 20, Paris/Brussels, 1938.

———. "Une comparaison chez Aristote, Alexandre et Plotin." *Les sources de Plotin, Entretiens sur l'Antiquité Classique* (Fondation Hardt), 429–44. Vandoeuvres-Geneva, 1960.

———. "Introduction." In *Enneads,* edited by S. MacKenna. London 1962, 1969.

Hershbell, J. P. "Plutarch's 'De animae procreatione in Timaeo': An Analysis of Structure and Content." *Aufstieg und Niedergang der Römischen Welt,* II, 36.1, 234–47.

Hick, J. *An Interpretation of Religion.* New Haven, Conn., 1989.

Huber, G. *Das Sein und das Absolute, Studia Philosophica* (suppl. 6). Basel, 1955.

Hunt, D. P. "Contemplation and Hypostatic Process in Plotinus." *Apeiron* 15 (1981): 71–79.

Igal, J. "Commentaria in Plotini 'De Bono sive de Uno' librum (Enn. VI, 9)." *Helmantica* 22 (1971): 273–304.

———. "The Gnostics and 'The Ancient Philosophy' in Plotinus." In *Neoplatonism and Early Christian Thought. Essays in Honour of A. H. Armstrong,* edited by H. J. Blumenthal and R. A. Markus, 138–49. London, 1981.

Inge, W. R. *The Philosophy of Plotinus,* 2 vols. London, 1929.

Jackson, B. D. "Plotinus and the Parmenides." *J. Hist. Phil.* 5 (1967): 315–27.

Jansen, H. L. "Die Mystik Plotins." *Numen* 11 (1964): 165–88.

Jerphagnon, L. "Exigences noétiques et objectivité dans la pensée de Plotin." *Revue de Métaphysique et de Morale* 79 (1974): 411–16.

Jevons, F. R. " 'Lumping' in Plotinus' Thought." *Archiv für Geschichte der Philosophie* 47 (1965): 132–40.

Jonas, H. "The Soul in Gnosticism and Plotinus." *Le Néoplatonisme,* Colloques internationaux du Centre National de la Recherche Scientifique, 45–53. Paris, 1971.

Jones, R. M. *The Platonism of Plutarch,* edited by Leonardo Taran. New York, 1980.

———. "The Ideas as Thoughts of God." *Classical Philology* 21: 317–26.

Kahn, C. *The Verb 'Be' and Its Synonyms: The Verb 'Be' in Ancient Greek.* Dordrecht, 1973.

———. "On the Terminology for Copula and Existence." In *Islamic Philosophy and the Classical Tradition.* 154ff. Oxford, 1972.

———. "Why Existence Does Not Emerge as a Distinct Concept in Greek Philosophy." *Archiv für Geschichte der Philosophie,* 58 (1976): 323–34.

Kélessidou-Galanou, A. "L'extase plotinienne et la problématique de la personne humaine." *Revue des Études Grecques* 84 (1971): 384–96.

———. "Plotin et la dialectique platonicienne de l'absolu." *Philosophia* 3 (1973): 307–338.

———. "Preuves de l'existence et nature du Premier chez Plotin." *Philosophia* 5–6 (1975–76): 353–69.

Kenney, J. P. "Monotheistic and Polytheistic Elements in Classical Mediterranean Spirituality." In *Classical Mediterranean Spirituality*, edited by A. H. Armstrong, 269–92. New York, 1986.

———. "Divinity and the Intelligible World in Clement of Alexandria." In *Studia Patristica* (vol. 21). Leuven, 1989.

———. "Theism and Divine Production in Ancient Realist Theology." In *God and Creation*, edited by D. Burrell and B. McGinn. Notre Dame, Ind., 1990.

Kenny, A. J. P. *The Five Ways*. Oxford, 1977.

Kneale, W., and M. Kneale. *The Development of Logic*. Oxford, 1962.

Kordig, D. R., "The Mathematics of Mysticism: Plotinus and Proclus." In *The Structure of Being: A Neoplatonic Approach*, edited by R. B. Harris, 114–21. New York, 1982.

Krämer, H. J. *Der Ursprung der Geistmetaphysik*. Amsterdam, 1964.

———. *Platon und hellenistiche Philosophie*. Berlin, 1972.

Kremer, K. *Die Neuplatonische Seinsphilosophie und ihre Wirkung auf Thomas von Aquin: Studien zur Problemgeschichte der antiken und mittelalterlichen Philosophie* (vol. 1). Leiden, 1966.

Kretzmann, N., A. Kenny, and J. Pinborg, eds. *The Cambridge History of Later Medieval Philosophy*. Cambridge, 1982.

Kristeller, P. O. *Renaissance Thought* (vol. 1). New York, 1961.

———. *Medieval Aspects of Renaissance Learning*. Durham, N.C., 1974.

Koch, H. *Pronoia und Paideusis*. Leipzig, 1932.

Langerbeck, H. "The Philosophy of Ammonius Saccas and the Connection of Aristotelian and Christian Elements Therein." *Journal of Hellenic Studies* 77:67–74.

Lee, E. N. "Plato on Negation and Not-Being in the Sophist." *Philosophical Review* 81 (1972) 267–304.

Lee, J. S. "The Doctrine of Reception According to the Capacity of the Recipient in Ennead VI.4–5." *Dionysius* 3 (1979) 79–97.

———. "Omnipresence and Eidetic Causation in Plotinus." *The Structure of Being: A Neoplatonic Approach*, edited by R. B. Harris, 90–103. New York, 1982.

Leff, G. *Gregory of Rimimi*. Manchester, 1961.

———. *William of Ockham*. Manchester, 1975.

———. *The Dissolution of the Medieval Outlook*. New York, 1976.

Leslie, J. *Value and Existence*. Oxford, 1979.

———. "Mackie on Neoplatonism's 'Replacement for God.'" *Religious Studies* 22 (1986) 325–42.

Lilla, S. *Clement of Alexandria*. Oxford, 1971.

Lloyd, A. C. "Neoplatonic Logic and Aristotelian Logic." *Phronesis* 1 (1955–56) 58–79, 146–60.

———. "Plato's Description of Division." In *Studies in Plato's Metaphysics*, edited by R. E. Allen, 219–30. London, 1965.

———. "The Later Neoplatonists." In *The Cambridge History of Later Greek and Early Medieval Philosophy* (pt. 4), edited by A. H. Armstrong. Cambridge, 1967.

———. "Non-discursive thought—an enigma of Greek philosophy." *Proceedings of the Society* 70 (1969–70): 261–74.

———. "The Principle That the Cause Is Greater Than Its Effect." *Phronesis* 21 (1976): 146–56.

———. "Plotinus on the Genesis of Thought and Existence." *Oxford Studies in Ancient Philosophy* 5 (1987).

Loenen, J. H. "Albinus' Metaphysics: An Attempt at Rehabilitation." *Mnemosyne* 9:35–56.

Louth, A. *The Origins of the Christian Mystical Tradition*. Oxford, 1981.

Lovejoy, A. *The Great Chain of Being*. Cambridge, Mass., 1936.

MacKenna, S. *The Enneads*. London, 1962.

Mackie, J. L. *The Miracle of Theism*. Oxford, 1982.

Mamo, P. "Forms of Individuals in the *Enneads*." *Phronesis* 14 (1969): 77–96.

———. "Is Plotinian Mysticism Monistic?" In *The Significance of Neoplatonism*, edited by R. B. Harris, 199–216. New York, 1976.

Manchester, P. "Time and the Soul in Plotinus, III, 7[45], 11." *Dionysius* 2 (1978): 101–36.

———. "The Religious Experience of Time and Eternity." In *Classical Mediterranean Spirituality*, edited by A. H. Armstrong, 384–407. New York, 1986.

Mann, W. E. "The Divine Attributes." *American Philosophical Quarterly* 12 (1975): 151–59.

———. "Divine Simplicity." *Religious Studies* 18 (1982): 451–72.

———. "Simplicity and Immutability in God." *International Philosophical Quarterly* 23 (1983): 267–76.

———. "Simplicity and Properties: A Reply to Morris." *Religious Studies* 22 (1986): 343–53.

Martin, R. M. "On Logical Structure and the Plotinic Cosmos." In *The Structure of Being: A Neoplatonic Approach*, edited by R. B. Harris, 11–23. New York, 1982.

Matter, P. P. *Zum Einfluss des platonischen Timaios auf das Denken Plotins*. Winterthur, 1964.

McCumber, J. "Anamnesis as Memory of Intelligibles in Plotinus." *Archiv für Geschichte der Philosophie* 60 (1978): 160–67.

Merlan, P. *From Platonism to Neoplatonism*. The Hague, 1960.

——. *Monopsychism, Mysticism, Metaconsciousness*. The Hague, 1963.

——. "Monismus und Dualismus bei einigen Platonikern." In *Parusia: Studien zur Philosophie Platons und zur Problemgeschichte des Platonismus*, edited by K. Flasch, 143–54. Frankfurt/Main, 1965.

——. "Greek Philosophy from Plato to Plotinus." In *The Cambridge History of Later Greek and Early Medieval Philosophy* (pt. 1), edited by A. H. Armstrong. Cambridge, 1967.

Miller, C. L. "Union with the One, Ennead 6, 9, 8–11." *The New Scholasticism* 51 (1977): 182–95.

Moody, E. A. *The Logic of William of Ockham*. London, 1935.

Moravscik, J. M. E. "The 'Third Man' Argument and Plato's Theory of Forms." *Phronesis* 8 (1963): 50–62.

Moreau, J. *Plotin ou la gloire de la philosophie antique*. Paris, 1970.

——. "Origine et expressions du beau suivant Plotin." In *Neoplatonisme: Mélanges offerts à Jean Trouillard. Cahiers de Fontenay* (1981): 249–263.

Morris, T. "On God and Mann: A View of Divine Simplicity." *Religious Studies* 21 (1985) 299–318.

Morrow, G., and J. M. Dillon. *Proclus' Commentary on Plato's Parmenides*. Princeton, N.J., 1987.

Mortley, R. "Negative Theology and Abstraction in Plotinus." *American Journal of Philology* 96 (1975): 363–77.

——. *From Word to Silence*, 2 vols. Bonn and Frankfurt/Main, 1986.

Mossé-Bastide, R. *La pensée philosophique de Plotin*. Paris/Brussels/Montreal, 1972.

Moutsopoulos, E. "L'évolution du dualisme ontologique platonicien et ses conséquences pour le néoplatonisme." *Diotima* 10 (1982): 179–81.

Nasr, S. H. *Knowledge and the Sacred*. New York, 1981.

Nehamas, A. "Plato on the Imperfection of the Sensible World." *American Philosophical Quarterly* 12 (1975): 105–17.

——. "Self-predication and Plato's Theory of Forms." *American Philosophical Quarterly* 16 (1979): 93–103.

Obermann, H. *Harvest of Medieval Theology: Gabriel Biel and Late Medieval Nominalism*. Cambridge, Mass., 1963.

O'Brien, D. "Plotinus on Evil: A Study of Matter and the Soul in Plotinus' Conception of Human Evil." *Downside Review* 87 (1969): 68–110.

——. "Le volontaire et la nécessite: Réflexions sur la descente de l'âme dans la philosophie de Plotin." *Revue Philosophiques de la France et de Pétranger* 167 (1977): 401–22.

——. "Plotinus and the Gnostics on the Generation of Matter." In *Neoplatonism and Early Christian Thought: Essays in Honour of A. H. Armstrong*, edited by H. J. Blumenthal and R. A. Markus, 108–23. London, 1981.

O'Daly, G. J. P. *Plotinus' Philosophy of the Self*. Dublin, 1973.

——. "The Presence of the One in Plotinus." *Atti del Convegno internazionale sul tema (Ottobre 1970): Problemi attuali di scienza e di cultura 198*, 159–69. Rome, 1974.

O'Meara, D. J. "Structures hiérarchiques dans la pensée de Plotin: Étude historique et interprétative." In *Philosophia antiqua* (vol. 27). Leiden, 1975.

——. "A propos d'un témoignage sur l'expérience mystique de Plotin (Enn. IV, 8[6] 1, 1–11)." *Mnemosyne IV* 27 (1974): 238–44.

——. "Being in Numenius and Plotinus: Some Points of Comparison." *Phronesis* 21 (1976): 120–29.

——. "Gnosticism and the Making of the World in Plotinus." In *The Rediscovery of Gnosticism: Proceedings of the International Conference on Gnosticism, March 28–31, 1978*, 365–78. Leiden, 1980.

——. "The Problem of Omnipresence in Plotinus, Ennead VI, 4–5: A Reply." *Dionysius* 4 (1980): 61–73.

——, ed. *Neoplatonism and Christian Thought*. New York, 1982.

Osborn, E. F., *The Philosophy of Clement of Alexandria*, Cambridge, 1957.

Owen, G. E. L. "Aristotle on the Snares of Ontology." In *New Essays on Plato and Aristotle*, edited by R. Bambrough. London, 1965.

——, "The Place of the *Timaeus* in Plato's Dialogues." In *Studies in Plato's Metaphysics*, edited by R. E. Allen, 313–38. London, 1965.

Owen, H. P. *Concepts of Deity*. New York, 1971.

Patterson, R. *Image and Reality in Plato's Metaphysics*. Indianapolis, Ind., 1986.

Peck, A. L. "Plato versus Parmenides." *Philosophical Review* 71 (1962): 159–84.

Pépin, J. "Éléments pour une histoire de la relation entre l'intelligence et l'intelligible chez Platon et dans le néoplatonisme." *Revue Philosophique de la France et de l'étranger* 146 (1956): 39–55.

——. "Cosmic Piety." In *Classical Mediterranean Spirituality*, edited by A. H. Armstrong, 408–35. New York, 1986.

Pinès, S. "The problem of 'otherness' in the Enneads." *Le Néoplatonisme*, Colloques internationaux du Centre National de la Recherche Scientifique. 303–17. Paris, 1971.

Plantinga, A. *The Nature of Necessity*. Oxford, 1974.

——. *Does God Have a Nature?* Milwaukee, Wis., 1980.

Puech, H.-C. "Plotin et les Gnostiques." In *Les sources de Plotin*, Entretiens sur l'Antiquité Classique (Fondation Hardt), 161–74. Vandoeuvres-Geneva, 1960.

Reeve, C. D. C. *Philosopher Kings*. Princeton, N.J., 1988.

Rich, A. N. M. "Reincarnation in Plotinus." *Mnemos*, ser. 4.10 (1957): 232–38.

——. "The Platonic Ideas as the Thought of God," *Mnemosyne*, ser. 4, 7 (1954) 123–33.

————. "Body and Soul in the Philosophy of Plotinus." *Journal of the History of Philosophy* 1 (1963): 1–15.

Rist, J. M. *Eros and Psyche*. Toronto, 1964.

————. *Plotinus: The Road to Reality*. Cambridge, 1967.

————. "Human Value: A Study in Ancient Philosophical Ethics." In *Philosophia Antiqua* (vol. 40). Leiden, 1982.

————. "Plotinus on matter and evil." *Phronesis* 6 (1961): 154–66.

————. "The Indefinite Dyad and Intelligible Matter in Plotinus." *Classical Quarterly*, n.s. 12 (1962): 99–107.

————. "The Neoplatonic One and Plato's *Parmenides*." *Transactions of the American Philological Association* 93 (1962). 389–401.

————. "Theos and the One in Some Texts of Plotinus." *Mediaeval Studies* 24 (1962) 169–80.

————. "Forms of Individuals in Plotinus." *Classical Quarterly*, n.s. 13 (1963): 223–31.

————. "Mysticism and Transcendence in Later Neoplatonism." *Hermes* 92 (1964): 213–25.

————. "Monism: Plotinus and Some Predecessors." *Harvard Studies in Classical Philology* 70 (1965) 329–44.

————. "Integration and the Undescended Soul in Plotinus." *American Journal of Philology* 88 (1967) 410–22.

————. "Ideas of Individuals in Plotinus: A reply to Dr. Blumenthal." *Revue Internationale de Philosophie* 92(2) (1971): 298–303.

————. "The Problem of 'Otherness' in the *Enneads*." In *Le Neoplatonisme*, edited by P. Schuhl and P. Hadot, 77–87. Paris, 1971.

————. "The One of Plotinus and the God of Aristotle." *Revue de Métaphysique et de Morale* 27 (1973): 75–87.

————. "Plotinus and Augustine on Evil." *Accademia nazionale dei Lincei. Problemi attuali di scienza e di cultura 198*, 495–508. Rome, 1974.

————. "Prohairesis: Proclus, Plotinus et alii." *De Jamblique à Proclus*, edited by H. Doerrie, 103–22. Vandoeuvres-Geneva, 1975.

————. "Metaphysics and Psychology in Plotinus' Treatment of the Soul." *Graceful Reason: Essays in Ancient and Medieval Philosophy*, edited by L. P. Gerson, 135–51. Toronto, 1983.

————. "Back to the Mysticism of Plotinus: Some More Specifics." *Journal of the History of Philosophy* 27 (1989): 183–98.

Robin, L. *La théorie platonicienne de idées et des nombres d'après Aristote*. Paris, 1908.

Ross, D. *Plato's Theory of Ideas*. Oxford, 1951.

Runia, D. T. *Philo of Alexandria and the Timaeus of Plato*. Leiden, 1986.

————. "A Note on Albinus/Alcinous Didaskalikos XIV." *Mnemosyne*, ser. 4, 39 (1986): 131–38.

————, ed. *Plotinus amid Gnostics and Christians*. Papers presented at the Plotinus Symposium held at Free University, Amsterdam, 1984.

Russell, B. "The World of Universals." In *Universals and Particulars*, edited by M. Loux, 128–58. New York, 1970.

Ryle, G. *Plato's Progress*. Cambridge, 1966.

Sambursky, S. *The Physical World of Late Antiquity*. London, 1962.

Schlette, H. *Das Eine und das Andere: Studien zur Problematik des Negativen in der Metaphysik Plotins*. Munich, 1966.

Schroeder, F. M., "Ammonius Saccas." In *Aufstieg und Niedergang der Römischen Welt*, II, 36.1, 493–526.

————. "Conversion and Consciousness in Plotinus, 'Enneads' 5, 1 (10), 7." *Hermes* 114 (1986): 186–95.

————. "The Self in Ancient Religious Experience." In *Classical Mediterranean Spirituality*, edited by A. H. Armstrong, 337–59. New York, 1986.

————. "Synousia, Synaisthaesis and Synesis: Presence and Dependence in the Plotinian Philosophy of Consciousness." *Aufstieg und Niedergang der Römischen Welt*, II, 36.1, 677–99.

Schwyzer, H.-R. *Ammonius Saccas, der Lehrer Plotins*. Opladen, 1983.

————. "Die pseudoaristotelische Theologie und die Plotin-Ausgabe des Porphyrios." *Rheinisches Museum* 90 (1941): 216–36.

————. "Die zwiefache Sicht in der Philosophie Plotins." *Museum Helveticum* 1 (1944): 87–99.

————. "Plotinos." In *Paulys Real–Encyclopädie*, 21.1. Stuttgart, 1951.

————. "Bewußt und Unbewußt bei Plotin." *Les sources de Plotin*, Entretiens sur l'Antiquité Classique (Fondation Hardt), 343–78. Vandoeuvres-Geneva, 1960.

————. "Zu Plotins Deutung der sogenannten Platonischen Materie." In *Zetesis*. 266–80. Antwerp/Utrecht, 1973.

————. "Plotinos." Paulys Real-Encyclopädie, Supplement 14. Munich, 1978, 316–19.

Seeberg, E. "Ammonius Sakkas." *Zeitschrift für Kirchengeschichte* 61 (1942): 136–70.

Seidl, H. "L'union mystique dans l'explication philosophique de Plotin." *Revue Thomiste* 85 (1985) 253–64.

Sells, M. "Apophasis in Plotinus: A Critical Approach." *Harvard Theological Review* 78 (1985).

Sheldon-Williams, I. P. "The Greek Christian Platonist Tradition from the Cappadocians to Maximus and Eruigena." In *The Cambridge History of Later Greek and Early Medieval Philosophy* (pt. 6), edited by A. H. Armstrong. Cambridge, 1967.

Shiner R. "Self-predication and the 'Third Man' Argument." *Journal of the History of Philosophy*, 8, 371–86.

Simons, J. M. "Matter and Time in Plotinus." *Dionysius* 9 (1985): 53–74.

Sinnige, T. G. "Metaphysical and Personal Religion in Plotinus." In *Kephalaion*, edited by J. Mansfeld and L. M. de Rijk, 147–54. Assen, 1975.

———. "Gnostic Influences in the Early Works of Plotinus and in Augustine." In *Plotinus amid Gnostics and Christians. Papers presented at the Plotinus Symposium held at Free University*, edited by D. T. Runia, 73–79. Amsterdam, 1984.

Sleeman, J. H., and G. Pollet. *Lexicon Plotinianum*. Ancient and Medieval Philosophy, ser. 1, vol. 2. Leiden, 1980.

Smith, A., *Porphyry's Place in the Neoplatonic Tradition: A Study in Post-Plotinian Neoplatonism*. The Hague, 1974.

———. "Unconsciousness and Quasiconsciousness in Plotinus." *Phronesis* 23 (1978): 292–301.

———. "Potentiality and the Problem of Plurality in the Intelligible World." In *Neoplatonism and Early Christian Thought: Essays in Honour of A. H. Armstrong*, edited by H. J. Blumenthal and R. A. Markus, 99–107. London, 1981.

———. "Did Porphyry Reject the Transmigration of Human Souls into Animals?" *Rheinisches Museum* 127 (1984): 276–84.

Sorabji, R. *Time, Creation and the Continuum*. London, 1983.

———. "Myths about Non-Propositional Thought." In *Language and Logos: Studies in Ancient Greek Philosophy Presented to G. E. L. Owen*, edited by M. Schofield and M. C. Nussbaum, 295–314. Cambridge, 1982.

Stace, W. T. *Mysticism and Philosophy*. London, 1960.

Straaten, M., "On Plotinus IV.7[2], 8." In *Kephalaion*, edited by J. Mansfeld and L. M. de Rijk, 164–70. Assen, 1975.

Strang, C. "Plato and the Third Man." In *Plato* (vol. 1), edited by G. Vlastos, 184–200. New York, 1971.

Sweeney, L. "Infinity in Plotinus." *Gregorianum* 38 (1957): 515–35, 713–32.

———. "Another Interpretation of *Enneads* VI.7.32." *Modern Schoolman* 38 (1961): 289–93.

———. "Plotinus Revisited." *Gregorianum*, 40 (1959): 327–31.

Swinburne, R. *The Coherence of Theism*. Oxford, 1978.

———. *The Existence of God*. Oxford, 1979.

Szlezak, T. A., *Pseudo-Archytas über die Kategorien*. Berlin, 1972.

———. *Platon und Aristoteles in der Nuslehre Plotins*. Basel, 1979.

Tarán, L. *Speusippus of Athens*. Leiden, 1981.

Tarrant, H. "Middle Platonism and the Seventh Epistle." *Phronesis* 28(1) (1983): 75–103.

Taylor, A. E. *A Commentary on Plato's Timaeus*. Oxford, 1928.

Teloh, H., and D. J. Lonzecky. "Plato's Third-Man Argument." *Phronesis* 17 (1972): 80–94.

Theiler, W. *Die Vorbereitung des Neuplatonismus*. Berlin, 1930.

──── . *Forschungen zum Neuplatonismus*. Berlin, 1966.

Thesleff, H. *An Introduction to the Pythagorean Writings of the Hellenistic Period*. Abo, 1961.

──── . *The Pythagorean Texts of the Hellenistic Period*. Abo, 1965.

──── , ed., *Pseudopythagorica I. Entretiens Hardt* 11, Vandoeuvres-Geneva, 1972.

Thevenaz, P. *L'âme du monde, le devenir, et la matière chez Plutarque*. Paris, 1938.

Tigerstedt, E. N. *The Decline and Fall of the Neoplatonic Interpretation of Plato*. Helsinki, 1974.

Trouillard, J. *La Procession plotinenne*. Paris, 1955.

──── . *La Purification plotinienne*. Paris, 1955.

──── . "L'impeccabilité de l'esprit selon Plotin." *Revue de l'Histoire des Religions* 143 (1953) 19–29.

──── . "La Présence de Dieu selon Plotin." *Revue de Métaphysique et de Morale* 59 (1954) 38–45.

──── . "La genèse du Plotinisme." *Revue Philosophique de Louvain* 53 (1955) 469–81.

──── . "The logic of attribution in Plotinus." *International Philosophical Quarterly* 1 (1961) 125–38.

──── . "Valeur critique de la mystique plotinienne." *Revue Philosophique de Louvain* 59 (1961) 431–44.

──── . "Raison et mystique chez Plotin." *Revue des études augustiniennes* 20 (1974) 3–14.

Vlastos, G., ed. *Plato* (vols. 1 and 2) New York, 1971.

──── , "Disorderly Motion in the *Timaeus*" and "Creation in the *Timaeus*: Is It a Fiction?" In *Studies in Plato's Metaphysics*, edited by R. E. Allen, 379–420. London, 1965.

──── . "The Third Man Argument in the *Parmenides*." In *Studies in Plato's Metaphysics*, edited by R. E. Allen, 231–64. London, 1965.

──── . "Postscript to the Third Man." In *Studies in Plato's Metaphysics*, edited by R. E. Allen, 279–92. London, 1965.

──── . "Degrees of Reality in Plato." In *New Essays on Plato and Aristotle*, edited by R. Bambrough, 58–75. London, 1965.

Vignaux, P. *Nominalisme au 14e siécle*. Montreal and Paris, 1948.

Wagner, M. F. "Vertical Causation in Plotinus." In *The Structure of Being: A Neoplatonic Approach*, edited by R. B. Harris, 51–72. New York, 1982.

Wainwright, W. *Mysticism*. Madison, Wis., 1981.

Wallis, R. T. *Neo-Platonism*. London, 1972.

──── . "The Spiritual Importance of Not Knowing." In *Classical Mediterranean Spirituality*, edited by A. H. Armstrong, 460–80. New York, 1986.

Warren, E. W. "Consciousness in Plotinus." *Phronesis* 9 (1964) 83–97.

——. "Memory in Plotinus." *Classical Quarterly* n.s. 15 (1965) 252–60.

——. "Imagination in Plotinus." *Classical Quarterly* n.s. 16 (1966) 277–85.

Weber, K.-O. *Origenes der Neuplatoniker, Zetemata* 27. Munich, 1962.

Westra, L. "The Soul's Noetic Ascent to the One in Plotinus and to God in Aquinas." *The New Scholasticism* 58 (1984) 99–126.

Whittaker, J. *God Being Time*. Oslo, 1971.

——. *Studies in Platonism and Patristic Thought*. London, 1984.

——. "EPEKEINA NOU KAI OUSIAS." *Vigiliae Christinaea* 23 (1969): 91–104.

——. "The 'Eternity' of the Platonic Forms." *Phronesis* 13 (1968): 131–44.

——. "Neopythagoreanism and Negative Theology." *Symbolae Osloenses* 44 (1969): 109–25.

——. "Neopythagoreanism and the Transcendent Absolute." *Symbolae Osloenses* (1973): 77–86.

——. "Numenius and Alcinous on the First Principle." *Phoenix* 32 (1975): 144–154.

——. "Parisinus gr. 162 and the Writings of Albinus." *Phoenix* 28 (1979): 320–54, 450–56.

——. "Philological Comments on the Neoplatonic Notion of Infinity." In *The Significance of Neoplatonism*, edited by R. B. Harris, 155–72. New York, 1976.

——. "Platonic Philosophy in the Early Centuries of the Empire." *Aufstieg und Niedergang der Römischen Welt*, II, 36.1, 81–123.

Wiggins, D. *Identity and Spatio-Temporal Continuity*. Oxford, 1971.

Witt, R. E. *Albinus and the History of Middle Platonism*. Cambridge, 1937.

Wolfson, H. A. *Philo* (vols. 1, 2). Cambridge, Mass., 1947.

——. *The Philosophy of the Church Fathers*. Cambridge, Mass., 1956.

——. *Religious Philosophy*. New York, 1965.

Wolterstoff, N. *On Universals*. Chicago, 1970.

Wurm, K. *Substanz und Qualität: Ein Beitrag zur Interpretation der plotinischen Traktate, VI 1, 2, und 3*. Berlin, 1973.

Abrahamic tradition, 151; and divine
simplicity, 101–102; and Neoplatonism, 156
Aëtius, 167 n. 74
Aitai, 5, 15, 37
Albinus, 74; *Introduction to Plato's
Dialogues*, 74
Alcinous, 74–85, 106, 113, 123, 124;
and Aristotle, 77, 78–79; and being-
intellect, 90;
Didaskalikos, 163, 3–4, p. 74
    163, 21–22, p. 74
    163, 29–31, p. 75
    163, 34–164, 1, p. 76
    164, 16ff., p. 76
    164, 17–18, pp. 78, 79
    164, 22–23, p. 78
    164, 26–27, p. 78
    164, 35–165, 3, pp. 80–81
    164, 37–165, 1–3, p. 82
    169, 8–14, p. 78
and divine thoughts, 75; and divine
will, 81–82; and finite theism, 85;
and first god, 77–78, 80–81, 83–85,
89; and ideas, 74–76; and negative
theology, 83–85, 139
Alexander of Aphrodisias, 179 n. 45
Alexander Polyhistor, 35
Alkimos, 23
Amelius, 177 n. 24
Ammonius, 74, 93–94
Anagogy, 84–85

Analogy and divine naming, 84–85
Anamnēsis, 3
Antiochus of Ascalon, 15, 26, 28–31,
52, 168 n. 93; and divine thoughts
doctrine, 29–31
Apeiron, 33
Aphairesis, 84–85, 139, 145
Apophasis, xx, 84, 181 n. 65
Apophatic theology, x, xii, xx, 3,
42, 72; and Hellenic monotheism,
40, 42, 43; and Plotinus, 42, 102,
134–35, 139–40, 148–49, 153–55
Apophēmi, xx
Archai, 36, 70, 103
Archē, 37, 103; and the One, 135, 145
Archytas, 34
Aristotle: and Alcinous, 77, 78–79;
and *aphairesis*, 84; and causality,
30; and divine thoughts doctrine,
27–28; and dualism, 33–34, 41; and
forms, 41;
Metaphysics, I.5, 985b23ff., p. 33
    I.6, p. 24
    I.6, 987a29ff., p. 33
    I.6, 987b18–22, pp. 26–27
    XII, p. 77
    XII, 1075b18ff., p. 41
    XII.7, 1072b30, p. 33
and monad and dyad, 26–27; on
Plato, 24
Armstrong, A. H., 77, 78, 180 n. 47
Aseity, 101–102, 105

Athenian school, 76, 83; and exemplarism, 85–88
Atticus, 76, 83, 93, 120; and divine thoughts, 87–88; and exemplarism, 86–88, 89–90, 95; and Plotinus, 98, 120
Aubenque, P., 135
Augustine, xv, 43
Axiarchism, 104–105

Becoming: and being, 54, 69; and demiurge, 49, 52; and forms, 47; and ideas, 52; and Plato, 20–21, 69; and Plutarch, 46, 47, 52–53, 54
Being: and Alcinous, 90; and becoming, 54, 69; and classical Greek period, 5–7; degrees of, xvi, xvii, 4–7, 9–10, 136–37, 139–40; and degrees of reality, 7, 8–9, 11–12, 14–15; and demiurge, 2, 22, 49, 52, 79–80; and divinity, xviii, 10; and first god, 70–71; and forms, 10; and the Good, 63; and intellect, 78–80, 82–83, 86, 90, 111, 117–22, 129–34; and Numenius, 62–63, 70–71; and the One, 45, 102, 111, 112, 128–31, 134, 142–43, 147; and Plato, 4–7, 9–10, 55, 69; and Plotinus, 98, 102, 111, 117, 120–21, 127, 137, 139–40, 147; and Plutarch, 45, 56, 71; transcendence of, 42, 134–40
Berchman, R. M., 159 n. 12
Boethius, 43
Boulēsis, 80, 81–82
Brotinus, 35
Bussanich, J., 179 n. 44

Causality, 30–31; and divine will, 82; and forms, 5, 15; and realist theology, xviii–xix
Cicero, 28–29; *Posterior Academics*, 28–29
Classical theism, xvi, xxviii, 43, 104
Clement of Alexandria, 159 n. 12
Conceptualism, 32, 116; and divine thoughts doctrine, 23–24, 28, 29, 31; and forms, 19–20, 23–24; and transcendence, xi
Contemplation, x–xi; and forms, 9–10, 11; and Plato, 9

Cosmology, 16, 75–76
Creatio ex nihilo doctrine, 148, 149

Decad, 28
Degrees of being, xvi, xviii, 4–7, 9–10, 136–37, 139–40
Degrees of divinity, 152; and degrees of reality, 51; and Middle Platonism, 51–52, 55–56; and Numenius, 59–74, 89; and Plato, 9, 52, 68; and Plutarch, 52–54
Degrees of reality, xvi–xvii; and being, 7, 8–9, 11–12, 14–15; and degrees of divinity, 51; and Hellenic monotheism, 40; and Middle Platonism, 58; and the One, 130–31, 137–38; and Plotinus, 95, 105, 130–31, 137–38, 146–47, 156; and Plutarch, 54; and subordination, 65–67, 70, 72
Deism, xxvii
Demiurge, 16–17; and becoming, 2, 22, 49, 52, 79–80; and causality, 30–31; as craftsman, 17–18, 19–20, 23; demotion of, 39, 57–90; and first god, 60; and forms, 19, 22–23, 44–45, 47, 50, 52, 54, 57, 86–87, 88–89, 93; and the Good, 86–87; and Longinus, 93; and Neopythagoreans, 59–60; and Plato, 10, 16–22, 44, 57, 76, 93, 97; and Plotinus, 97–98, 125–26; and Plutarch, 44–54, 56, 88; and realist theology, 67–90; in *Timaeus*, 10, 16–22, 44, 57, 76, 93, 97; and world soul, 18–19, 21, 29, 81
Deus, 29
Diairesis, 5
Diakritikon hautou, 110
Dianoia, 97
Dillon, J., 26, 27, 53, 77, 87
Divine first principle, xxvi, 35, 40, 41–42; and Plotinus, 96, 97, 111, 113
Divine happiness, 48
Divine ideas, 78–80. *See also* Ideas
Divine immanence, 82
Divine mind, 22
Divine names, 83–85
Divine simplicity: and Abrahamic

tradition, 101–102; and perfection, 102–103, 104–105, 108; and Plotinus, 98–111, 131–32, 133, 146, 151; and production, 103–105, 108

Divine thoughts doctrine, 22–24, 54–55, 56, 58, 106; and Alcinous, 75; and Antiochus, 29–31; and Aristotle, 27–28; and Atticus, 87–88; and conceptualism, 23–24, 28, 29, 31; and exemplarism, 30–32; and forms, 23–24, 46, 47; and Old Academy, 23–24, 27–28, 31–32; and Plotinus, 119; and Plutarch, 54–55, 56; and Xenocrates, 26–27

Divine will, 80–81; and causality, 82

Dodds, E. R., 37, 66, 96, 173 n. 21, 179 n. 44

Dualism: and Aristotle, 33–34, 41; and forms of value and disvalue, 14–15; and Neoplatonists, 3; and Neopythagoreans, 40, 41; and Plato, 33; and Plutarch, 51–52; and Pythagoreans, 33, 40; and Xenocrates, 24, 34

Dunamis pantōn, 104, 108, 129

Dyad: and Aristotle, 26–27; and monad, 35–37; and numbers, 26–27; and Numenius, 60; and the One, 35, 39, 48; and Plotinus, 107; and world soul, 24, 25–26, 37; and Xenocrates, 34

Eckhart, Meister, xi

Eidē, 95, 122, 134

Einai, 6

Epistēmē, 48

Epistemology, 14

Eriugena, xi

Essentialism, 8

Eternalism, xxvii

Euclidean geometry, 84

Eudorus of Alexander, 36–37, 38, 61, 107

Evil, problem of, 67

Exclusive monotheism, xxiv, xxv

Exemplar, 30–31

Exemplarism, 46; and Athenian school, 85–88; and Atticus, 86–88, 89–90, 95; and divine thoughts doctrine, 30–32; and forms, 16–17,

46–47; and Plato, 4–5, 16–17, 21–22, 31, 32, 33, 49, 71, 76, 81, 86, 94; and Plotinus, 97–98, 112, 115, 125–26, 130

Finite theism, 43, 55; and Alcinous, 85; and Numenius, 73–74

First god, 59, 60–61, 67–68, 72, 77–78; and Alcinous, 77–78, 80–81, 83–85, 89; and being, 70–71; and demiurge, 60; epithets, 83–84; and forms, 70–71; and intellection, 61–68, 69, 70, 78–79, 89; and self-contemplation, 89; and self-production, 64, 77–78; and will, 80–81

Forms, 161–62 n. 36; and Aristotle, 111; and artifacts, 13, 25; and beauty, 5, 10; and becoming, 5, 15, 46, 47; and being, 10; and causality of particulars, 5, 15; and conceptualism, 19–20, 23–24; contemplation of, 9–10, 11; and demiurge, 19, 22–23, 44–45, 47, 50, 52, 54, 57, 86–87, 88–89, 93; of disvalue, 12–15, 75; as divine thoughts, 23–24, 46, 47; and exemplarism, 16–17, 46–47; and first god, 70–71; immanent, 52–53; of individuals, 124; and intellect, 118, 126; mathematical, 12, 62–63, 162 n. 37; and natural species, 12; negative, 124–25, 163–64 n. 40; as paradigms, 4 (*see also* Exemplarism); and Plato, 3, 44–45, 100, 137, 162–65, 246; and Plotinus, 115–16, 118–19, 122–23, 124–26, 131, 144–45, 146, 147; and Plutarch, 45–48, 52–53, 54; and realist theology, 45–46; self-predication of, 7–8; transcendence of, 28–29, 47, 131; valuational, 9–10, 12; and Xenocrates, 24–25, 164 n. 40

Freudenthal, 74

Galen, 74

Gnosticism, 82, 98

God, first. *See* First god

God, second. *See* Second god

God, third. *See* Third god

Good, the, 20; and being, 63; and forms, 86–87; and intellect, 130, 143; and the One, 33, 35, 130, 143

Hellenic metaphysics, xi, xii
Hellenic monotheism, xxviii–xxix; and apophatic theology, 40, 42, 43; and degrees of reality, 40; and divine simplicity, 101–102, 151; and dualism, 40, 41, 42; emergence of, 32–43; and mysticism, 150–56; and Plato's *Timaeus*, 43, 46, 54
Hierarchical structure of divinity, 65–67, 70, 72–73
Horasis, 106
Hyle, 150–51
Hypostases, 37, 42, 58, 73; and degrees of divinity, 152; and Plotinus, 91, 112–13, 130, 134, 142, 144, 152

Iamblichus, 66, 115; Fragment 41, 66
Ibn 'Al 'Arabi, xi
Idea-numbers, 25–26
Ideas, 39; and Alcinous, 74–76; and becoming, 52; and cosmology, 75–76; and monad, 25–26, 28; transcendence of, 47; and Xenocrates, 74–75
Inclusive monotheism, xxiv, xxv, xxvi, 91
Inge, Dean, xxii
Intellection, xix, 21; and being, 78–80, 82–83, 86, 90, 111, 117–22, 129–34; and first god, 61–66, 69, 70, 78–79, 89; and forms, 118, 126; and the Good, 130, 143; and Numenius, 61–66, 69, 70, 89, 96, 107–109; and second god, 61–63, 66, 69
Intelligibles, xi, 18–19; and living creature, 18–19, 94–95; and Longinus, 94, 95; and mutual immanence doctrine, 66–67; and the One, 107–11, 129–31, 132–36, 143; and Plato, 1; and Plotinus, 1–2, 93–111, 115, 121, 148

John Philoponus, 43

Katanoēsis autou, 110
Kataphatic theology, 139–40, 149

Krämer, H. J., 53

Living creature, 93; and first god, 63; and intelligibles, 18–19, 94, 95; and *nous*, 95, 130; and Numenius, 108, 130; and Plato's *Timaeus*, 63, 68, 81, 87, 94–95
Logoi spermatikoi, 29, 32, 52
Logos, 29, 32; and the One, 38–39
Longinus, 88; and the demiurge, 93; and the intelligibles, 94, 95; and Plotinus, 59, 93, 98, 120

Mackie, J. L., 104
Matter, 44, 60; and first god, 89; and Plotinus, 182–84 n. 2
Merlan, P., 37–38
Middle Platonism: and degrees of reality, 58; and demiurge, 47, 57, 88–89; and exemplars, 86–88, 89; and forms, 47, 57, 88; and Plotinus, xxx, 90, 92–93, 99–100, 107, 119–20, 121, 123, 127, 128; and realist theology, 58, 59
Mind in activity, 77
Mind in passivity, 77
Moderatus of Gades, 37–38, 53, 59, 61, 68, 69, 107, 128
Monad, 24, 26, 53; and Aristotle, 26–27; and dyad, generation of, 35–37; and ideas, 25–26, 28; and *nous*, 34; and numbers, 26–27, 35; and the One, 35, 39, 42; and Xenocrates, 24, 28
Monism, xxii, xxiii–xxiv, xxv; and Plotinus, xxiii–xxiv, 91, 156
Monotheism, xxi–xxix; and cosmology, xxvii; exclusive, xxiv–xxv; inclusive, xxiv, xxv, xxvi, 91; mystical, xxix–xxx, 150–56; and ontological generation, xxv–xxvi; qualitative, xxiv–xxv, xxviii–xxix
Mortley, R., 84, 181 n. 65
Muein, xx
Musterion, xx
Mustikos, xx
Mutual immanence, 66–67
Mystical monotheism, xxix–xxx, 150–56
Mysticism, xix–xxii; common-core

hypothesis, xx–xxii, 158–59 n. 9; and contextualism, xxi

Necessary declension, 103
Negative theology, 71–72, 73; and Alcinous, 83–85, 139; and Numenius, 71–72, 73; and Plotinus, 85, 102, 127–28, 138, 144
Neoplatonists, xi, 3; and Plotinus, 155–56
Neopythagoreans, 32–33, 71, 88; and demiurge, 59–60; and dualism, 40, 41; and monotheism, 34; and the One, 34, 36–42; and Plotinus, xxx, 90, 99, 120; and realist theology, 59
New Academy, 26, 38
Nicomachus of Gerasa, 172 n. 6
Noēma, form as, 23
Noeron, 75
Noēsis noēseōs doctrine, 77, 78–79
Noēton, 95, 96
Nominalism, xv, 140, 157 n. 1, 176; and realism, xvii–xviii
Nondemiurgic theology, 67–71. *See also* Demiurge, demotion of
Nous, 20, 32, 61, 75; and contemplation, 130–31; and demiurge, 114–15; and living creature, 95, 130; and monad, 34; and *noēton*, 96; and the One, 129–33; and Plotinus, 96, 97, 98, 103, 105–106, 107, 111, 112–13, 114–15, 119–21, 127–31, 152
Numbers, monad and dyad generation of, 26–27, 35
Numenius of Apamea, 53; and being, 62–63, 70–71; and degrees of divinity, 59–74, 89; and dyad, 107; and finite theism, 73–74; Fragment 11, 59, 71; Fragment 12, 60, 61; Fragment 13, 60; Fragment 15, 62; Fragment 16, 63, 65, 70; Fragment 18, 60; Fragment 22, 108, 130; and intellection, 61–66, 69, 70, 89, 96, 107–109; and living creature, 108, 130; and matter, 172–73 n. 8; and negative theology, 71–72, 73; and Plotinus, 59, 74, 94, 96, 97, 98, 105, 106, 107–108, 111, 113, 128, 130, 131

Ockham, 157 n. 1

Old Academy, 52; and divine thoughts doctrine, 23–24, 27–28, 31–32; and dualism, 33–34, 107; and the One, 48, 107; and paradigmatism, 28
The One, 33–35, 151–52; and *archē*, 135, 145; aseity, 101–102, 105; and being, 45, 102, 111, 112, 128–31, 134, 142–43, 147; and being-intellect, 129–31; contemplation of, 141–42; and degrees of reality, 130–31, 137–38; and dyad, 35, 39, 48; and the good, 33, 35, 130, 143; and intelligibles, 107–11, 129–31, 132–36, 143; and monad, 35, 39; and *nous*, 129–33; and Old Academy, 48, 107; and Plutarch, 47–48; production, 147–48; and Pythagoreans, 34–35, 37–38, 48, 107; self-discernment, 110; simplicity, 98–111, 131–32, 133, 144, 146, 151; and the soul, 145; terms for, 139; transcendence of, 134–40, 144–47, 153–54, 155; unity of, 145–46
Ontological derivation, xvii
Ontological type thesis, 111, 132–33, 135, 137–38
Opsis, 106
Origen, xxviii, 74, 94, 159 n. 12

Paradigms, 16, 76. *See also* Exemplarism
Particulars, xvii
Peras, 33
Peri archōn, 35
Philo Judaeus, xxviii, 32, 159 n. 12
Philolaus, 34
Phronēsis, 48
Plato and Platonism: and becoming, 20–21, 69; and being, 4–7, 9–10, 55, 69; and contemplation, 9–10, 11; *Cratylus*, 389b1–d3, p. 13; and degrees of being, 4–7, 9–10; and degrees of divinity, 9, 52, 68; and divine ideas, 15–34; and dualism, 33; *Euthyphro*, 5d2–5, p. 13; and exemplarism, 4–5, 16–17, 21–22, 31; and forms, 3, 44–45, 100, 137, 162–65, 246; *Laws* IV, 709b, p. 49; *Laws* X, pp. 21, 30; *Laws* XII. 967a, p. 80; middle period dialogues, xvi,

Plato and Platonism: (*continued*)
  2, 4, 5, 137; and numbers, ideal and
  mathematical, 25;
  Parmenides, 4, 24, 37–38, 71, 100,
  101, 137, 138
    129e, p. 12
    130a–e, pp. 11–12
    130b, p. 12
    130c5–7, pp. 12–13
    130d5–6, p. 13
    132b, pp. 19, 23
    160d–ereff., p. 133
  Phaedo, 3, 9
    74d–75c, p. 160 n. 14
  Phaedrus, 9–16, 48, 155
    247cff., pp. 9–10
    249c1–8, p. 10
    250a4, p. 10
    250b–c, p. 10
    250b6–7, p. 10
    265e1–3, p. 164 n. 40
  Philebus, 33
    15a, p. 12
    23c–30e, p. 20
    26e–30e, p. 41
  and Plotinus, 92, 94–95, 96, 97,
  100–102, 103, 104, 106, 110–11, 115–
  16, 121, 124, 125–26, 128, 135–40,
  146–47, 148, 153, 154, 156;
  Protagoras, 330–d–e, pp. 4–5;
  Republic, 3, 8–9, 11, 86, 130
    Book 6, p. 9
    250c2–3, p. 10
    476a4–7, p. 13
    490b, p. 9
    500cff., p. 9
    504e7–509c4, p. 20
    507ff., p. 48
    507c6, p. 20
    509, p. 65
    509b, pp. 33, 137
    53oa6, p. 20
    596, p. 163 n. 4
    596a5–7, p. 13
    596b3ff., p. 13
    597bff., pp. 19–20, 93, 164 n. 40
    599a–b, pp. 8–9
  Sophist, 4, 122
    248cff., pp. 20, 166 n. 57
    250aff., p. 55

    251cff., p. 12
    257–258, p. 163 n. 40
    265a–266d, p. 166 n. 57
    265c3–5, p. 20
  Statesman
    262c8–263e1, p. 163 n. 40
    263a2–11, p. 164 n. 40
    270a3–5, p. 20
  Symposium, 5, 10, 11, 48
    210aff., p. 10
    210eff., p. 5
    211b1, p. 5
    211e, p. 5
  Theaetetus
    176e3–177a2, p. 13
    185aff., p. 12
  Timaeus, 24, 30, 43, 54, 104
    28aff., p. 16
    28c, p. 21
    28c–29a, 39e, p. 81
    29a2–b1, p. 16
    29a3, p. 17
    29d7–30c1, p. 17
    29e, pp. 19, 39, 81, 82
    29e–30a, p. 80
    30a, p. 19
    30c–d, p. 39
    30c–31a, p. 166 n. 57
    30c1–31a1, p. 18
    31a2–b3, p. 18
    35aff., p. 25
    36e5–37a2, pp. 18–19
    39e, pp. 7–9, 18, 63, 94
    39e–40a, p. 97
    41a, p. 19
    48a, p. 17
    48eff., p. 49
    51b, p. 12
    92c7, p. 19
Plotinus, 21, 43, 91–149; and apophatic theology, 42, 102, 134–35,
  139–40, 148–49, 153–55; and artistic
  production, 123; and Atticus, 98,
  120; and being, 98, 102, 111, 117,
  120–21, 127, 137, 139–40, 147; and
  degrees of reality, 95, 105, 130–31,
  137–38, 146–47, 156; and demiurge,
  97–98, 125–26; and divine simplicity, 98–111, 144, 146, 151; and
  divine thoughts, 119; and dyad,

107; education, 93–94;
Enneads, xxx, 74, 92, 154
  II.9[33]1 and 6, p. 98
  II.9.10–12, p. 82
  III.9[13], p. 93
  III.9.1, pp. 94–97, 98, 113, 115
  V.1.[10], pp. 93, 112, 129
  V.1.4, 26–33, 34–41, pp. 121–22
  V.1.7, 1ff., p. 143
  V.1.7, 13–24, pp. 129–30, 132
  V.1.7, 18–20, p. 133
  V.2[11], pp. 93, 129
  V.2.2, 24–29, p. 144
  V.4[7], pp. 93, 98, 99
  V.4.1, 20–21, 23–26, 32–42, pp.
    103–104
  V.4.2, pp. 105–106
  V.4.2, 37–44, pp. 110–11, 112
  V.7.[18], p. 124
  V.9.2, 23–27, p. 129
  V.9.3, p. 98
  V.9.5, pp. 93, 98
  V.9.5, 1–13, pp. 112–13
  V.9.5, 19–29, pp. 114–15
  V. 9.5, 32–36, 42–46, pp. 116–17
  V.9.6, 1–3, 7–9, p. 117
  V.9.7, 14–18, p. 119
  V.9.8, 1–4, pp. 118, 119
  V.9.8, 7–19, p. 120
  V.9.10, 1–3, p. 123
  V.9.11, pp. 123–24
  V.9.14, 8–9, pp. 124–25
  VI.8[39], p. 109
  VI.8.13, p. 80
  VI.9[9], pp. 93, 129
  VI.9.1, p. 135
  VI.9.3, 1–6, p. 144
  VI.9.3, 36–45, pp. 133–34
  VI.9.3, 49–54, p. 141
  VI.9.4, 3, p. 141
  VI.9.4, 11–16, p. 141
  VI.9.5, 38–46, p. 141
  VI.9.6, 1–20, pp. 145–46
  VI.9.9, 7–12, pp. 146–47
and exemplarism, 97–98, 112, 115,
125–26, 130; and forms, 115–16,
118–19, 122–23, 124–26, 131, 144–
45, 146, 147; and hypostases, 91,
112–13, 130, 134, 142, 144, 152; and
inclusive monotheism, 91; and

intelligibles, 1–2, 93–111, 115, 121,
148; and the living creature, 94–
95; and Longinus, 59, 93, 98, 120;
and matter, 182–84 n. 2; Middle
Platonic background of his thought,
xxx, 90, 92–93, 99–100, 107, 119–
20, 121, 123, 124, 127, 128; and
monism, xxiii–xxiv, 91, 156; and
negative theology, 85, 102, 127–
28, 138, 144; and Neoplatonism,
155–56; and Neopythagoreans, xxx,
90, 99, 120; and *nous*, 96, 97, 98,
103, 105–106, 107, 111, 112–13, 114–
15, 117, 119, 121, 127–31, 152; and
Numenius, 59, 74, 94, 96, 97, 98,
105, 106, 107–108, 111, 113, 128, 130,
131; and the One, 92, 100–11, 149;
and pantheism, 91; and Platonism,
92, 94–95, 96, 97, 100–102, 103, 104,
106, 110–11, 115–16, 121, 124, 125–
26, 128, 135–40, 146–47, 148, 153,
154, 156; and Porphyry, 92, 93, 94,
98; and *psyche*, 152, 153; and realist theology, 95, 104, 118–19, 121,
123, 124, 125–26, 131, 137, 146–47,
148; self-contemplation, 113; and
theism, xxviii–xix, 154
Plutarch of Chaeroneia, 25, 44–54;
and becoming, 46, 47, 52–53, 54;
and being, 45, 56, 71;
  De Defectu, 423d, pp. 49–50
    428f–429a, p. 48
    429b, p. 48
    435eff., p. 49
  De E Apud Delphos, 393b–c, p. 47;
  De Facie, 927b–d, p. 49; *De Genio
  Socratis*, 591b, p. 53; and degrees
of divinity, 52–54; and degrees of
reality, 54;
  De Iside, 351d–e, p. 48
    373a–b, p. 52
    382b–c, p. 49
and demiurge, 48–54, 56, 88; and
divine thoughts doctrine, 54–55, 56;
and dualism, 51–52; and forms, 45–
48, 52–53, 54; *Moralia*, 44; and the
One, 47–48;
  Platonicae Quaestiones, 1001ef, p. 46
    1001cff, p. 47
on *Timaeus*, 46, 55

Polytheism, xxii–xxiii, 40, 159 n. 13; dualistic, xxviii; and Numenius, 72–73; and ontological origins, xxvi–xxvii

Porphyry, 1, 37–38, 87, 88, 155; Matter, 38; and Plotinus, 92, 93, 94, 98; and *Vita Plotini*, 17, 18, 59, 95

Prepositions, metaphysics of, 76, 81

Proclus, 33–34, 61, 63, 66, 93, 155; and Atticus, 86–87; *Commentary on the Parmenides*, 34–35; Fragment 22, 63, 65–66;
  In Timaeus, I.305, 6ff., p. 86
    I.322, 24, p. 93
    I.394, p. 88
    I.431, 14ff., p. 87
  Platonic Theology, 94

Proschrēsis, 65–66, 67, 96

Ps-Archytas, 35, 37, 38

Ps-Brotinus, 37, 38, 169–70 n. 109

Psyche, 152, 153

Pythagoreans, 32–34, 53, 172–73 n. 8; and dualism, 33, 40; and forms and numbers, 64; and the One, 34–35, 37–38, 48, 107

Qualified theism. *See* Finite theism

Realist theology, x–xi, xvi–xix; ancient sources, xv; and causality, xviii–xix; and degrees of divinity, xvii–xviii; and demiurgic theology, 69–70; and forms, 45–46; and Middle Platonism, 58, 59; modern neglect of, xv–xvi; and Plato, 3–15; and Plotinus, 95, 104, 118–19, 121, 123, 124, 125–26, 131, 137, 146–47, 148; and Plutarch, 45–46

Receptacle, 16, 17

Rist, J. M., 110, 178–79 n. 44

Ross, D., 150, 162–65 n. 40

Scholasticism, x, 55

Second god, 59–61, 67, 77; and intellection, 61–63, 66, 69; and self-production, 64, 65, 70

Self-predication, 7–8, 101

Self-production, 64; and first god, 64, 77–78; and second god, 64, 65, 70

Seneca, 30–31; *Epistulae*, 65, p. 30

Sextus Empiricus, 35

Simplicius, 36

Socrates, 3, 4, 12–13

Sophia, 48

Speusippus, 28, 33–34

Stoicism, 24, 28–29, 32, 47; Plutarch contra, 19

Subordination, 65–67, 70, 72, 73

Sunaisthēsis, 110

Syrianus, 34–35, 173 n. 23; *Commentary on the Metaphysics*, 37

Tertullian, 158 n. 2

Theism, xxii–xxiii, xxvii–xxviii; and Plotinus, xxviii–xix, 154

Theoprepēs, 100

Third god, 59–61, 67, 77

Tillich, Paul, 159 n. 13

Transcendence: of forms, 28–29, 47, 131; of ideas, 47; monism's denial of, xxiii–xxiv; of the One, 134–40, 144–47, 153–54, 155

Unitary Logos, 38

Unum-plenum paradox, 107

Via eminentiae, 143, 145–46, 148

Via negativa, 143, 148

Vis, 29

Whittaker, J., 84

Witt, R. E., 77

Wolfson, H. A., 84

World soul: and demiurge, 18–19, 21, 29, 67, 81; and dyad, 24, 25–26, 27; and intellection, 25–26; and Xenocrates, 24–27, 167 n. 74

Xenocrates, 15, 52, 123; and divine thoughts, 26–27; and dualism, 24, 34; and dyad, 34; and forms, 24–25, 164 n. 40; and ideas, 74–75; and monad, 24, 28; and world soul, 24–27, 167 n. 74

Zeno, 12

UNIVERSITY PRESS OF NEW ENGLAND publishes books under its own imprint and is the publisher for Brandeis University Press, Brown University Press, Clark University Press, University of Connecticut, Dartmouth College, Middlebury College Press, University of New Hampshire, University of Rhode Island, Tufts University, University of Vermont, and Wesleyan University Press.

Library of Congress Cataloging-in-Publication Data

Kenney, John Peter.
  Mystical monotheism : a study in ancient Platonic theology / John Peter Kenney.
    p. cm.
Includes bibliographical references and index.
ISBN 0–87451–541–6
    1. Monotheism—History. 2. Platonists. 3. Plotinus—Contributions in mystical monotheism. 4. Neoplatonism. 5. Mysticism—History. 6. Philosophical theology—History. 7. Philosophy, Ancient. I. Title
B187.T5K46 1991   90–50314
211'.34'0938—dc20   ∞   CIP